INSIDE
HITLER'S
GERMANY

INSIDE HITLER'S GERMANY

LIFE UNDER THE THIRD REICH

CHARTWELL
BOOKS, INC.

MATTHEW HUGHES & CHRIS MANN

This edition published in 2010 by
CHARTWELL BOOKS, INC.
A division of BOOK SALES, INC.
276 Fifth Avenue Suite 206
New York, New York 10001
USA

ISBN-13: 978-0-7858-2653-8
ISBN-10: 0-7858-2653-X

Produced by
The Brown Reference Group Ltd
First Floor
9-17 St. Albans Place
London N1 ONX
www.brownreference.com

Editor: Chris Westhorp
Picture research: Antony Shaw
Design: Colin Woodman
Production Director: Alastair Gourlay

Printed in China

Pages 2–3: An early Nazi Party rally in Nuremberg, 1929

CONTENTS

ADOLF HITLER

Like many Nazis, Adolf Hitler, born on 20 April 1889, came from Austria. He was also a misfit. His early years are well documented. He was born at Branau am Inn in Austria on the border with Germany in 1889, the son of an Austro-Hungarian customs official, Alois Hitler, aged 52, and a peasant girl, Klara Pölzl, some 30 years his junior. In 1876, Alois had changed his name from Schicklgruber to Hitler because the former sounded coarse and rustic. In this region of the Austro-Hungarian Empire, the names Hiedler, Hietler, Hüttler, Hütler and Hitler, denoting

"smallholder", were all used interchangeably. Alois was illegitimate, and Hiedler was the surname of his stepfather.

Hitler's childhood was not easy. While his mother doted on him, his father was a strict and difficult man. Alois was the archetypal middle-ranking provincial civil servant: he was frugal,

6

strict, pedantic, pompous, lacking in humour and status-conscious. Alois took little interest in his family, preferring to spend time in the bar drinking and smoking, or indulging his passion for beekeeping. Thrice married, Alois was an unsympathetic man and his use of physical punishment may well have had a profound impact on his son Adolf. It probably contributed to Adolf's patronizing contempt for submissive women, a desire to dominate, his inability to form deep personal relationships, and his immense capacity for hatred. From an early age, Adolf's strong will clashed with his father's, a clash that invariably led to the young Adolf being thrashed. As Adolf's younger sister Paula later remembered: "It was especially my brother Adolf who challenged my father to extreme harshness and who got his sound thrashing every day … How often, on the other hand, did my mother caress him and try to obtain with her kindness what my father could not succeed [in obtaining] with harshness."

A DIFFICULT CHILDHOOD

Neither was Adolf's education a success. His father moved as part of his job, which disrupted the children's schooling. Eventually, in 1900, Adolf moved from elementary to secondary school. Hitler's father had opted for the *realschule* rather than the *gymnasium*. The *realschule* had a more vocational and less traditional emphasis, and reflected Adolf's father's view that classical and humanistic subjects were of little use in looking for a job. At secondary school Hitler did not excel; he performed poorly academically, was unruly and in constant trouble with teachers who attempted to control him. Hitler left school with an unbending dislike of schooling and teachers. This contempt for academic endeavour and all things intellectual would find its fullest expression in Nazism. "Most of my teachers," Hitler remarked, "had something wrong with them mentally, and quite a few of them ended their days as honest-to-God lunatics." The only subject that Hitler did find of interest during and after school was Germany: he soaked up books in the public library on all things German.

In 1907 Hitler went to Vienna where he attempted to enter the Vienna Academy of Fine Arts. However, he failed the entrance test – another blow to him and a further source for his hatred of teachers and intellectuals. The following year his mother died, and in the years afterwards through to the outbreak of World War I Hitler eked out an existence in Vienna (and Munich from 1913 to 1914). The future chancellor of Germany was reduced to sleeping in dosshouses, and with his long overcoat, long hair and unshaven appearance, fellow down-and-outs gave him the nickname of "Ohm Paul Krüger", after the Boer leader of the period. Hitler was, however, not the down-and-out he liked to subsequently portray. His standard of living improved with some handouts from his aunt, a legacy from his mother and

Below: A portrait of Hitler's father, Alois. An exacting and unforgiving father, he died when Adolf was a boy. He is seen here with Franz Joseph moustache and side-whiskers.

Above: The famous shot of a jubilant Hitler in the Munich crowd following the outbreak of World War I. The future Nazi leader joined the German Army in 1914.

with the proceeds from his sketches, for which he could get five kronen per picture. At times his income was equivalent to that of a junior teacher; at other times he was short of money. Looking overall at the six years that Hitler spent in Vienna, one would have to conclude that his life in the Austrian capital was not easy.

The traditional view is that Hitler developed his anti-semitism in Vienna. However, it is not as clear cut as this. Many of the art dealers through whom Hitler sold his pictures were Jews. Hitler himself felt that the Jews he dealt with were better business people and more reliable than the "Christian" dealers; he even struck up a good friendship with one Jewish dealer, Josef Neumann. However, Hitler later claimed in *Mein*

Kampf that he became anti-semitic after coming to Vienna from Linz. Hitler remarked on one particular episode: "Once as I was strolling through the inner city, I suddenly encountered an apparition in a black caftan and black hair locks. 'Is this a Jew?' was my first thought. For to be sure, they had not looked like that in Linz. I observed the man furtively and cautiously, but the longer I stared at this foreign face, scrutinizing feature for feature, the more my first question assumed a new form: 'Is this a German?'" Following this encounter, Hitler began to see Vienna in a different light: "Wherever I went, I began to see Jews, and the more I saw, the more sharply they became distinguished in my eyes from the rest of humanity." Gradually, everything Hitler hated about the decaying Austro-Hungarian Empire he associated with the machinations of Jewry. Hitler also began to associate Marxism with Jewry through what he called "the Jewish doctrine of Marxism".

There is, however, little reliable confirmation of Hitler's anti-semitism in this period, while his friendships with some Jews actually point in the other direction. Hitler's World War I comrades also attested to the fact that he expressed no notable anti-semitic views. Therefore, the current view on Hitler is that his rabid anti-semitism, that he claimed was formed in pre-war Vienna, was, in fact, largely a product of post-1918 Germany. To bolster the image that Hitler portrayed of himself as a self-made man brought up in poverty, it suited his purposes to stress his days of trial in Vienna. In fact, his pathological hatred of Jews (and Marxists) seem to have stemmed more from his experience of a defeated Germany in 1918 and his life as a rabble-rouser in Weimar Germany than his pre-war years in the decaying Austro-Hungarian Empire.

In August 1914, following the assassination of the Archduke Franz Ferdinand, war erupted in Europe. The war shattered the old world and proved to be a formative experience for men drawn into the conflict, such as Hitler and Benito Mussolini in Italy. Ex-servicemen formed the backbone of the post-war fascist movements. Had war not broken out in 1914, Hitler would probably have eked out the rest of his life as a second-rate, obscure painter. But fated dictated otherwise.

As an Austrian (and someone who had avoided military service in the Austro-Hungarian Army), Hitler had to petition the ruler of Bavaria, King Ludwig III, to join the Bavarian part of the German Army. All-in-all, the war was a Godsend for Hitler and marked the end of his period of idleness after leaving home in 1907. For the first time, Hitler had a cause, comrades and discipline. It was

Below: German soldiers with Pickelhaube helmets and crude gas masks in the trenches in World War I. Hitler looked back fondly on his Western Front days.

his first real job. He was desperate to stay with his regiment, the Bavarian Reserve Infantry Regiment 16 (known as the "List" Regiment after its commander), even after he had been wounded. Hitler later referred to the war years as "the greatest and most unforgettable time of my earthly life".

Hitler spent the war as a dispatch runner, and never lacked for courage. His superiors thought him lacking in leadership potential and he never rose above the rank of corporal. Having said this, Hitler seems to have shown no interest in rising through the ranks. As a runner, Hitler was in the thick of the action and he courted many risks. In November 1914 a French shell exploded in the regimental forward command post minutes after Hitler had left, killing or wounding almost the entire staff. On 2 December 1914 Hitler was awarded the Iron Cross, Second Class. It was, he

Below: Post-war discontent in Germany: strikers demonstrating in 1919. In Munich Hitler witnessed the crushing of the Bavarian socialist government by *Freikorps*.

said, "the happiest day of my life". Through all of this Hitler was serious and humourless. When it was suggested by his comrades that Hitler might want to date a French girl, his horrified response was: "I'd die of shame looking for sex with a French girl." This was a portent for Hitler's uneasy relationships with women after the war. He was, however, loyal to his comrades from the war years. Those who served with Hitler were usually well cared for after the war. Having said this, actions such as the "Night of the Long Knives" in 1934 (see Chapter Eight) proved that Hitler was willing to kill war veterans and erstwhile comrades within the Nazi movement if he considered them a threat.

In the trenches, Hitler received few parcels from home; he neither smoked nor drank and he never visited brothels. Instead, he spent his time brooding or reading, the source of some amusement to his comrades, who ribbed him for his seriousness. In the frontline, Hitler grew attached to Foxl, a small white terrier. Any affection that

Above: Hitler in civilian dress, 1921. He was employed by the army after the war to monitor extremist organizations, including the *Deutsche Arbeiterpartei*.

Hitler had amidst the horrors of the trenches was lavished on Foxl, and when the dog was lost Hitler was, for once, emotional. There were echoes here of Hitler's later attachment to his Alsatian dog Blondi. Hitler felt more for dogs than human beings, perhaps because of their ability to give unswerving loyalty and obedience. Albert Speer, Hitler's master architect and war-planner, remembered that Hitler's love for his dog seemed his only human emotion.

Although an Austrian, Hitler was excessively patriotic and took Imperial Germany's fight to heart. He disapproved of the Christmas fraternization in 1914 and was easily provoked by any defeatist comments from comrades. Interestingly, and as noted above, Hitler's comrades remember few hostile comments about Jews. A few off-the-cuff anti-semitic remarks were the sum total of a man who would go on to preside over the Holocaust.

THE END OF THE WAR

In 1916 Hitler was wounded by a British shell and spent time in hospital near Berlin. He was shocked to see the low morale and malingering behind the lines, and this image later provided the Nazis with their "Stab-in-the-Back" myth for why Germany lost the war. Hitler was eager to get back to the front, and so in March 1917 he rejoined the "List" Regiment near Vimy. On 4 August 1918 Hitler was awarded the Iron Cross, First Class (*Eisernes Kreuz* – EK1), a rare distinction for an ordinary soldier in the Imperial German Army. Ironically, Hitler was nominated for the medal by a Jewish officer, Lieutenant Hugo Gutmann. It was subsequently claimed that Hitler had won the EK1 for single-handedly capturing 15 soldiers. In truth, Hitler received the EK1 for delivering a message through heavy fire. Gutmann had promised two dispatch runners, one of them Hitler, the medal if they made the journey. The courageous if not striking actions of the runners meant that Gutmann spent several weeks petitioning divisional headquarters before the award was agreed. In October 1918, a month before the Armistice, Hitler was gassed with mustard gas and partially blinded. When the war ended he was convalescing in hospital in Pomerania. The news of Germany's defeat shattered him. He recalled from his hospital bed how he "knew everything was lost. Only fools – liars or criminals – could hope for mercy from the enemy. In these nights my hatred grew against the men who had brought about this crime. I, however, decided to go into politics."

World War I traumatized Europe and provided the foundations for the success of communism and fascism. For many veterans of the trenches, the return to civilian life proved an impossible adjustment. Many of these veterans found a new home in the uniformed and disciplined ranks of the

Above: An early Nazi Party meeting. The Nazi on the right wears an Iron Cross and the Swastika armband, an ancient symbol appropriated by the Nazis.

emerging fascist movements. In Germany, many future senior Nazis, men such as Hermann Göring and Rudolf Hess, had fought in the war and they took the martial life of the front with them into fascist politics. As for Hitler, the Germany that he returned to was being torn apart by a Left-versus-Right political battle as communists and right-wing paramilitary *Freikorps* units fought for control. As a devoted noncommissioned officer (NCO), Hitler was kept on the payroll of the "List" Regiment and given the task of spying on political parties in Munich. This represented his only proper peacetime employment with regular pay. It was one of these political parties that he was supposed to spy

on, the German Workers' Party (*Deutsche Arbeiterpartei – DAP*), that attracted Hitler's attention most. In September 1919 the 30-year-old Hitler joined as member number seven following an excoriating intervention by him at a *DAP* meeting. Or did he?

MEMBER NUMBER SEVEN?

One of the recurring themes of Hitler's life is deception. As has been seen, in Vienna Hitler dealt with Jews and seems to have shown no exceptional anti-semitism. The anti-semitism Hitler developed in the 1920s needed some root, and so Hitler claimed that he had developed the idea of anti-semitism from his formative time in Vienna. This was not the case: Hitler, like many others, was profoundly anti-semitic in the 1920s because of the sense of betrayal and hatred felt by many Germans after their defeat in the war. Rather than ascribe his ideology to the prosaic ideas of 1919, ideas shared by many in Germany, Hitler needed to be different; he needed to have had vision. This is why he later lied about his days in Vienna, which he subsequently stated had made him into "something special".

The same is true for Hitler's membership of the *DAP*. Hitler was actually reacting to events and joining an already established party rather than leading from the front and forming his own party. Thus, Hitler was perhaps a pragmatist more than a visionary. In fact, Hitler joined the *DAP* as member number 555, but the Nazis subsequently buried this fact and claimed that Hitler was member number seven. Anton Drexler, the founder of the *DAP*, even wrote to the Führer in 1940: "Nobody knows better than yourself, my Führer, that you were never the seventh member of the party, but at best the seventh member of the committee when I asked you to step in as propaganda representative. A few years ago I was forced to complain about this

at a party meeting, that your first German Workers' card which carried Shüssler's signature had been falsified whereby the number 555 had been deleted and the number seven inserted … How much better and more valuable it would be for posterity if the course of history had been portrayed as it really happened." (Drexler became a background figure in the party and died, forgotten, in Munich in 1942).

What Hitler proved good at was talking. His speeches attracted new members for the *DAP*, and in 1921 he moved to take over the party and give it a new name: the National Socialist German Workers' Party (*Nationalsozialistische Deutsche Arbeiterpartei – NSDAP*). This was shortened to the acronym "Nazi" from the first syllable of NAtional and the second syllable of SoZIalist (a similar process happened with "Gestapo" from *Geheime Staatspolizei*). With the term "Nazi" came all the

Below: Nazi storm troopers in 1923, the year of the "Beer Hall Putsch". These men, armed with rifles and truncheons, are mostly dressed in World War I-style clothing.

symbols of fascism that helped draw in new recruits. There were uniforms and a new greeting to replace Guten Tag: "Heil Hitler!" Eventually, school study periods in Germany were opened with "Heil Hitler!" and every child was expected to say "Heil Hitler!" over 100 times per day. Along with the greeting went the infamous raised right-arm salute. The Nazis also appropriated a powerful symbol in the Swastika (or Hakenkreuz). This was an ancient symbol that appeared on ceramics as far back as the fourth millennium B.C. Under the Nazis, the black Swastika on a white circular background against red came to denote the superior "Aryan" race, and the Nazi propaganda machine under Dr Josef Göbbels popularized the symbol as the official Nazi emblem.

Below: Adolf Hitler in civilian dress at a Nazi Party rally in Nuremberg in 1923, before his abortive Putsch. By this date the Nazis had 70,000 members in Bavaria.

The use of symbols and greetings was complemented by Hitler's programme of simple political slogans backed up by the use of newspapers and Storm Troopers – the *Sturmabteilung* or *SA*, headed by another war veteran, the brutal Ernst Röhm – for battles on the streets with communists and social democrats. Hitler pushed the message that all Germany's woes were the result of international Jewry and Marxists, and his message was eagerly received by many in a population angered by the Treaty of Versailles and suffering from economic dislocation. Hitler's ideas of racial superiority and extreme nationalism were not new, but he coloured them with showmanship and eloquence, all carefully contrived to build up a myth status around the former Austrian corporal and failed painter. Hitler certainly had a presence. When Hitler walked into a student cafe in Munich in 1921, Herbert Richter recalled: "He was wearing an open-necked shirt and he was accompanied by

Above: Hitler with Ernst Röhm, the head of the *SA*. While a close associate of Hitler in the 1920s, he came to be seen as a threat and was assassinated in 1934.

guards or followers … And I noticed how the people with whom he arrived – there were about three or four of them – how their eyes were fixed on Hitler. For many people there must have been something fascinating about him."

THE "MAN OF DESTINY"

Such an image was encouraged by Heinrich Hoffman, Hitler's official photographer, who produced a series of portraits that gave a "naturalistic" flavour and the sense of a "man of destiny" staring out of the crowd with a keen gaze and invariably surrounded by attentive, devoted acolytes. Hitler saw his personality as one of the Nazis' biggest assets. He cultivated "great man" mannerisms, such as staring intently into the eyes of those with whom he spoke. Fridolin von Spaun recalled an encounter with Hitler at a Nazi Party dinner: "Suddenly I noticed Hitler's eyes resting on me. So I looked up. And that was one of the most curious moments of my life. He didn't look at me suspiciously, but I felt that he was searching me

somehow … It was hard for me to sustain this look for so long. But I thought: I mustn't avert my eyes, otherwise he may think I've something to hide. And then something happened which only psychologists can judge. The gaze, which at first rested completely on me, suddenly went straight through me into the unknown distance. It was so unusual. And the long gaze which he had given me convinced me completely that he was a man with honourable intentions. Most people nowadays would not believe this. They'd say I'm getting old and childish, but that's untrue. He was a wonderful phenomenon." As is so often the way with politics, Hitler proved the maxim of Hans von Seeckt, the German Army commander of the 1920s: *"Mehr seins als Schein"* ("Be more than you appear to be").

THE "BEER HALL PUTSCH"

The creation of a "myth" around Hitler accelerated when, in 1923, he led an attempted coup (the so-called "Beer Hall Putsch") in Munich as a prelude to a national revolution against the Weimar Republic. Again, all was not what it seemed at first sight. The putsch failed, and Hitler and the other ringleaders were put on trial in February 1924. Hitler stood up and claimed full responsibility for the putsch, which had claimed the lives of three policemen. His speech and behaviour before the court made him known across Germany. He became a national figure. Before the judges, Hitler proclaimed: "Gentlemen, it is not you who pronounce judgment upon us, it is the eternal court of history which will make its pronouncement upon the charge which is brought against us [high treason] … You may pronounce us guilty a thousand times, but the goddess who presides over the eternal court of history will, with a smile, tear in pieces the charge of the Public Prosecutor and the verdict of this court. For she acquits us." These were brave words that in normal circumstances would have angered the judges and led to a heavier sentence. But in courting publicity, Hitler was not taking any real risk for the judge who presided at his trial, Georg Neithardt, had sat on an earlier trial in 1922 where Hitler had been charged with violent affray. At that trial Neithardt had passed the minimum sentence possible of three months. Neithardt then wrote to the superior court asking that the three-month sentence be reduced to a fine. In 1924, when Hitler made his courageous stand, he was doing so in front of a sympathetic judge. Hitler knew he could say what he liked. Once in power in January 1933, the Nazis quickly tried to seize all the evidence of this trial (as they did with evidence detailing Hitler's time in Vienna before the war). At the "Beer Hall Putsch' trial, Hitler was not so much making history as reading from a script.

Sentenced to the minimum term of five years' imprisonment, Hitler served his sentence in a comfortable cell in Landsberg prison (he even got rather fat from over-eating). He was out after 10

Below: A Nazi Party rally in 1923 in Munich. Note how the speaker is being protected by an armed guard as he addresses the large audience.

months, having written his manifesto while in prison. Hitler's original title for this manifesto was *Four and a Half Years of Struggle against Lies, Stupidity and Cowardice*. This was reduced to the snappier *Mein Kampf* ("My Struggle") by Hitler's publisher, Max Amann (who was later to become President of the Reich Press Chamber). The turgid, rambling discussion in *Mein Kampf* has been seen by many as a blueprint for Hitler's later actions. The pragmatic and reactive policies of Hitler suggest otherwise. Soon, however, every home in Germany had to have a copy of *Mein Kampf* (even if few Germans actually read it) and the royalty sales from the book were the main source of Hitler's personal income. After the war, Hitler's income tax file was discovered and it revealed that his income was 19,843 marks in 1925, 15,903 in 1926, 11,494 in 1927, 11,818 in 1928 and 15,448 in 1929. These figures tally closely to the royalties he received from sales of the book.

Hitler's career after Landsberg is well documented. After a period in the late 1920s when the Nazis did very badly in elections, the depression following the Wall Street Crash helped bring the Nazis to prominence. Aided by wealthy German politicians and businessmen who thought they could control Hitler and use him to smash communism and organized labour, Hitler became chancellor in January 1933. This was the beginning of Hitler's Thousand-Year Third Reich. This would, in the end, last for a mere 12 years and leave Germany defeated, destroyed and occupied.

HITLER AND DEVOLVED POWER STRUCTURES

In the development of the Nazi state, Hitler's personality and ideas naturally played an important role. One of his most critical beliefs was in social Darwinism – the idea that within society or politics constant struggle would lead the fittest to survive. Thus, Hitler encouraged his subordinates to use their initiative and carve out their own power bases. If they were the "strongest and fittest" they would succeed. In a speech in 1928 at Kulmbach, Hitler told the audience that the "idea of struggle is as old as life itself". He went on to say: "In this struggle the stronger, the more able, win while the

Above: German Army cavalry clearing the streets in Munich after the failed Nazi coup of 1923. Both Hitler and Göring were wounded in the abortive Putsch.

less able, the weak, lose. Struggle is the father of all things." Thus, when, in 1925, Gustav Seifert had written to Nazi Party HQ asking to be reappointed as leader of the Hanover branch, he had received the following reply: "Herr Hitler takes the view on principle that it is not the job of the party leadership to 'appoint' party leaders. Herr Hitler is today more than ever convinced that the most effective fighter in the National Socialist movement is the man who wins respect for himself as leader through his own achievements. You yourself say in your letter that almost all the members follow you. Then why don't you take over leadership of the branch? Why don't you '*take over*'? What command could be more exciting to a young man? If you don't like it, change it, don't come to us for orders, if you are stronger than your enemies you'll win."

This devolution of power has helped generate nonsensical and offensive arguments that Hitler knew nothing about the Holocaust. The Wannsee Conference of 1942 that decided on the "Final

Solution", for example, was chaired by Reinhard Heydrich (Chief of the Reich Security Office and Protector of Moravia) as Hitler's plenipotentiary. This fitted in with Hitler's style of government from the early days of the Nazi Party – though ultimately the Führer always maintained iron control over his subordinates.

On a personal level, Hitler was a vegetarian and neither smoked nor drank alcohol; a doctor, Theodor Morell, prescribed him various "medicines", many of which had the effect of slowly poisoning the Führer. In terms of his relationships with the opposite sex, Hitler only seems to have had one relationship that was at all serious and involved any real emotional attachment. This was

with his niece, Geli Raubal, who came to live with "Uncle Alf" in 1929. In 1931 she was found, aged 23, shot dead with Hitler's pistol. The suicide of Geli had a profound impact on Hitler and confirmed his already awkward attitude to women. While he liked to flirt and made occasional clumsy physical advances, Hitler viewed women with little interest. Hitler's relationship with Geli, however, appears to have been different. Hitler was obsessively jealous and carefully controlled her movements and who she saw. She was chaperoned wherever she went and was effectively a prisoner. Hitler's political enemies made much of his supposed physical maltreatment of Geli, but there is no definite evidence of this. In *The Rise and Fall of the Third Reich* William Shirer suggests that a masochistic sexual urge in Hitler might have repelled Geli, but there is no tangible proof. But Hitler's psychological abuse was such that Geli

Below: Hitler in *NSDAP* uniform with fellow Nazi Gregor Strasser (fourth from right), 1927. Strasser eventually came to be seen as a threat to Hitler and was assassinated in 1934.

Above: Hitler as demagogue. Hitler made much use of hand gestures to increase the effect of his speeches.
Left: A well-orchestrated Nazi mass rally. Each rally was designed to demonstrate support to Hitler and Nazism.

took her own life. While depressed and near hysterical at Geli's death, Hitler soon got over her suicide and got back into politics and the business of getting into power. In the final days of the Third Reich, Hitler married Eva Braun, his close female companion for many years. But she was an intellectually slight women whose role in Hitler's life was as a pretty blond companion who would not disagree with the Führer.

In the end, it is hard not to disagree with the conclusions of the historian Hugh Trevor-Roper who described Hitler's mind as: "A terrible phenomenon, imposing indeed in its granite harshness and yet infinitely squalid in its miscellaneous cumber – like some huge barbarian monolith, the expression of giant strength and savage genius, surrounded by a festering heap of refuse – old tins and dead vermin, ashes and egg shells and ordure – the intellectual detritus of centuries." Alan Bullock in his magisterial book, *Hitler: A Study in Tyranny*, concluded with an equally sombre assessment that emphasized Hitler's profound impact on European history: "He [Hitler] was in revolt

Right: Geli Raubal, his niece, was perhaps Hitler's only real love. Hitler, however, was fanatically jealous and in 1931 Geli committed suicide.

against 'the System' not just in Germany but in Europe, against the liberal bourgeois order, symbolized for him in the Vienna which had once rejected him. To destroy this was his mission, the mission in which he never ceased to believe; and in this, the most deeply felt of his purposes, he did not fail. Europe may rise again, but the old Europe of the years between 1789, the year of the French Revolution, and 1939, the year of Hitler's War, has gone forever – and the last figure in its history is that of Adolf Hitler, the architect of its ruin. *Si monumentum requiris, circumspice* – "If you seek his monument, look around."

However important Hitler's personality, he was not a *deus ex machina*. His success in dominating Germany and then leading it down the road to ruin also owed much to the recent history of Germany itself, and in particular to conflicts within Germany and problems of the legitimacy of German institutions.

The Germany that Hitler ruled and then destroyed had not become a unified nation until the last quarter of the nineteenth century, and up to the mid-nineteenth century to talk of a single German state would have seemed nonsensical. Politically, religiously and socially, Germany was a far more disparate state in the late nineteenth century than France or Great Britain, and many fundamental institutions lacked national, as opposed to regional, acceptance. For example, Germany was the one major European power where neither Catholicism nor Protestantism was dominant in religious terms. Thus, Bavaria was a mainly Catholic area, whereas Prussia was overwhelming-

ly Protestant. Such regional divisions came out in other ways – the Rhineland was more liberal than, say, Schleswig-Holstein, for example.

These regional differences had been disguised, in the late nineteenth century, by a strong authoritarian tradition. Prussia, whose military victories over Denmark, the Austro-Hungarian Empire and France lay behind German unification, expanded throughout the century. From 1823 she formed a series of customs unions with other small German states; in 1864 she defeated Denmark and annexed Schleswig-Holstein; in 1866, the Austro-Hungarian Empire was defeated and excluded from the North German Confederation, a Prussian-dominated union of German states north of the River Main. Then, in 1870, France was defeated, and Alsace and Lorraine were annexed.

Above: Eva Braun. Hitler's mistress for 12 years, she married the Führer in April 1945. A day later they both committed suicide as Soviet troops rolled into Berlin.

The German states south of the Main then joined the German Reich, a new political entity, ruled by a Kaiser (emperor) of the Prussian ruling house, with Otto von Bismarck as his chancellor. Ostensibly, the new empire had a liberal constitution with power in the hands of elected deputies. However, the Prussian state had an authoritarian tradition, and there was no real experience of parliamentary government to call on.

To the outside world the new Germany was a modern, dynamic state, with an expanding population and economy. Germany's population was 45 million in 1880, 56 million in 1900 and 70 million by 1914. The expansion of the population was accompanied by an even more rapid expansion of industry. By 1910 Germany's urban population was 60 percent of the total. Internally these changes created huge social problems. The industrial explosion disrupted traditional ways of life, and helped create the conditions whereby political

institutions were discredited. "To a people sentimental about nature and their ancient towns, the sudden rise of monstrously big and ugly cities was distressing. Nor did Germany do things by halves; by 1910, it had almost as many large cities as the entire rest of the Continent." (Fritz Stern, *The Politics of Cultural Despair*).

Hand-in-hand with this disillusion was the anti-liberal flavour of much German nationalism. A typical reaction to these changes, especially among the middle classes for example, was a kind of nostalgic mysticism. People hearkened back to a pre-modern age, to a "folk" community where German peasants had been close to the earth (the Nazis would later apply the phrase Blood and Soil – *Blut und Boden* – as an expression of an anti-urban, anti-industry and anti-capitalist doctrine). Many Germans looked back 1000 years before, when individuals such as Henry the Fowler (876-936) defended German lands against raiders from the east.

"Folk" characteristics easily lent themselves to racism. As in most European states, anti-semitism was common in the late nineteenth century. The German authorities were also not averse to using anti-semitism for political ends. In the 1870s, for example, a number of financial scandals in which Jews were involved had been exploited by Chancellor Bismarck to attack his liberal political enemies.

Just how far any of these elements were crucial in the rise to power of Hitler is debatable. However, what is clear is that the problems of legitimacy that underlay the German Reich founded in 1870 were of long-term importance. For during the period 1914 to 1930 a series of events swept over this large, powerful German state that had a disastrous impact, partly because of the immaturity and weakness of this state's most basic institutions. The slaughter of World War I, German defeat in 1918, the fall of the monarchy, revolution, the impact of the Versailles Treaty, the catastrophic inflation of the early 1920s, the problems experienced by democracy under the Weimar Republic, and finally the Great Depression – all these subjected German society to strains and disruptions that created the atmosphere in which a politician like Hitler could come to power.

A PEOPLE WITHOUT HOPE: GERMANY IN THE 1920S

Above: German sailors and soldiers during the attempted revolution in 1919. These gunners are from the sailors' and soldiers' soviets that sprang up after World War I.

It is often argued that German discontent and resentment in the 1920s stemmed from the unfairness of the post-war peace settlement and the Treaty of Versailles that Germany signed in 1919. With hindsight, the "unfairness" of Versailles is an argument difficult to sustain when one compares it with the swingeing treaties of Bucharest and Brest Litovsk of 1918 that Germany imposed on the defeated states of Romania and Russia, and with the plans that the Germans had for European dominance if they had won the war, expressed in documents such as Bethmann Hollweg's "September Programme" of 1914. It is also the case that a close examination of the Treaty of Versailles shows that the compensa-

Opposite top: Hitler using his considerable oratory skills at a meeting in Germany in the interwar years.
Opposite below: A Workers' Defence Force militia unit deployed for action, somewhere in Germany in 1921.

tion that Germany was to pay for starting and prosecuting the war was not unreasonable. It was within Germany's means to pay the reparations agreed, but German unwillingness to pay led to a series of compromises which culminated in Hitler's abrogation of the treaty in the 1930s.

However, the perception of many in Germany *at the time* was that Versailles was unfair. It was, in their eyes, a punitive "Carthaginian Peace" designed to crush German strength for ever. There were those in Britain, such as the economist John Maynard Keynes, who supported this view in books such as the *Economic Consequences of the Peace*, published in 1919. The treaty was not overly harsh, and its critics would have done well to consider what the peace would have looked like had

Germany won the war. Nonetheless, for a population trying to come to terms with defeat and economic depression, the idea of a punitive peace soon took hold. Many in Germany even questioned whether they had been defeated at all. After all, Germany was not occupied when the war ended in November 1918, and the German Army had withdrawn from the front in France and Belgium at the war's end in good order. This was the basis of the Nazis' later "Stab-in-the-Back" myth: the idea that it was Marxists and Jews on the home front who had betrayed the army. It would take another war, another defeat and occupation by British, French, American and Soviet forces to prove that Germany had been comprehensively defeated.

When World War I ended, many German frontline veterans (or *frontkämpfer*), including the Austrian corporal Adolf Hitler, could not face defeat. "We did wonder," recalled war veteran Herbert Richter, "because we didn't feel beaten at all. The frontline troops didn't feel themselves beaten, and we were wondering why the armistice was happening so quickly, and why we had to vacate all our positions in such a hurry, because we were still standing on enemy territory and we thought all this was strange." Richter vividly remembered his feelings at the war's end: "We were angry because we did not feel we had come to the end of our strength."

THE WEIMAR REPUBLIC

It was in this climate of defeat and anger that the short-lived Weimar Republic was born. As soon as it was proclaimed, forces from the Left and the Right moved to seize power. The National Assembly met in Weimar for the first time in February 1919. Berlin was not selected because it had been the scene of the abortive left-wing Spartacus Revolt in January 1919. Led by Karl Liebknecht and Rosa Luxemburg, it was brutally suppressed by the *Freikorps* (see below), who murdered both leaders of the revolt.

The kaiser had abdicated and moved to the Netherlands; Allied forces moved into Germany and set up permanent occupation zones in the Rhineland; German POWs were not repatriated;

and the British naval blockade remained in place. The blockade, which continued into 1919, prevented foodstuffs from entering Germany and starved the German population into agreeing to the Versailles settlement. For the German people all these woes were the fault of the Weimar Republic. Though its constitution contained many democratic elements, the republic was perceived by some as being the illegitimate child of defeat. It was given little support from the Allies, was attacked by internal opponents and lasted only until Hitler came to power in 1933. It was small comfort that the short-lived Weimar Republic still lasted longer than Hitler's Third Reich.

THE *FREIKORPS*

The struggle for power in the early 1920s saw the frontline veterans organized into the right-wing, paramilitary *Freikorps* ("Free Corps") to fight the threat of a communist take-over. The men of the *Ehrhardt* Brigade of the *Freikorps* brought a traditional symbol with them from their fighting in the Baltic, which they wore on their helmets: the Swastika. In the Bavarian capital of Munich the battle was particularly intense, as both sides sought to outmanoeuvre the other in a series of bitter street battles and assassinations of rival leaders. In May 1919 a communist soviet was overthrown by the forces of reaction as regular troops moved in, with *Freikorps* support, and brutally suppressed the left-wing government. This suppression by military and paramilitary forces marked a decisive shift to the Right in Bavarian politics. In 1920 a right-wing coup in Berlin, the "Kapp Putsch", took place. In March the *Ehrhardt* Brigade, protesting against the government's acceptance of the Versailles Treaty (which would have required the brigade's disbandment), marched into Berlin and installed the right-wing journalist Wolfgang Kapp as chancellor. However, a general strike of workers in the capital ended the Putsch after five days. Though it had failed and marked the end of the immediate threat to the Weimar Republic from the Right, it did reveal how unreliable the military, which had done nothing, was in the defence of the republic. The seeds of political hatred had been sown among a wide sec-

tion of the German populace, and it would be these people who would be drawn into the Nazi Party. Disgruntled ex-soldiers were still dedicated to destroying the hated Weimar democracy and its perceived "Bolshevik republicanism".

Four years after the end of the war, Germany was a divided and disgruntled nation. The imposition of the terms of the Treaty of Versailles made matters worse. The sum of reparations was fixed at £6600 million, and chunks of territory in the east were lost to Poland. The policy of the Weimar Republic of keeping to the terms of the treaty was unpopular in Germany.

The French occupation forces in Germany exacerbated German anger at the consequences of the war. In 1923, Germany defaulted on reparation repayments. As a punishment, French forces occupied the industrial Ruhr area of the Rhineland. The

Above: A demonstration against the Treaty of Versailles' terms passes the Hotel Adlon, where the Allied Commission that would enforce the treaty were staying, May 1919.

occupation was intended as a humiliation for the Germans. The sense of shame was increased by the behaviour of the French troops sent in to occupy the Ruhr. As Jutta Rüdiger, the woman who would go on to lead the female branch of the Hitler Youth (the *BdM*: see Chapter Four), recalled: "That was when we found out that the French ruled with an iron hand. Perhaps they simply wanted their revenge. Revenge is an emotion I do not know at all." With perhaps a touch of unintended irony considering what the Nazis did once they achieved power, Rüdiger concluded: "But the French have a slightly different character, don't they? Perhaps there is a tiny bit of sadism there."

Private armies – THE *FREIKORPS*

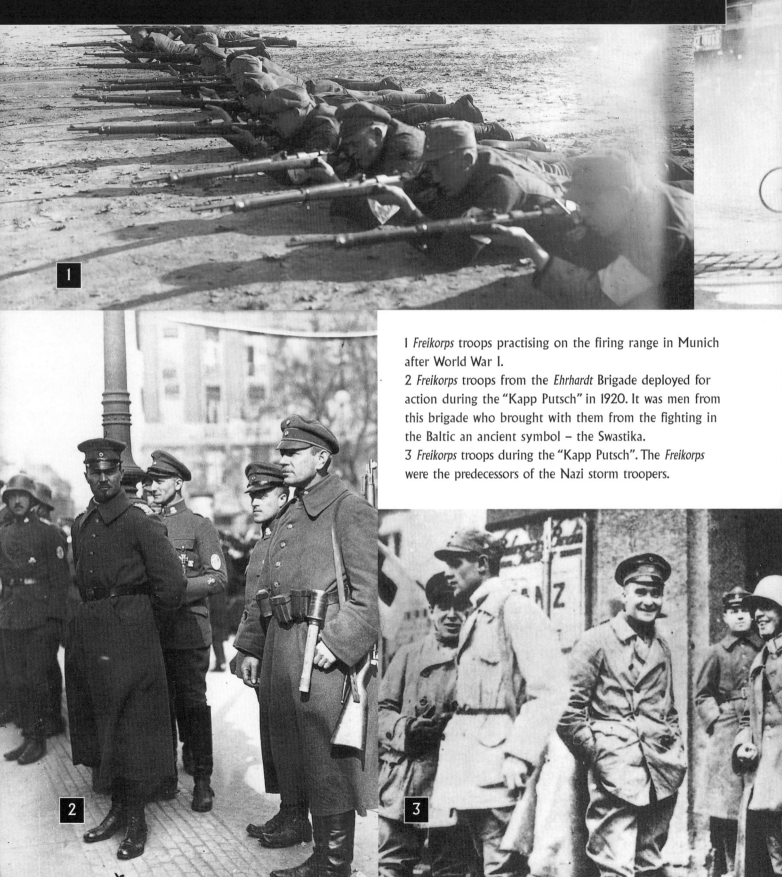

1 *Freikorps* troops practising on the firing range in Munich after World War I.

2 *Freikorps* troops from the *Ehrhardt* Brigade deployed for action during the "Kapp Putsch" in 1920. It was men from this brigade who brought with them from the fighting in the Baltic an ancient symbol – the Swastika.

3 *Freikorps* troops during the "Kapp Putsch". The *Freikorps* were the predecessors of the Nazi storm troopers.

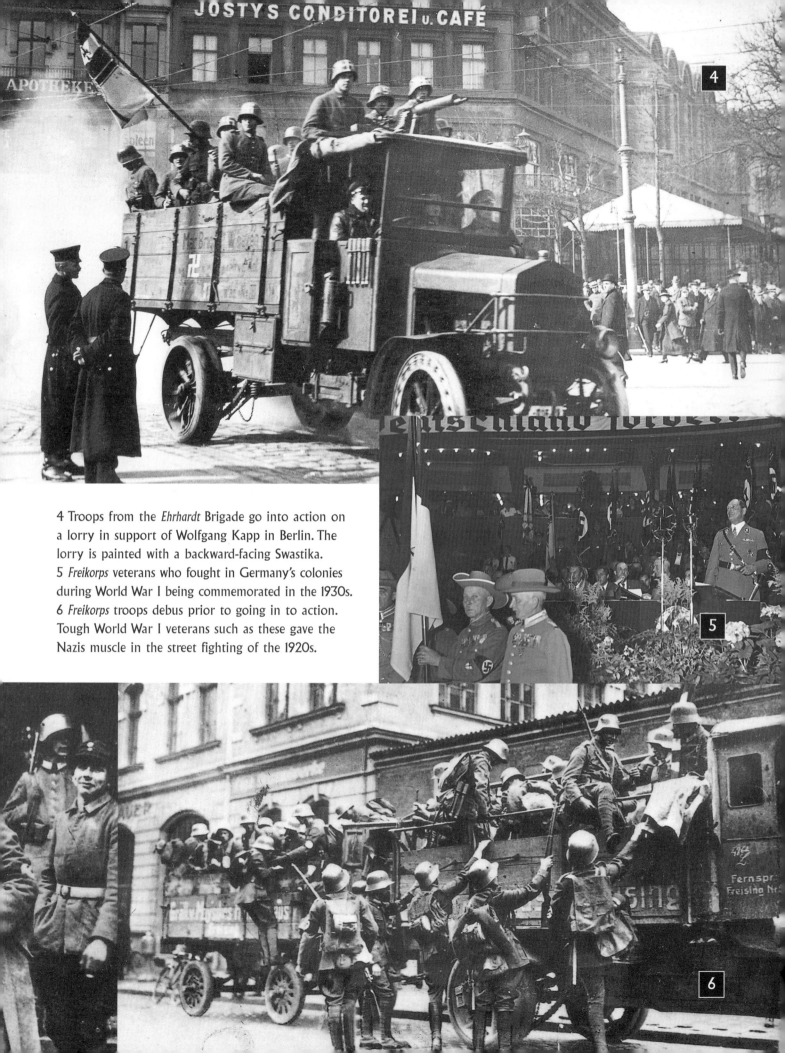

4 Troops from the *Ehrhardt* Brigade go into action on a lorry in support of Wolfgang Kapp in Berlin. The lorry is painted with a backward-facing Swastika.
5 *Freikorps* veterans who fought in Germany's colonies during World War I being commemorated in the 1930s.
6 *Freikorps* troops debus prior to going in to action. Tough World War I veterans such as these gave the Nazis muscle in the street fighting of the 1920s.

In the Ruhr the humiliation of French occupation bred a sense of disquiet that extremist groups like the Nazis could feed upon. Bernd Linn was only five when he saw French troops entering his town. As the French soldiers marched past, he stood watching them in a child's army uniform "armed" with a toy gun. As he later remembered: "I turned around and then a Frenchman came and disarmed me – apparently he needed this for his children. And I felt very hurt." It was perhaps then no coincidence that when Linn grew up he became a colonel (a *standartenführer*) in the *SS*.

The French occupation of the Ruhr united Germans against a common enemy. The German

Below: Hitler addressing a Nazi Party rally in the palace park at Tiefurt. These early rallies were a foretaste of the well-planned rallies after the Nazis came to power.

government called for a campaign of passive resistance and this soon spread from the Ruhr to the other French and Belgian occupation zones in the Rhineland. Before long, this became a state of undeclared war as French troops tried to make the Germans keep up with their reparation repayments. On one side the Germans employed strikes, sabotage and dissent; on the other side, the French used arrests, deportations and economic blockade.

To compound the humiliation of defeat and occupation, the French garrisoned African colonial troops in Germany. This was intended as a slight to the Germans, who saw these troops as "racially inferior". The result of these garrison occupations, however, was a series of liaisons between the colonial troops and local German women, and when the Nazis came to power the resultant mixed-race

Right: Berlin Jews gather in the street. The economic problems Germany experienced in the interwar period allowed the Nazis to whip up anti-semitism as part of their racist policies and the search for scapegoats.

offspring were an obvious target for Nazi policies of racial hatred. Even under the Weimar Republic, these *Rheinlandbastarde* (there were some 500 of them) suffered discrimination. Once the Nazis were in power, these children were ordered to register with the health authorities. Once this was complete they were forcibly sterilized.

ECONOMIC COLLAPSE

As the Ruhr was occupied, Germany's economy collapsed. The most obvious sign of this was hyperinflation. The German mark became useless. "I once paid four billion marks for a sausage roll," recalled Emil Klein, who attended his first Nazi meeting in 1920. It was this economic collapse which drew ordinary people into extreme parties such as the Nazis. Klein again: "And this collapse naturally supported the Hitler movement and helped it grow, because people said, 'It can't go on like this!' And then slowly emerged the decision about the need for a strong man. And this stuff about a strong man grew more and more because democracy achieved nothing." With runaway inflation and a worthless mark, employees were forced to keep their wages in laundry baskets as there were so many notes. On one occasion, a thief came, tipped out the money and stole the basket: it at least had some barter value. The German mark which had stood at the rate of four to the US dollar in 1918 rapidly lost its value. In the summer of 1922, the dollar was worth 400 marks, by the beginning of 1923 more than 7000. In the hyper-inflation

of 1923–24, the Weimar Republic was forced to overprint banknotes to create fantastic notes valued at 20 million and 10 billion marks.

The collapse of the currency not only resulted in an end to trade, bankrupt businesses, food shortages and unemployment; it also reached down and touched every single German citizen. The hardearned savings of the middle and working classes were wiped out at a stroke; simultaneously, the

Above: Bread being passed out by Nazis in the 1920s. The Nazi Party was always careful to appear as the benefactor of former service personnel.

purchasing power of the weekly wage was reduced to almost zero. Ordinary Germans could work until they dropped but it was still impossible to feed and clothe the family. For many Germans, though, this was academic as there was no work anyway.

The inflation of the early 1920s was another blow to the emerging Weimar Republic. The runaway inflation destroyed not only money and property, but faith in the meaning of money and property. People were now willing to turn to extremes, and Hitler's attacks on the supposedly corrupt, "Jew-ridden" Weimar system found a following in the misery and despair of large sections of the German people.

In the devalued Germany of the 1920s, parties like the Nazis offered a sense of pride and belonging to many. "It was exciting," recalled Nazi Storm Trooper Wolfgang Teubert, "there was the comradeship, the being-there-for-each-other, that for a young man is something outstanding – at least it was then." Membership of the brown-shirted Storm Troopers also gave young men like Teubert a sense of importance: "We marched behind the Swastika flag, marching through the towns. Outside working hours there was nothing but the Storm Troopers." There was also the danger and

excitement of fighting with the opposition. Teubert again: "There was the danger, the threats from other people. Night after night we increasingly provided protection at hall meetings not just in our town but in many other towns to strengthen the Storm Troopers there. We had no weapons, the most we could do was defend ourselves with our fists and only work the enemy over with our fists – where it was necessary. And it was necessary more often than not!" For Teubert and his storm trooper comrades, it was the Communist Party that typically provided the opposition: "Breaking up the chairs in the halls and then fighting with the chair legs, that happened quite a lot ... Both sides did that, each as much as the other."

For many, memories of the defeat of 1918 and Germany's subsequent humiliation drew them into the Nazis. Bruno Hähnel joined the Nazis by way of the *Wandervogel*, a "folklorical" group which wanted a return to nature. Hähnel decided to join the Nazis in 1927, following a discussion in a youth hostel: "There was one [a discussion] about the subject of internationalism and among other things it was said that one had to reach the point of being able to marry a Negress. And I found that thought very uncomfortable." In addition, Hähnel felt, like many Germans, an anger at the Versailles settlement and the "November criminals" who had surrendered in 1918. Hähnel had a strong dislike of international movements like communism: "Many of us said simply, 'We are Germans first', and now there was a group who said 'Germany first'. They shouted 'Germany awake!'"

ANTI-SEMITISM

The anti-semitism of the Nazis played little part in the decision of those like Hähnel to join the party: "I still remember those statements which frequently occurred, that 50 percent of all Berlin doctors were Jews, 50 percent of Berlin lawyers, that the whole press in Berlin and in Germany was in the hands of the Jews and this had to be done away with." However, while Hähnel gave tacit support to this anti-semitism, he had little difficulty reconciling it with the realities of his own life, which included Jewish friends: "I had relatives who were Jews and we would meet at family gatherings. I had a very warm relationship with two cousins who were Jewish. It didn't stop me from agreeing with the other things which the party demanded."

Many young people rejected the Nazis, at least at first. For Alois Pfaller, the Nazis' obsession with anti-semitism drove him away from the party: "That was something very strange, this extreme anti-semitism, the Jews being held responsible for everything. I knew Jews and I had friends with whom I used to spend time and I absolutely didn't understand what difference there was supposed to be – we're all humans ... I have always stood up for justice – what is just and reasonable, that was my problem, and also fighting injustice, that was my problem, and

not somehow persecuting other races or other people." Pfaller turned his back on the Nazis and turned instead to another radical solution to Germany's malaise: the German Communist Party (*Kommunistische Partei Deutschlands – KPD*).

Below: The German communist Ernst Thälmann, a prime target for the Nazis. Put into a concentration camp in 1933 after the Reichstag fire, he was executed in 1944.

Above: Dr Josef Göbbels casts his vote in Berlin, 1933. The organizational abilities of Hitler's propaganda supremo gave the Nazi Party many votes in the elections in the 1920s.

Beginning in about 1925 and lasting until the Wall Street Crash of 1929, the German economy picked up. This had a dramatic effect on the fortunes of the Nazis, and emphasizes the importance of economic factors in Hitler's eventual success. For the first time since the war, unemployment fell below a million. These were lean years for Hitler and the Nazis. The lower middle classes, on whom Hitler depended for much of his support, shared in Germany's economic revival. Some of this economic upswing was a result of American loans. The effect was dramatic: in Germany there was a boom in artistic and intellectual life. Berlin became the entertainment capital of Europe. Hitler was sidelined, and in the elections of 1928 the Nazi Party polled 810,000 votes out of 31 million cast. This amounted to a paltry 2.6 percent of the vote. Germany no longer needed the Nazis, and in the sort of Darwinian world of struggle and survival of the fittest that the Nazis were so keen to promote they were about to be made extinct.

But then, in 1929, Wall Street "crashed", the Americans called in their loans to Germany and across the world an economic recession hit hard.

The brief flourishing of the Weimar Republic in the mid-1920s ended with another collapse of the German economy. Unemployment again began to grow, as the Nazi Bruno Hähnel recalled: "In those days our unemployed would stand in huge queues in front of the labour exchange every Friday, and they would receive five marks at the counter. This was a new and different situation – there were many who simply did not have the means to buy food." Alois Pfaller, who had joined the *KPD*, remembered: "It was a hopeless business. People walked around with spoons in their pockets because they got a meal for a mark [from charity soup kitchens]."

And it was not only the working class who suffered. Middle class families such as Jutta Rüdiger's were hit too: "My father did not become unemployed but he was told he had to agree to a lower salary." Rüdiger's chances of going to university were dashed until an uncle stepped in with an allowance. Across middle class Germany the experiences of the Rüdigers were mirrored as families cut back and made do. After the Wall Street Crash, unemployment in Germany rose to over five million. The unemployed and those in work but in much tightened circumstances now looked for a radical solution.

It was in this depressed and uncertain climate that the Nazis' fortunes improved. In September 1930 their share of the vote increased to 18.3 percent; at the same time, the *KPD* increased its share of the vote to over 13 percent. The German people were turning to extremes as Weimar democracy seemed to be failing. At the labour exchanges, "signing-on" times were the occasion for fights between rival factions. Pfaller remembered how everybody met at the dole office, "and then the discussions would start and the fights". A young woman, Gabriele Winckler, recalled how she felt uncomfortable when she crossed the road – "You felt uneasy when you were alone in the woods and so on. The unemployed lay in the ditches and played cards."

In this climate, Hitler thrived. Jutta Rüdiger heard him talk for the first time: "There was a huge crowd and you got the feeling he was aiming

Below: Hitler with the German President Paul von Hindenburg. Germany's ruling élite hoped to control Hitler and use him to smash the forces of revolution.

for electrifying tension. Today I can probably only explain it with the poverty the people had been suffering and were suffering … In that context Hitler with his statements seemed to be the bringer of salvation. He said, 'I will get you out of this misery, but you all have to join in.' And everybody understood that."

HITLER COMES TO POWER

The economic depression after 1929 gave Hitler his opportunity. And Hitler was not someone to let a chance pass. Like most great revolutionaries, Hitler thrived in difficult times, and with the masses in Germany unemployed, hungry and desperate the Nazis moved to seize power. They were helped in this by skillful propaganda campaigns, by divisions on the Left and by rich German industrialists and conservative politicians lending their support to the Nazis. In January 1933 the former Austrian down-and-out, Adolf Hitler, became chancellor of Germany. He had come to power legally, within a democratic, constitutional system. In the election of September 1930, for example, the Nazis polled 6,371,000 votes, giving them 107 Reichstag seats. In 1932 the Nazi Party polled 13,732,779 votes, giving it 230 Reichstag seats. Though another election in the November reduced this number to 196 seats, Hitler had enough seats to make him chancellor (he was sworn in by Hindenburg on 30 January 1933). He had, however, no intention of keeping the democratic system in place, and moved to destroy the legacy of the Weimar Republic and replace it with his own Third Reich.

The *KPD*, the Nazis' long-standing rivals, reacted slowly to the news of Hitler's success in 1933. One member recalled: "The Communist Party line, to which I still belonged, was that it didn't matter if Hitler came to power. That's good. He'll soon have proved himself incompetent and then it's our turn … For some extraordinary reason they didn't realize that he was going to change the law once he came to power." Many viewed this change with equanimity. Eugene Leviné, a Jew and communist, was fearful because of his political leanings rather than his Jewish parentage. He remembered how there "were quite a few Storm

Right: A Nazi rally at Nuremberg in 1934. In the centre of the picture are Hitler (middle), Heinrich Himmler (left, the head of the SS) and Victor Lutze (right, chief of the SA).

Troopers who had Jewish girlfriends and therefore a lot of Germans just thought, 'Oh well, it's not going to be so bad – they have Jewish girlfriends they can't hate us all.'" Leviné also thought that the Nazis would act with some restraint: "At one of the schools I was in there was a Nazi and he said to me, 'You really should be one of us.' I said, 'Look, I can't, I'm a Jew,' and he would say: 'We don't mean you, decent chaps like you will be perfectly all right in the new Germany.'"

VERDICT ON THE WEIMAR REPUBLIC

Though the Weimar Republic achieved some notable results, such as superior health provision and public spending on housing (over 300,000 new houses were being built by the late 1920s), it had powerful enemies within Germany. The political foundation of the republic was attacked by Germany's élite institutions and groups. Most judges, for example, handed out lenient sentences to right-wing activists brought before them, such as Hitler (see Chapter One). Universities were bastions of conservatism and élitism, and the school system itself, even during the Weimar period, used textbooks filled with nationalist and anti-democratic sentiments which glorified war. Teachers themselves tended to be authoritarian.

The military was a powerful bulwark against democracy. For example, General Kurt von Schleicher, head of the political bureau of the *Reichswehr*, backed rearmament and looked favourably on the Nazis. In addition, many military leaders believed the republic to be too submissive to the demands of the Allies.

From the first elections in 1919, no single party was able to gain a clear mandate for governing in the National Constituent Assembly. Thus the only way for the democratic process to work was to form coalition cabinets. In the end, though, the Weimar Republic, tarnished with the stigma of Versailles and hampered with massive social and economic problems, had too few supporters and too many enemies.

THE NAZI ECONOMIC MIRACLE

Above: Necessity over ideology. Women at work: female factory workers supporting the German war effort.
Below: Chancellor Adolf Hitler at the VW motor car factory in May 1938.

Under the Nazis, the German economy picked up dramatically. However, the durability of the Nazis' economic miracle is questionable for war broke out in 1939 and the economy moved to a "total war" footing. It is, therefore, unclear whether the Nazis could have sustained Germany's recovery into the 1940s. It is also unclear who led the recovery of the 1930s. Hitler neglected many areas of domestic policy, including the economy. This is explained by the Nazi decision-making process which can be termed "working towards the Führer". Most political parties have carefully thought-through economic policies that are outlined in their party manifestoes. This was not the case with the Nazis. Hitler wanted to rid Germany of unemployment and he wanted to rearm the German armed forces, but he had little idea of how exactly he would achieve these goals. Therefore, to meet his objectives Hitler delegated and left subordinates to "work towards the Führer" and achieve what they thought were Hitler's objectives. The German economic recovery of the 1930s occurred within this system.

HYBRID ECONOMY

The Nazi economy in the 1930s was a hybrid. The economy was only marginally socialist, since big business and private enterprise were left, in many ways, untroubled by government control. Yet neither was the German economy after 1933 fully capitalist either as the state controlled key areas of production. In the end, the Nazis produced an

Right: The imagery of industry in the Third Reich was one of power and inexorable forward movement, such as this picture of stone drilling.

economy that was neither socialist nor capitalist. It was, in essence, an economy geared for war but operating in peacetime.

Hitler had never seriously considered an economic future for Germany through increased productivity and peaceful trade with other countries. Hitler's objective seems to have been *Lebensraum* (or "living space") in eastern Europe, to be achieved by military conquest. The German economy, therefore, needed to be tailored for this end, even if actual state control of day-to-day production was minimal. Hitler saw the economy as a means of achieving a political end, and was not overly concerned about what the economy was like. As a consequence, Hitler tolerated different types of economic structures in Germany as long as they produced for him the weapons to wage war. With this in mind, the Nazis were willing to encourage big business while simultaneously eliminating inefficient small businesses and subsidizing some industries. These policies appeared contradictory, but the Nazis were willing to be ideologically inconsistent if it produced increased output for a possible war.

UNEMPLOYMENT AND HJALMAR SCHACHT

When Hitler came to power in 1933, the most pressing economic problem was high unemployment. Those on the socialist side of the Nazi Party pushed for nationalization and state control. Hitler, however, had no intention of dismantling large industrial enterprises that would be useful for his war economy. To reassure big business, Hitler brought into his government a former president of the Reichsbank and a brilliant economist, Hjalmar Schacht, to run the economy. Nazi economic theory was slender and therefore Hitler turned to Schacht, who had resigned in 1930 in

protest at reparation repayments and turned to the Nazis. "I desire a great and strong Germany and to achieve it I would enter into an alliance with the Devil," Schacht exclaimed.

After 1933, Schacht followed a policy of reflation financed on credit. Alongside this reflation, he implemented a compulsory public works programme for the unemployed. Well over a billion marks went on public works schemes: the *Autobahnen* motorway system, grants to private companies for building and renovation, and tax concessions to industry and agriculture for expansion. As the historian A.J.P. Taylor has argued, this policy was similar in many ways to President F.D. Roosevelt's "New Deal" in America that tackled America's Great Depression. The effect of these policies in Germany was dramatic and immediate. The jobless were cleared off the streets and unemployment began to fall. With some "massaging", unemployment fell from a high of six million in January 1932 to 2.4 million by the summer of 1934. The unemployed were used in a variety of schemes, but none was such an obvious symbol of Germany's renewed strength as the building of the *Autobahnen*. Although plans had been laid by the Weimar Republic for a motorway system, Hitler was quick to see the propaganda value of the building plan. Under the organizational talents of Hitler's Minister of Armaments, Fritz Todt,

3000km (1860 miles) of motorway black-top were laid down between 1933 and 1938. With their usual propaganda skill, the Nazis capitalized on the building programme. Official pictures showed thousands of eager workers building the "Führer's roads". This had the added impact of suggesting a united community in which class and privilege had been sacrificed for the greater good. The perception of the German people was that life was safe again. As one "ordinary" German exclaimed: "My wife and all my daughters can walk through the park in darkness and not be molested."

For Germans who lived through this economic recovery the memories were vivid. Erna Kranz was a teenager at the time and remembered the Nazi

years as "a glimmer of hope … not just for the unemployed but for everybody because we all knew that we were downtrodden … I can only speak for myself … I thought it was a good time. I liked it. We weren't living in affluence like today but there was order and discipline." Such public works schemes stimulated the economy, they provided jobs and, more specifically, helped revitalize the German motor industry. The new highways gave a sense of equal opportunity among a workforce with reinvigorated morale. This buoyant mood was reinforced by a government announcement in 1938 that the new motorways were open for everybody's use. Simultaneously, a new car, the *Volkswagen* ("People's Car") came off the production line. Costing the modest sum of 990 Reichsmarks, and designed by Ferdinand Porsche, the new car was aimed at the popular market. It was priced so as to be within the range

Below: Reichsbank President Dr Hjalmar Schacht (front row, second from right) attending a Nazi meeting. After World War II he became an adviser to Colonel Nasser of Egypt.

Above: The Nazis built up Germany's transport network during the 1930s. Here, Rudolf Hess opens a new stretch of canal under the glare of the cameras.

of the ordinary German family (see Chapter Six). This ideal of the *Volkswagen* was, however, quite different from the reality: although 100,000 *Volkswagen* were planned for 1940, the factory that produced them had by then switched to war production.

German business in general was happy to go along with this new regime. The Nazis smashed organized labour, left-wing revolution and restored "order". In return, German big business was expected to help finance the Nazis. This they did following a meeting between the top Nazis and leaders of big business in February 1933. Hitler began it with a long speech: "Private enterprise cannot be maintained in the age of democracy; it is conceivable only if the people have a sound idea of authority and personality … All the worldly goods we possess we owe to the struggle of the chosen … We must not forget that all the benefits of culture must be introduced more or less with an

iron fist." Hitler promised the assembled businessmen that he would "eliminate" Marxism and would rearm the German armed forces. This latter promise appealed to the industrialists from arms-based industries, such as Krupp, United Steel and I.G. Farben, promising as it did big contracts. Hitler promised an end to democracy. This promise was met with an enthusiastic response from the assembled industrialists: like Hitler they had no need for elections, democracy and disarmament. Krupp, the munitions king, jumped up and expressed his "gratitude" to Hitler "for having given us such a clear picture". Schacht, Hitler's economist, then passed the hat. "I collected three million marks," he later recalled when on trial at Nuremberg after World War II.

Above: Dr Fritz Todt, Reich Minister for Armaments and Munitions. Killed in an air crash in 1942, he was replaced by Albert Speer, who later wrote *Inside the Third Reich*.

Karl von Clausewitz famously said that "war is a continuation of policy but by another means". For Hitler the classic dictum of Clausewitz is best turned on its head – "policy is a continuation of war by other means". With war as a necessary, indeed positive, means of gaining foreign policy goals and restoring German prestige, Hitler needed to rearm. Initially much of the rearmament was just rhetoric from Hitler, but after 1936 arms manufacturing accelerated and became a central part of government policy. To achieve his aim of rearmament and expansion, Hitler needed a powerful economy.

Schacht's deficit spending would not of itself have solved the problem of unemployment, but alongside a policy of massive rearmament, steady progress towards full employment was achieved.

Only three days after assuming office, Hitler promised Germany's military chiefs that he would increase the armed forces and smash the restrictive provisions of the Treaty of Versailles. Hitler's aim seems to have been to conquer eastern Europe as part of a *Drang nach Osten* into the Soviet Union. As part of this military expansion, Hitler wanted Germany to have an autarkic economy (that is, one that was self-sufficient in basic raw materials). This was difficult as Germany lacked crucial reserves such as rubber, copper, base metals and oil. To overcome this, Hitler ordered Wilhelm Keppler, as special adviser on economic matters, to look into the possibility of developing substitute synthetic (or *ersatz*) goods to replace those that Germany lacked. Keppler's organization promptly began to look into the development of synthetic rubber, oil, fats and metals. This achieved some success: oil, man-made from brown coal, and developed by Braunkohle Benzin A.G., was essential for Germany's war effort during the war. This drive for self-sufficiency helped stimulate areas of German industry and research.

HERMANN GÖRING

In 1936, Hitler prepared a secret memorandum on economic strategy and rearmament. This memorandum concluded that Germany needed to be ready for war within four years. Annoyed by the caution of Schacht, Hitler appointed Hermann Göring as director of a new four-year plan and gave him great powers to subordinate the German economy to the need to prepare for war. Under Göring's leadership, German industry was cajoled into expanding into areas such as synthetic production, vital for any war. This culminated in the establishment of the *Hermann Göring Werke* – industrial plants set up to exploit low-grade iron ores in central Germany (75 percent was owned by the government, while the private sector was forced to buy the remaining shares).

Göring's policies were popular with ordinary Germans but almost bankrupted the country. He had little understanding of economics, but he threw himself into his task for he realized that he had an opportunity to become economic dictator of Germany. Imports were curtailed and wage and

Above: Robert Ley, National Socialist leader of the German Labour Front. He committed suicide in October 1945.
Right: Walther Funk, the Nazi Minister for Economics and Schacht's successor as President of the Reichsbank.

price controls were instituted. Public expenditure between 1933 and 1939 reached 101.5 billion marks, of which 60 percent was spent on rearmament. During the same period, government revenues accounted for only 62 billion marks.

Schacht came up with a system to cover the remaining deficit. These were state credits called *Mefo-weschel* ("*Mefo* exchange"), named after a fake institution called *Mettallurgische Forschungs GmbH* (Metallurgical Research Ltd.). "*Mefo* Bills" were a form of deficit financing that could be kept secret and permitted the Nazis to pay for rearmament on credit. Hitler knew little about the mechanics of this, but he was delighted with the results. The German Army was equally delighted to be allowed to expand and absorb new equipment that the

Göring – THE PLAYBOY NAZI

1 A portrait of Göring in his younger, thinner days as a war hero sporting his many medals won as a fighter ace during World War I.
2 A fatter Göring getting married to Emmy Sonnemann, his second wife, in 1935. The wedding was one of the greatest social events of the Third Reich, combining as it did Christian and Nazi-pagan ritual.
3 Göring pictured in January 1935 outside his palace in Berlin. Göring developed a great desire for the arts and amassed a huge collection of some of the most expensive works of art. Many of these were stolen from European states during the Nazi occupation.

5

6

4 Göring passing a guard of honour at the beginning of the hunting season. He was given the title of Reich Master Hunter, an honour he was most pleased to receive.

5 Göring gives an after-dinner speech. Göring was a *bon viveur* and became increasingly corpulent over the years. His health was not helped by a drug addiction developed after a period of morphine treatment in the 1920s.

6 November 1937, the era of appeasement. A well-wrapped Göring accompanied by the British Foreign Secretary, Lord Halifax.

7 Göring handing out pictures of his master, Hitler, at a dinner party (he was considered attractive by many German women).

8 Göring indulging one of his hobbies, hunting, in a forest near Hanover in 1934. His rise to power within the armed forces, economy and politics was meteoric: Commander-in-Chief of the Luftwaffe in 1935, Commissioner Plenipotentiary for the Four-Year Plan in 1936, Minister of the Economy in 1937, created a field marshal in 1938, Chairman of the Reich Council for National Defence and named as Hitler's successor in 1939. Finally, in 1940, Hitler gave him the unprecedented rank of *Reichsmarschall*.

8

7

Treaty of Versailles had forbidden. Four major defence contractors underwrote the system with one billion marks, and this allowed government contractors to receive payment in *Mefo* notes that would be discounted by the Reichsbank.

After 1936 Schacht and Göring disagreed on economic policy. Schacht, while supporting rearmament, felt that Germany's economy could not support both a "guns" and "butter" policy. Schacht felt that imposing a permanent wartime economy on Germany was crippling the country. For Schacht, German resources were not infinite and they could not provide both rearmament and higher living standards for ordinary Germans. Göring, on the other hand, felt that an autarkic

(self-sufficient) policy was possible that would allow a self-sufficient Germany to create a rearmed and rich economy. In November 1937 Schacht resigned as Minister of Economics (although he was kept on as a Minister-without-Portfolio) and his place was taken by Walther Funk. Funk, a man without any strong ideas, tied his economic ministry closely to Göring's office and Schacht's restraining influence disappeared. Funk was also not averse to lining his own pockets. After the war he was implicated in plundering the wealth of conquered territories and hoarding gold, jewellery and money from millions of murdered Jews. He was tried as one of the 22 major war criminals at Nuremberg, where an interrogator described him as a "tubby homosexual suffering from diabetes and afflicted at the moment with bladder pain". He received a life sentence, though was released after 20 years due to ill health.

Below: Hitler inspecting the latest German automobile technology. The Nazis' willingness to crush trade unionism endeared them to German industrialists.

Above: German shipping in the port of Hamburg. While German international trade picked up in the 1930s, Nazi economic policies stressed self-sufficiency and autarky.

The results of the economic policies of the 1930s were, in the short term, largely successful. By 1936 it was possible for a neutral observer in Amsterdam to publish a book entitled *The German Economic Miracle*. By 1939 Hitler had massively rearmed and had, arguably, the best armed forces in Europe. Simultaneously, he kept consumer satisfaction high, unemployment low, inflation low and wages stable. Whether this boom would have lasted is debatable. It has been argued (by T.W. Mason) that Germany was on the brink of an economic crisis in 1939, and only escaped it through war.

How did these economic changes affect the German population? The Nazis' rearmament policies were a big boost for German business and to a lesser extent for the German bourgeoisie. Big business not only received lucrative arms contracts but was not held back by any trade union agitation because the Nazis had crushed organized labour organizations. On the other hand, benefits for German business were accompanied by increased government intrusion into business affairs. Nazi central authorities now told business what it should produce and in what quantities. Profits, wage levels and future plant construction were all set centrally. While big business put up with these intrusions as the economy boomed, the benefits for smaller businesses were less obvious. Those small firms that supplied defence contractors profited, but those small firms not producing for the arms industry did less well from the Nazis' economic policies of the 1930s. However, many businesses benefited from the "Aryanization" programme that confiscated Jewish businesses and homes. Skilled craftsmen also gained from the boom in armaments building. Their skills were much in demand and the Nazis protected the position of the independent artisan. German artisans were also quick to organize themselves into a Nazi-sponsored craft estate (a *stand*) made up of guilds

45

representing the various skilled trades. In November 1933, the Nazis passed a tradecrafts bill that said that artisans could only operate if their employer belonged to the appropriate guild, possessed a certificate of qualification and was politically reliable. In return for protected employment, skilled workers were drawn tightly into the Nazi state machine. The new guild structure resembled on one level a medieval guild system; however, the Nazis subjected the guilds to tight political control as Nazi functionaries supervised the system at all levels.

THE *DAF*

German industrial workers did consistently well economically from Nazism. Workers lost their right to strike and the ability to organize into unions, but unemployment fell and many Germans felt that the loss of union protection was worthwhile when the rise in employment was taken into account. Skilled labour was also in high demand, especially in the defence industries. The workers also benefited from new social programmes such as *Kraft durch Freude* (*KdF* – "Strength through Joy", see Chapter Six). These programmes were headed by Robert Ley, who led the *Deutsche Arbeitsfront* (*DAF* or German Labour Front). Ley proclaimed: "Workers, your institutions are sacred and unassailable to us National Socialists. I myself am a poor son of peasants and have known poverty. I swear to you that we shall not only preserve everything you have, we shall extend the rights of the worker in order that he might enter the new National Socialist state as an equal and respected member of the nation." Ley, an alcoholic megalomaniac, was nicknamed the "Reich drunkard". Hitler trusted him to the end, however, giving him the command of the non-existent *Freikorps Adolf Hitler* in April 1945.

Ley's *DAF* was a monolithic labour front, established in May 1933 by the Nazis, that took the place of trade unions. The aim, as Ley often said, was the end of class struggle. All workers, whether "white collar" or "blue collar", were included in

Left: Newly built motorways snake through the mountains. Building the *Autobahns* in Germany helped ease the chronic unemployment of the early 1930s.

the *DAF*. Instead of strikes, the new system called for workers to pull together for the common good. The *DAF* had over 20 million members, a huge budget and extensive property. Along with the *KdF*, the *DAF* provided a security net for workers. It distributed financial assistance, organized workers' education classes and stabilized wages. Along with leisure organizations like the *KdF*, the *DAF* provided a holistic service for the country's workers. In 1938, some 180,000 Germans went on cruises, with a further 10 million participating in other *KdF* activities. A typical *KdF* one-week holiday, including travel expenses, meals, accommodation and guides, would cost 43 marks for a holiday to Mosel or 39 marks for a trip to Upper Bavaria. For the sum of 155 marks, German workers could take a two-week holiday to Italy. These affordable holidays did much to sell Nazi economic policies. There was even a "Beauty of Labour" section of the *DAF* organized to make the Nazis' policies on labour more attractive; it was designed as a welfare unit to plan holiday trips, festivals, factory celebrations, folk dancing and political education. It worked closely with the *KdF*. The *DAF* was, in the end, an attempt to win labour over to the Nazi cause.

WORKERS' INDEPENDENCE

The price for full employment, welfare provision and affordable holidays was that the Nazis took away any workers' independence. Workers could no longer rely on their trade union but looked instead to Trustees of Labour to protect their interests. The Nazis introduced new arrangements in which employer and employee worked for the common good on the basis of mutually acceptable goals. This was a feudal-style system with Councils of Trust and Labour Courts of Honour to settle disputes. But these courts were run by pliant Nazis who typically found in favour of the employer.

The Nazis also brought in controls to restrict the choice of jobs for workers, and the free movement of workers was curtailed. All workers needed a "work book" (*Arbeitsbuch*) to secure employment. Without this book, which contained details of qualifications and employment history, no

Above: German agricultural workers harvesting in the late 1930s. Once war broke out in 1939, military manpower needs left women and forced labour to tend the land.

German worker could secure gainful employment. The Nazis regimented German workers in the same way that they ordered other areas of German society. Young German men between the ages of 18 and 25 were forced to complete six months' labour service. This labour service was dreaded by many young German males, especially those from the upper classes who had to spend six months with other young Germans they considered to be their social inferiors (until 1939, women had the option of volunteering for labour service).

What of agriculture under the Nazis' economic boom of the 1930s? When the Nazis took charge in 1933, German agriculture was in a state of crisis. To reverse this, the Nazis laid out three goals:

firstly, self-sufficiency in agriculture through a policy of protectionism; secondly, revitalization of agriculture through the creation of a new peasant order; finally, a new organization to represent farmers' needs. The Nazis replaced the free market with state control. Agricultural markets and prices were regulated by government; land ownership was brought under a Reich Entail Farm Law that aimed to protect farmers in debt from bankruptcy and loss of their farms. In addition, the Nazis regulated inheritance in favour of one heir and they forbade the sale of entailed farms. The government also encouraged new farms with a land-planning programme.

The Nazis' plans for agriculture were supervised by Richard Walter Darré. In April 1933 Hitler appointed Darré *Reichsbauernführer* (Reich Agricultural Leader) and *Reichsernährungsminister* (Reich Food Minister). He set up the Reich Food

Estate in 1933. A former member of the Artamans – a group of young Germans who believed in the back-to-the-soil movement and the creation of a "racially pure" Teutonic peasant class – great power corrupted him. Enriching himself on a grand scale, he was dismissed in 1942 for being involved in large-scale black market food deals.

Below Darré, peasant leaders filled positions at the state, district and local levels. The results of Darré's policies were not entirely satisfactory. The protectionism and self-sufficiency policies were not ideal and shortages developed in many areas of German agriculture. Some smaller farmers benefited from the new policies, but the large landed estates were not redistributed among smaller farmers. This meant that there was little land available for new farmers. Therefore, the drift of

Below: Richard Walter Darré (left), Nazi agricultural and food leader. *SS* chief of the race and resettlement bureau, he was also a prolific author on race, Marxism and agriculture.

labour from the countryside to the cities continued throughout the 1930s. By 1939, German agriculture had lost around 1.4 million workers to the industries in the cities. This caused a labour shortage in agriculture that was met by impressing German youth into working in the countryside in the summer months. German agriculture under the Nazis was not a great success story.

The Nazis' economic recovery of the 1930s brought down unemployment. Jobs, wage stability, restored prestige and *KdF* welfare policies made the new regime appealing to German workers. Many Germans regarded the 1930s as a golden age. However, these benefits were short-lived as Hitler was gearing the economy for a future conflict to satisfy his policy aims. This conflict, when it began in 1939, would be Germany's ruin and would destroy the German economy. With hindsight, it is clear that the short-term gains of the 1930s were not worth the war that engulfed Germany in the 1940s.

THE CONTROL OF YOUTH

From the beginning the Nazis were determined to subvert German youth to their own aims. They made great efforts to incorporate individuals into the Hitler Youth and the so-called *Volksgemeinschaft* ("racial community'). In general, the younger section of the population was usually receptive to the benefits offered by a policy of rearmament, as well as to the ideas of the *Führerstaat* ("leadership state") with its promise to end the fighting of the 1920s and to restore German "greatness".

Young people who became teenagers after 1936 had no memories of the pre-Hitler days and went through a schooling process steeped in National Socialism. For this cohort of teenagers there seemed to be no alternative. The other group of teenagers who came to adolescence during World War II experienced the most extreme and brutal forms of National Socialism for youth; it included conscription into defence units and, for some, action with the 12th *SS HitlerJugend* (Hitler Youth) Division. This élite *Waffen-SS* division fought fanatically and was all but wiped out in the fighting in Normandy in 1944.

Above left: The Nazi ideal: a German blond, blue-eyed "Aryan" girl sporting a Swastika and pigtails.
Left: A Hitler Youth rally. The Nazis wanted to turn children into future soldiers and Nazi technocrats.

It was through the Hitler Youth that young people learned about Nazism. It was an alternative centre of authority to home and school. The Hitler Youth became more organized as the 1930s unfolded and with its bureaucracy came increased membership. However, for many schoolchildren life under Nazism contained many contradictions. The following extract shows how children could ignore yet not ignore the new system: "No one in our class ever read *Mein Kampf*. I myself only took quotations from the book. On the whole we didn't know about Nazi ideology. Even anti-semitism was brought in rather marginally at school – for example via Richard Wagner's essay *The Jews in Music* – and outside school the display copies of *Der Stürmer* made the idea questionable, if anything ... Nevertheless, we were politically pro-

Above: Young girls learn the Nazi salute at a celebration in Coburg. From an early age, German children were taught to revere Hitler and greet each other with "Heil Hitler".

grammed: to obey orders, to cultivate the soldierly 'virtue' of standing to attention and saying 'Yes, Sir', and to stop thinking when the magic word 'Fatherland' was uttered and Germany's honour and greatness were mentioned." As we will see, while many young people duly joined organizations such as the Hitler Youth, many others opposed the control of their lives by the Nazis.

By the end of 1933 all other youth organizations had been either banned or subsumed into the Hitler Youth. The only exception to this were Catholic groups that had some protection under the Concordat agreed between the Nazis and the

Vatican. The groups that were incorporated into the Hitler Youth included the non-political *bündisch* ("youth") organization and the Protestant youth groups. Therefore, by early 1934 the Hitler Youth contained 47 percent of all German boys aged between 10 and 14 (in the *Deutsches Jungvolk* – German Young People) and 38 percent of all boys aged between 14 and 18 (in the Hitler Youth proper). The figures for girls were not as high, but still impressive: 15 percent of girls aged between 10 and 14 had joined the *Jugendmädelbund* (Young Girls' League) while eight percent of the 14–18 age group were in the *Bund Deutscher Mädel* (League of German Girls – *BdM*).

Hitler believed that the survival of the Third Reich depended on the education of its youth. He

proclaimed: "A violently active, dominating, brutal youth – that is what I am after. Youth must be indifferent to pain ... I will have no intellectual training. Knowledge is ruin to my young men." With this in mind, the Hitler Youth for both boys and girls was brought together under the central direction of the Reich Youth Leader, Baldur von Schirach (during the war he was Gauleiter of Vienna, and was sentenced to 20 years' imprisonment at the Nuremberg Trials for his administration of foreign workers and his treatment of Jews in Vienna). At the September 1935 Nuremberg rally, 54,000 Hitler Youth members paraded before Hitler. The Führer addressed them, saying he required a new generation "swift as the greyhound, tough as leather, and hard as Krupp steel".

The education of the Hitler Youth was carefully regulated. By 15 March during the year that a German boy would become 10, he would have to register with the Reich Youth Headquarters. After

Below: Hitler meets German boys. The Führer realised the importance of influencing the children of Germany to turn them into good Nazis.

a thorough investigation of the youth's background for racial purity, he was admitted to the *Jungvolk*. The celebration admitting the new entrants took place on 20 April, Hitler's birthday. In the *Jungvolk*, the boy was a *pimpf* and was required to undergo an initiation test where he recited Nazi dogma, all the verses of the "Horst Wessel Song" (a Nazi anthem in honour of an *SA* man killed in a street fight with communists), ran 60 metres (180ft) in 12 seconds and completed a one-and-a-half day cross-country hike. As a *pimpf*, he was expected to learn semaphore, to lay telephone wires and to participate in small arms drill. If successful at his tests as a *pimpf*, at 14 the boy entered the Hitler Youth proper and at 18, as a young adult, Hitler Youth members entered the *NSDAP*. At 19 there was entry to the State Labour Service before joining the armed forces. The Hitler Youth, therefore, provided a means of

Above: Hitler takes the raised-arm salute in 1938. Note the girls are in the background – the Nazi view was that a girl's place was in the home nurturing children.

indoctrinating and forming young boys for Nazism and military service.

To increase the recruitment figures for the Hitler Youth, the Nazi authorities passed the Hitler Youth Law of 1 December 1936 that aimed for the incorporation of all German youth into the Hitler Youth, and this was backed up with growing "pressure" on those outside the Nazi youth organizations to join "voluntarily". In 1939, two executive orders ancillary to the 1936 Law made "youth service" compulsory. During World War II, the Hitler Youth collected blankets and clothes for the troops. The Nazis monopolized every free hour and parents dared not object lest they were seen to be troublemakers. Youngsters, living more

Above: Excited girls, members of the *Bund Deutscher Mädel*, attending a Nazi rally in Potsdam in 1932, a year before Hitler became German leader.

and more with their comrades, were gradually being weaned away from their families.

The *BdM* for girls was organized along similar lines to the Hitler Youth for boys. It was also under the overall control of the Reich Youth Leader and took in girls at the age of 10 into the *Jugendmädelbund*. The girls' groups were organized along military lines, with the smallest group being the *Mädelschaft*, two or four of which made up a *Mädelschar*. Two to four *Mädelscharen* constituted a *Gruppe*, and five *Gruppen* made up a *Ring*. Five to six *Ring* then formed an *Untergau*, of which there were 684. Finally came the *Obergau*. All girls in the *BdM* were constantly reminded that the whole task of schooling was to prepare them to be "carriers of the National Socialist *Weltanschaung* [worldview]". As *BdM* maidens they were to devote themselves to comradeship, service and physical fitness so as to become good German mothers. As Hitler outlined in *Mein Kampf*: "The one absolute aim of female education must be with a view to the future mother." On military style parades, they wore a uniform of navy blue skirts, white blouses, brown jackets and twin pigtails. When they became 17, *BdM* members became eligible for the *Glaube und Schönheit* (Faith and Beauty) organization where they were trained in domestic science and prepared for marriage. The Faith and Beauty organization was tailored to give spiritual and physical grace to young women between the ages of 17 and 21. These women were to become the prize exhibits of the Nazi conception of womanhood. By 1936, more than two million girls were enrolled in the *BdM*.

In the countryside and small towns of Germany, the Hitler Youth gave young people access, for the first time, to leisure activities and travel. Holiday trips widened the horizons of country children who would not normally have travelled; it gave them contact with young people from other regions of Germany. As the Nazi hold on Germany increased after 1933, these emancipatory parts to the youth movements began to fade. The Hitler Youth became another large-scale bureaucracy. The ageing of the first youth leaders and the purging of those tainted with the Weimar Republic made the movement less attractive to young people. It became a more disciplined and politicized youth movement. The campaign to bring all young people into the Hitler Youth also sucked into the organization young people who had previously opposed the whole idea by not joining. These new recruits led to an increased surveillance of youth. Everyday pleasures such as meeting friends became difficult, and in some instances criminal offences. Hitler Youth patrols, whose members were scarcely older than the youths they were policing, monitored the activities of all young people. With war approaching, the Hitler Youth also focused more on drill and less on the leisure and sports activities that had attracted youngsters originally.

THE 12TH SS *HITLERJUGEND* DIVISION

The ultimate expression of the martial virtues instilled by the Hitler Youth came with service in the 12th *SS Hitlerjugend* (Hitler Youth) Division. The division was originally formed as a panzergrenadier unit, changing to a full panzer division in time to fight in Normandy in June 1944. It was a peculiar formation, comprising members of the Hitler Youth trained by a cadre of battle-hardened NCOs and officers from the 1st *SS Leibstandarte* Division (originally Hitler's bodyguard). This gave the unit both ideological zeal and excellent training, and made them formidable and ruthless opponents in combat.

The training provided by the NCOs and officers of the *Leibstandarte* was realistic and prepared the *Hitlerjugend* for battle. The method was unconventional, but gave it the edge over its opponents in Normandy. The drill instructors from the *Leibstandarte*, veterans of the Eastern Front, eschewed drill and formal parades in favour of realistic battle training: every lesson and exercise

had a purpose and had to be conducted as if the squad were actually in battle. This was standard training for all Waffen-SS soldiers, but it was taken to an extreme with the *Hitlerjugend*. Thus, when the young panzergrenadiers went into battle in 1944 they were already accustomed to the noises and strains of battle. They had already been fired upon with live rounds on the training ground; indeed, a proportion of training deaths was considered "normal" and necessary to make the soldiers battle effective. The military historian Max Hastings recalled how one of the signals officers in the *Hitlerjugend* felt they had received a proper training in the Hitler Youth; they "had a sense of order and discipline ... and knew how to sing!" The youth of the men or boys of the division was striking: they were given a chocolate ration in lieu

Below: Baldur von Schirach, Reich Youth Leader. He flattered Hitler by writing him verse in the 1920s. In 1933, aged 26, he was appointed the leader of Germany's youth.

As hard as Krupp Steel – THE HITLER YOUTH

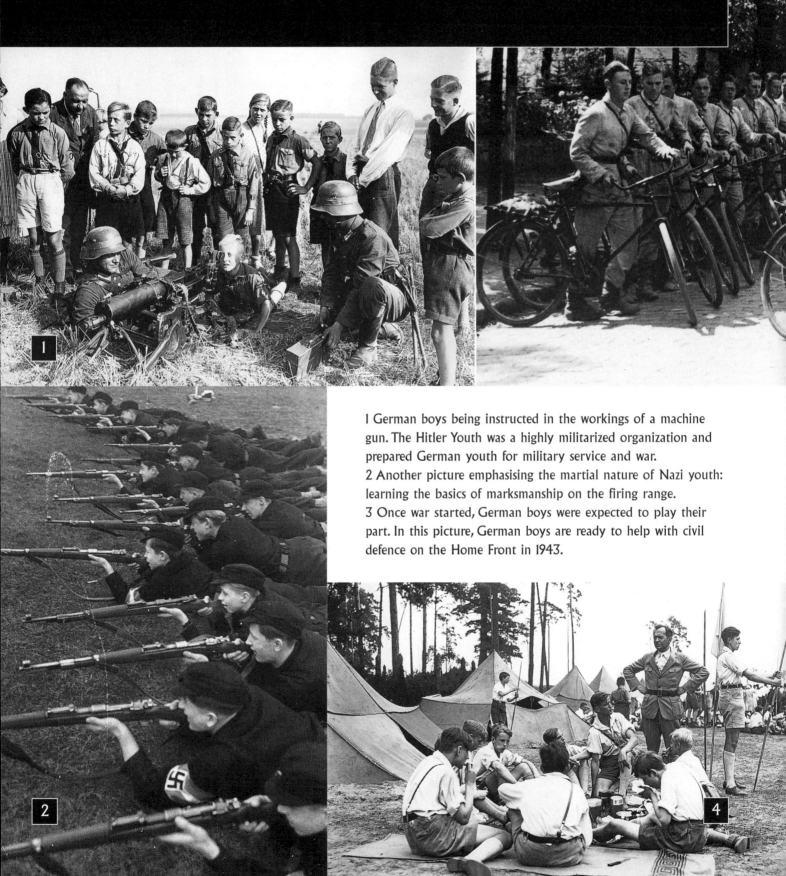

1 German boys being instructed in the workings of a machine gun. The Hitler Youth was a highly militarized organization and prepared German youth for military service and war.

2 Another picture emphasising the martial nature of Nazi youth: learning the basics of marksmanship on the firing range.

3 Once war started, German boys were expected to play their part. In this picture, German boys are ready to help with civil defence on the Home Front in 1943.

4 Under the watchful eye of their instructor (wearing the Iron Cross), these Hitler Youth enjoy a meal outdoors.
5 Basic military skills such as map reading were taught to the Hitler Youth to prepare them for service with the army.
6 The Hitler Youth at war: the 12th SS Hitler Youth Division going into action, 1944.
7 Everything about the Hitler Youth stressed the martial and physical. Here, German boys practise their marching.

Above: Hitler Youth playing at Hitler's residence high up in the mountains at Berchtesgaden in the Bavarian Alps before the outbreak of World War II.

of the more usual cigarette ration for everyone else. It was these ideologically driven, determined and well-trained panzergrenadiers who went with their tanks to the Normandy countryside around the town of Caen in 1944 to face the British and Canadians in the days after D-Day.

What happened to traditional education during the rise of the Hitler Youth? After all, Germany had long provided a model for good, modern education. During the 12 years of the Third Reich, schooling for German children became much less academic. Hitler, convinced that whoever has the children has the future, had definite ideas about education (perhaps influenced by his own academic failure: see Chapter One): "My teaching will

be hard. Weakness will be knocked out of them … There must be no weakness or tenderness in it. I want to see once more in its eyes the gleam of pride and independence of the beast of prey. I will have no intellectual training. Knowledge is ruin to my young men. I would have them learn only what takes their fancy. But one thing they must learn – self-command. They shall learn to overcome their fear of death under the severest tests. This is the heroic stage of youth. Out of it will come the creative man, the god-man!"

For the Nazis, education was about indoctrination and physical development. Education was there to teach children the importance of race and to prepare them for war. Hitler's hostility to edu-

Right: Nazi girls camping out and segregated according to age. As with the boys, the Nazi youth movement for girls was hierarchical and highly militarized.

cation permeated through the upper echelons of the Nazi hierarchy. Josef Göbbels, Minister for Public Enlightenment and Education, proclaimed: "Youth belongs to us, and we will yield them to no one." Once in power, the Nazis set about a Nazification of education from the nursery to the university. Under its regime, the first book a German child ever saw at school was the *Primer*. On the cover was a caricature of a Jew, with the words: "Trust no fox on the green heath! Trust no Jew on his oath!" Inside the *Primer*, the young child saw pictures of martial life and an accompanying text:

"He who wants to be a soldier,
That one must have a weapon,
Which he must load with powder,
And with a good hard bullet.
Little fellow, if you want to be a recruit,
Take good care of this little song."

German schools now emphasized sport and taught history, biology and Germanics. The biology and history taught were twisted to promote the party's racial and nationalist perspective. Students learned about the "Beer Hall Putsch" of 1923, of the evils of communism and the decadence of the Weimar Republic. Even mathematics was given a new spin. Maths tests involved sums and equations around artillery trajectories and fighter-to-bomber ratios. A typical question from a lower-grade test ran: "An airplane flies at a rate of 240 kilometres per hour [150mph] to a place at a distance of 210 kilometres [130 miles] in order to drop bombs. When may it be expected to return if the dropping of bombs takes 7.5 minutes?"

ADOLF HITLER SCHOOLS

Hitler also tried to move education into the Hitler Youth so that youths would gain a full Nazi education uncorrupted by any liberal teachers. Hitler also established "party" schools for the training of a future Nazi élite. First were the Adolf Hitler Schools, where young cadets were trained in physical exercise, racialism and loyalty to Hitler; secondly, there were the National Political Training Institutes to give a type of education formerly given in Prussian military academies, with the emphasis on soldierly virtues; finally, there came the Order Castles dedicated to the training of the highest echelons of the Nazi élite with a mix of physical activities and Nazi indoctrination. The aim of all these changes to education was to indoctrinate a whole generation of German youth and to discredit and destroy a fine, albeit inherently conservative, education system once renowned the world over.

OPPOSITION TO THE HITLER YOUTH

Faced with such complete control of their lives, many young people rebelled. By the end of the 1930s, many were turning away from the Hitler Youth and finding a more unconventional lifestyle in independent gangs. As the Hitler Youth patrols and *Gestapo* stepped up the pressure, these youth gangs defended their interests as best they could. By 1942, the Reich Youth Leadership was forced to admit: "The formation of cliques, i.e. groupings of young people outside the Hitler Youth, has been on the increase before and, particularly, during the war to such a degree that one must speak of a serious risk of the political, moral and criminal subversion of youth." It was also the case that by 1942 the Nazis no longer had the excuse of youth being corrupted by Weimar or communist influence, as these youth had been brought up on uncorrupted National Socialism.

Two groups in particular stand out in their rejection of the Hitler Youth: the "Edelweiss Pirates" (*Edelweisspiraten*) and the "Swing Youth" (*Swing-Jugend*). The "Edelweiss Pirates" first appeared at the end of the 1930s in western Germany. Their "uniform" was a badge of edelweiss flowers with a checked shirt, dark short trousers and white socks, and soon a variety of groups called themselves "Edelweiss Pirates": the "Roving Dudes" from Essen, "Kittlebach Pirates" from Oberhausen and the "Navajos" from Cologne. On weekend trips to the countryside, these groups would confront and fight Hitler Youth patrols. Alarmed by these "pirates", the Hitler Youth and *Gestapo* branded them "wild" *bündisch* organizations. The "Edelweiss Pirates" were aged 14 to 18 and tried to make the most of their lives outside of the Hitler Youth. With conscription into the National Labour Service at 18 and then the armed forces, the "Edelweiss Pirates" tended to have younger members. With the outbreak of war in 1939, the increased militarization of the Hitler Youth made these alternative groups even more attractive. The drill instructors in the Hitler Youth were scarcely older than the boys they were training, and so membership of the Hitler Youth could be particularly irksome.

In 1941 one adult tasked with training youngsters noted: "Every child knows who the 'Kittelbach Pirates' are. They are everywhere; there are more of them than there are Hitler Youth. And they all know each other, they stick close together ... They beat up the patrols, because there are so many of them. They don't

agree with anything. They don't go to work either." These gangs were territorial and consisted of a few dozen boys and girls. The fact that girls were involved at all distinguishes these groups from the strictly segregated Hitler Youth girls' groups. It was in these "pirate groups" that many German adolescents had their first sexual experience, because the Hitler Youth had an almost obsessive fixation on sexual repression.

Weekend trips to the country for these "pirates" was a way of avoiding the control of a totalitarian state. Once away from the built-up urban areas, these young people could escape the

Below: Indoctrinated *BdM* girls give the Nazi salute in a rally in Berlin. It was the aim to take adolescents out of their social class so they could be emersed in Nazism.

all-pervasive denunciations, spying and punishments of the National Socialist authorities. Some of these youngsters went on long hikes that took them across Germany. This was quite an accomplishment, especially once Germany was at war and the population was tightly controlled. These trips to the country provided the opportunity to sing proscribed songs and adapt existing Nazi songs with new words to give a subversive feel.

Once war had taken hold, though, the activities of these groups were suppressed with renewed vigour as rival factions clashed. In July 1943 the Düsseldorf-Grafenburg branch of the Nazi Party reported to the *Gestapo*: "Re: 'Edelweiss Pirates'. The said youths are throwing their weight around

again. I have been told that gatherings of young people have become more conspicuous than ever [in a local park], especially since the last air raid on Düsseldorf. These adolescents, aged between 12 and 17, hang around into the late evening with musical instruments and young females. Since this riff-raff is in large parts outside the Hitler Youth and adopts a hostile attitude towards the organization, they represent a danger to other young people. It has recently been established that members of the armed forces are to be found among these young people and they, owing to their membership in the *Wehrmacht*, exhibit particularly arrogant behaviour. There is a suspicion that it is these youths who have covered the walls of the pedestrian subway on the Altenbergstrasse with the slogans 'Down with Hitler', 'The *OKW* is lying', 'Medals for Murder', 'Down with Nazi Brutality' etc. However often these inscriptions are

Below: Torch-bearing young storm troopers. Such youths formed the backbone of the *SA* that fought on the streets of Germany in the early 1930s.

removed, within a few days new ones reappear on the walls."

In response to these acts of rebellion, the Hitler Youth and *Gestapo* brought the full weight of the Nazi state to bear. They issued individual warnings, arrested young people and raided the homes of suspects. Many of those arrested had their heads shaved as a public branding. Those unwilling to desist in their opposition were given weekend detention, corrective education, put on trial and even sent to youth concentration camps. Thousands were rounded up by the secret police. On 7 December 1942, the local *Gestapo* in Düsseldorf broke up 28 groups containing 739 adolescents, including the "Cologne Edelweiss Pirates". The ringleaders of the "Edelweiss Pirates" were publicly hanged in November 1944 as an example to other youths.

Just as the Third Reich was collapsing, the machinery of internal repression increased. Heinrich Himmler, the head of the *SS*, issued a

Above: War in 1939 meant labour shortages as men went to the front, and this forced *BdM* girls to register for factory work. Here, *BdM* girls enrol as apprentices.

decree in October 1944 on the "combating of youth gangs", the last in a long series of official attempts to defeat the youth protest movement. On the whole, the Nazi authorities were confused over how to treat these youth gangs. They needed these young Germans for the war effort, and the lack of any organized structure to the gangs made repression even more difficult. Therefore, the reaction of the state ranged from patronizing contempt to extreme repression.

As for the "pirates", they seem to have been a motley set of young people opposed to the conformity expected of them by the Nazis. Most were content with passive rejection of the Nazis, but some went to the extreme of posting Allied propaganda leaflets through letterboxes or even joining organized resistance groups. In 1942 in

Above: Involvement in the youth movement also meant, at least in the beginning, the chance for recreation and travel. Trips to the countryside and the sea were popular.

Düsseldorf, "Edelweiss Pirates" contacted the *KPD* leader Wilhelm Knöchjel, and subsequently some "pirates" offered shelter to German deserters, POWs, forced labourers and concentration camp escapees. They gathered supplies by way of military style raids on depots and even attacked the Cologne *Gestapo* in 1944.

Jazz music and the adoption of English and American dress was another way that many middle class adolescents made their statement against the Nazis; the jitterbug dance was a means of defying authorities which regarded jazz as decadent "negro" music. By using music, young people avoided the national folk music popular with the Nazis. The Hitler Youth became alarmed at this interest in foreign music, and an internal Hitler Youth report in 1940 on a "swing" festival lamented: "The dance music was all English and American. Only swing dancing and jitterbugging took place. At the entrance to the hall stood a notice on which the words 'Swing prohibited' had been changed to 'Swing requested'. Without

exception the participants accompanied the dances and songs by singing the English lyrics. Indeed throughout the evening they attempted to speak only English; and some tables even French. The dancers made an appalling sight. None of the couples danced normally; there was only swing of the worst sort. Sometimes two boys danced with one girl; sometimes several couples formed a circle, linking arms and jumping, slapping hands, even rubbing the backs of their heads together; and then, bent double, with the top half of the body hanging loosely down, long hair flopping into the face, they dragged themselves around practically on their knees. When the band played a rumba, the dancers went into wild ecstasy. They all leapt around and mumbled the chorus in English. The band played wilder and wilder numbers; none of the players was sitting any longer, they all 'jitterbugged' on the stage like wild animals. Frequently boys could be seen dancing together, without exception with two cigarettes in the mouth, one in each corner ... "

When the Nazis banned these public festivals, the emphasis shifted to private, informal gatherings. Like the "Edelweiss Pirates", the *Swing-Jugend* movement was a means of opposing the control of youth by the Nazis. Playing and dancing to the enemies' music was an act of rebellion. Even the dancing involved, which became more freestyle and spontaneous, was an affront to the regimented Germanic folk dancing favoured by the Hitler Youth. The state acted when it could: in Hamburg in 1940, over 500 *Swing-Jugend* were arrested for degeneracy while attending a "swing" festival.

The swing scene was a middle and upper class reaction to the Nazis, compared to the more working class "Edelweiss Pirates". They were able to gather in expensive nightclubs and wear more expensive English and American dress because their parents were better off. Nazi reports stressed the promiscuous sexual nature of the swing scene. In fact, the Nazi reports on the swing scene said

more about the Nazis' obsession with sex than the actual behaviour of the youngsters involved. Bragging by adolescents was taken as literal truth by Nazi spies; isolated incidents were blown up into general theories about the behaviour of youth. Himmler was so upset by the swing scene he tried to put the "ringleaders" of the movement into concentration camps where they could be beaten, punished and made to do forced labour.

All these protests by youth against the Nazis show that not all German youth went into the Hitler Youth without a protest. It is worth comparing the Hitler Youth panzergrenadiers in Normandy with the alternative forms of protest by other young Germans against the Nazis. It was not easy to protest, and the consequences could be fatal, but the alternative forms of protest within the Third Reich outlined above show that considerable sections of the young population resisted the Nazis' control of youth.

Below: The Nazi ideal: two blond youths. He would become a soldier in the army of the Third Reich, and she would stay at home and produce future good Nazis.

WOMEN AND THE THIRD REICH

Hitler was attracted to and respected women who were completely convention-al. He was simultaneously repelled and fascinated by sexual relations, and was himself reportedly sexually inexperienced. He described his ideal woman as a "cute, cuddly, naive little

Left: Wartime manpower needs meant agricultural work devolved to the women living in the countryside.
Below: A German *SS* officer dances carefully with Eva Braun (left), Hitler's mistress. The Führer did not dance.

Right: The Nazi leader for women, Frau Gertrud Scholtz-Klink. She embodied the sexism of the Third Reich, and the belief that a woman's place was in the home.

Right: The Nazi leader for women, Frau Gertrud Scholtz-Klink. She embodied the sexism of the Third Reich, and the belief that a woman's place was in the home.

thing – tender, sweet and stupid". Hitler's patronizing attitude found its fullest expression in Nazi policies towards women during the Third Reich. Women had little real influence in the Nazi decision-making process and their position was largely superficial. The women's movement under the Nazis was headed by Gertrud Scholtz-Klink as the "Reich Mother-in-Chief". Her liberating motto for women was "The German woman is knitting again!"

GERTRUD SCHOLTZ-KLINK

In 1934, Frau Scholtz-Klink was promoted from deputy leader of the National Socialist *Frauenschaft* ("women's organization") to leader (*führerin*) of all National Socialist women. Scholtz-Klink was an able and energetic worker who had cut her teeth in labour organizations. Her husband, a storm trooper, had died of a heart attack during a demonstration, leaving her with six children, two of whom died. She then married a doctor. Physically she was the stereotype of the ideal Aryan woman: tall, blond and able to bear children. From 1934, she was theoretically in charge of all women's organizations. These included the *Frauenwerk* (a federal organization of women), the Women's League of the Red Cross, the Women's League in the *Deutsche Arbeitsfront* (the German Labour Front), and the Women's Labour Service. The *Frauenschaft* was the overall body coordinating the women's organizations of the Third Reich. Other women's groups, especially any with democratic or

humanitarian tendencies, were accused of being Marxist, anti-family, unpatriotic or pro-abortion, and were closed down.

Behind all these women's organizations there was male authority and control. Scholtz-Klink was expected to tread softly and avoid difficult issues. Hitler was adamant that the primary role of women was reproduction. He regarded any kind of feminism or women's liberation as anathema. He

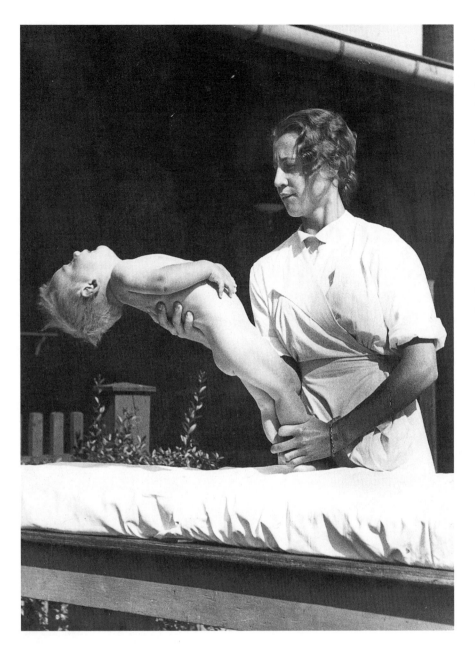

Above: Breeding tomorrow's soldiers: a shot of a woman exercising a baby in a gymnastics programme. Babies would fill the ranks of Germany's armed forces.

Female emancipation was, in the Nazi mind-set, another sign of decadent parliamentary democracy. Scholtz-Klink stated the goal of women in Hitler's Germany: "Woman is entrusted in the life of the nation with a great task, the care of man, soul, body and mind. It is the mission of the woman to minister in the home and in her profession to the needs of life from the first to the last moment of man's existence. Her mission in marriage is ... comrade, helper and womanly complement of man – that is the right of woman in the new Germany."

The correspondent of the *New York Times* asked Scholtz-Klink in 1937 what she felt about the possibility of Germany going to war: "She glances up at the Swastikas and across at the black boots of the uniformed men beyond the doorway and she turns quickly away to hide the tears in her eyes. 'I have sons,' she says quietly. Her eyes are as sad as the eyes of many other German mothers who know so well the German Labour Corps motto which says so plainly that sons must 'fight stubbornly and die laughing.'" Scholtz-Klink hid from the Allies for three years after the war, but was acquitted of war crimes in 1948.

WOMEN AS MOTHERS

For the Nazis, women were primarily reproductive units to generate soldiers and Nazis for the Third Reich. Such crude ideas were not publicized. Instead, the Nazis built up an ideal image of German women to achieve their objective. Nazi art portrayed a traditional image of women within the environment of the family. In the Nazi view, men, women and children all fulfilled an allotted role in the family. With this in mind, countless

expected women to play a subordinate role in German society. Women were there to bear the future generation of Nazis. The Nazis' cry was "*Kinder, Kirche, Küche*" ("Kids, Kirk/Church, Kitchen"). The idea that a "woman's place was in the home" was not new: similar ideas had been propounded during the Weimar period, but the Nazis put it into practice. The Nazi hierarchy actively believed in the inferiority of women.

posters were printed showing well-groomed blond children with their loving Aryan parents. The Nazi hierarchy was determined to increase Germany's birthrate as it was tailing off in the 1930s (the French Government was also encouraging French women to have larger families in the interwar years so as to match Germany's larger population).

In order to make German women have more babies, the state discouraged equal opportunities that could lead women away from the path of motherhood. German women were also denied access to abortion and contraception. At the same time, homosexuality and prostitution were repressed. In a more positive fashion, the Nazis offered a series of incentives to women to have larger families: marriage loans, child allowances and generous family subsidies. But not to everyone. Loans were granted only to women who were "genetically healthy". Those who did not meet the conditions were not only refused, but if they had, or were thought to have, hereditary diseases, they could be compulsorily sterilized in accordance with a law passed on 14 July 1933.

Those women and couples that resisted these blandishments were labelled "decadent" and "Western". Across Germany, Nazi authorities mounted exhibitions to extol the virtues of the family. Distinguished Germans such as J.S. Bach were praised for their large families. The phrase "blessed with children" (*kindersegen*) was used constantly. Alongside this emphasis on children, the Nazis launched a cult of motherhood. Hitler's mother's birthday, 12 August, was transformed into a day for mothers when the most fertile received special awards. There was an "Honours Cross" in three classes for those mothers with

Below: Practical Nazism for women: a shoe exchange programme where growing youths could exchange their shoes for larger, second-hand pairs.

Above: German Red Cross Sisters, both with the Iron Cross Second Class. Many women served as medical staff during World War II, serving at or near the front.

large families: bronze for five children, silver for more than six and gold for mothers with more than eight children. Not all women were interested in being baby factories, though. A report published in 1934 stated: "The reorganization and re-establishment of the pattern of female employment, however, on the basis of those occupational categories which are appropriate to the female nature and disposition – the basic aim of the change in the female labour market that is being sought by the state – is meeting obstacles which are rooted in the personal attitudes of the present-day generation of women rather than in objective economic causes."

The facade that the Nazis built up for women and family hid a more sinister reality. The Nazis saw women as a means to create more soldiers and Nazi functionaries. As has been seen in Chapter Four, the Nazis tried to wean young people away from their families with organizations such as the Hitler Youth. Women were needed to make babies, but once they were born the Nazi state increasingly intruded into the family to take control. This usurped traditional notions that the family was an autonomous unit protecting children from the heavy hand of the state. Like all totalitarian governments, the Nazis resented the independence of the family and the fact that it represented an alternative source of power for citizens. This Orwellian "Big Brother" approach attempted to replace biological ties with a new surrogate relationship. If necessary the state would divide families by setting members against each other. Once they were old enough, children were encouraged to inform on their parents to the *Gestapo*. As the Nazis were not in power long enough and the family in Germany was a sufficiently strong unit, this destructive trend ultimately failed.

The wife of Josef Göbbels was held up as a model for German women. Magda Göbbels was tall, blond and had produced six children. She was an ideal propaganda image. Her husband had this to say on women: "The mission of women is to be beautiful and to bring children into the world. This is not at all as rude and unmodern as it sounds. The female bird pretties herself for her mate and hatches the eggs for him. In exchange, the mate takes care of gathering the food, and stands guard and wards off the enemy." That Göbbels was a notorious womanizer and was forever arguing with Frau Göbbels over his mistresses, rows that Hitler frequently had to reconcile by telling Göbbels to behave himself, suggests a level

of hypocrisy in the Nazi ideal of women. The woman was not expected to "pretty" herself too much, though: lipstick and make-up were considered unnatural. A woman with too much powder was suggestive of the decadent Weimar period; she was someone who was not properly "German". The Nazis were, therefore, always comparing the fresh, healthy beauty of the Aryan woman with the heavily made-up women of other European countries. As many senior Nazis kept mistresses and wanted little to do with the Puritanism they propagated, it is readily apparent how this ideal for women was partly for show and

Below: German girls sewing for the Third Reich. Though Nazism stressed that a woman's place was in the home, of necessity German women were drawn into war work.

partly something only ordinary Germans would be expected to adhere to.

In 1936 Hitler made a speech to the *Frauenschaft* that summed up the new policy on women. Hitler proclaimed: "If today a female jurist accomplishes ever so much and next door there lives a mother with five, six, seven children, who are all healthy and well-brought-up, then I would like to say: From the standpoint of eternal values to our people the woman who has given birth to children and raised them and who thereby has given back our people life for the future has accomplished more and does more." With Hitler expressing sentiments such as these, it came as no surprise that women were excluded from the legal profession. Efforts were also made to exclude women from other traditionally male-dominated professions such as medicine and teaching. Women were even barred from jury service on the grounds that "they cannot think logically or reason objectively, since they are ruled only by emotion". Women interested in politics, even those actively Nazi, had few openings available for their talents and enthusiasm. National Socialism was very much a male event.

DOUBLE STANDARDS

Within the Nazi hierarchy itself, women suffered from this patronizing attitude. Magda Göbbels reluctantly put up with her husband's infidelities; Martin Bormann's wife, Gerda, accepted her husband's admission that he had finally seduced the actress Manja Behrens and made a remarkable offer. Frau Bormann was so accepting of the new order of women as subservient to men that she suggested a *ménage à trois* with Behrens as a situation likely to produce more children. Frau Bormann's view was that Behrens was too racially pure and valuable not to bear children. She suggested to her husband: "You can certainly be helpful to Manja, but you have to see to it that Manja has a child one year and I have one the next, so that you can always have one woman around who's in good shape." Gerda's suggestion, it has been pointed out, was similar to crop rotation in farming.

Everything about Nazism stressed male superiority. Males fought for the nation and safeguarded its values. For the family, the father was like a king ruling by divine right with the rest of the members accepting his rule unconditionally. The only forum where women had any power was in the home, where they were expected to maintain an ordered household that the man could return home to after work. The father was the breadwinner, the woman was the homemaker. This order was maintained with children, where girls were expected to imitate their mothers while boys prepared for an adult life of service for the state.

Under the pressure of state propaganda, many women inculcated their children with the values of National Socialism and played out the role assigned to them as females. Many women voted for Hitler, and the pictures of crowds of adoring followers saluting him attest to his popularity

Below: Frau Magda Göbbels. Divorced from her Jewish husband, she was a dutiful wife to her philandering, crippled husband and tolerated his many affairs.

Right: A *BdM* girl at war helping to prepare food for bombed-out German families after an Allied bombing raid in 1943.

among women. Many women, just as with the men, were taken in by the slogans and promises of the Nazi New Order after 1933. In 1981, when interviewed, an elderly Frau Scholtz-Klink confirmed the Nazi views she held in the 1930s. The Nazi line she had imbibed in the 1920s and 1930s was still strong long after the Third Reich had been destroyed. For her, Nazism in the 1930s had produced "one happy family" for women with the top Nazis behaving as perfect gentlemen. One suspects that this sort of denial was widespread among a population eager for an end to unemployment and the restoration of a strong Germany.

WOMEN AND REARMAMENT

One of the problems that the Nazis faced was the need for factory workers. With rearmament, and especially with war in 1939, women were needed to maintain industrial production. This need for female labour ran contrary to the policies outlined above that saw the woman's place to be in the home. After 1936, the rearmaments boom caused a labour shortfall. By the end of 1938 Germany's labour exchanges had one million vacancies on their books. Women without children, and those with older ones, were an obvious source of labour to meet this shortage. The Nazis were alarmed at how the labour shortage was creating a scarcity that male workers were using to secure higher wages and better conditions.

Because of these shortages, the Nazis instituted measures to encourage some women to enter the world of work. Yet this pragmatism ran into the problem that the thrust of Nazi policy was to keep the woman tied to the home. Therefore, these efforts to mobilize women were half-hearted, hesitant and mostly unsuccessful. Some progress was made in providing medical facilities, rest rooms and maternity facilities in factories that employed women. However, the Nazis still propagated an attitude of protective superiority towards women. Factory managers saw women as fragile and in need of attention. In the end, the patronizing attitude displayed towards women reinforced rather than challenged the traditional stereotypes of women. By 1939 the number of women in paid employment had risen from 11.5 million (in 1925 and 1933) to 12.7 million, a proportion of 37 percent. During the first half of the war this rose to 38 percent. However, the proportion of women in German armaments production remained below the World War I level. By contrast, in countries such as Britain and America rearmament and war resulted in a massive expansion in employment for women. In Germany the reluctance of the Nazis to countenance such a shift was partly compensated for by the employment of slave labour from occupied Europe in German factories during the war. Such a labour force was discontented, poorly fed,

badly treated and so, not surprisingly, had low productivity (there were also draconian fraternization rules to prevent any liaisons with local German women). This unwillingness to employ women in large numbers was one of the factors contributing to Germany's defeat in 1945.

WOMEN IN THE COUNTRYSIDE

Even with their stress on traditional family values, in the countryside, where the education of girls had always been a matter of preparing them for family life, the Nazis brought some changes to women's lives. The Nazis introduced rural women to a wider world. They founded separate women's organizations and they introduced a form of national service for girls. These nationally run bodies allowed women to travel beyond the confines of their villages and brought them into con-

Below: With the men in the armed forces, some women were forced to work in factories. Here, women help with the vital business of munitions production.

Above: The Nazis planned to take 800,000 women out of the workplace in the four years after 1933, but by the war's end thousands of women were working in industry.

tact with women from other villages. This also allowed women to meet men from other areas and broke the pattern of intra-village marriage.

THE REALITIES OF NAZI RULE

However, while Nazism brought a certain liberation for women in the countryside, the new regime also made demands. As the Third Reich moved towards war, women were expected to play their part. As men went off into the armed forces, women were forced to combine roles and fill the gap. Therefore, women were forced to take over management of the farm (only horse farmers were exempt from military service as the Germans needed horses for the army), and some even moved to industrial employment in towns. For example, before 1934 in the village of Körle in Hesse none of the village girls who left school had taken up an apprenticeship or received vocational training; after 1935 more and more girls took up

training and moved into the world of work. Once the war began to turn against Germany after 1942, the village women who had moved to factories were subjected to the full rigours of a militarized economy as they worked alongside POWs and forced labourers.

Despite the facade of Nazism cherishing the virtues of womanhood and femininity, those who failed to toe the line or who were deemed to have no place in the Thousand-Year Reich found themselves in the concentration camps. The first concentration camp for women, at Moringen, was opened in October 1933. Jewesses, Jehovah's Witnesses, socialist, communists, the racially unfit and other women the Nazis classed as "misfits" were sent there. By 1938 Moringen was unable to deal with the increasing numbers, so the Lichtenburg camp in Saxony became the second women's concentration camp, to be followed by Ravensbrück in Mecklenburg in May 1939. Originally built to hold 6000 prisoners, the number had doubled by 1944. Medical experiments were carried out at the camp, where a total of 92,700 perished.

EVERYDAY LIFE UNDER THE NAZIS

Above: There was no avoiding the trappings of Nazism in the Third Reich: Vienna after the Anschluss of 1938.
Below: For many Germans the perception was that the Nazis had cut unemployment and restored order.

For most Germans, memories of the 1930s were characterized not by terror, murder and repression, but by order, calm, employment and prosperity. Therefore, in 1951 almost half of the people questioned in the Federal Republic of Germany described the years from 1933 to 1939 as the best for Germany. A 1949 survey by the German Public Opinion Institute summarized the findings of its surveys: "The guaranteed pay packet, order, *KdF* [*Kraft durch Freude* – "Strength through Joy", the Nazis' leisure organization] and the smooth running of the political machinery … Thus 'National Socialism' makes them think merely of work, adequate nourishment, *KdF* and the absence of disarray in political life."

For many ordinary Germans, the Nazis brought a period of calm after the turbulence of the 1920s. One fitter for Krupp, Ernst Bromberg, compared the trouble of the 1920s with the calm after the Nazis came to power. In the 1920s life was hard; he was laid off from Krupp five times between 1927 and 1932 owing to a lack of work. The National Socialist period was marked by employment. Bromberg was also able to distance himself from Nazi control: "No time for it [political activity], when you're on three-shift working – with the Labour Front. Later on – oh God, yes – people kicked against it a bit and then it just carried on, you know! Yes, well obviously if you were on piece work, you didn't have time to make speeches, you got up in the morning when you had to, you didn't overstretch your break periods – because after all – the money was tempting … I didn't worry any more about the Nazis, put it that way, apart from my Labour Front contribution. I just didn't have anything to do with the Nazis, you know – and anyway I was tied up with my Protestant clubs all week … " For Bromberg, like many Germans, this was a period of economic boom when there was the opportunity to earn higher wages. His love of singing for the Protestant church choir shows how many Germans tried to find interests that took them away from Nazism. For Bromberg, the period from 1933 to the early years of the war were quiet years. The core of this peaceful phase was long-term economic prosperity.

For many Germans, everyday life was marked not only by an economic upswing, but also by the Nazi Party's *Kraft durch Freude* (Strength through Joy or *KdF*) holiday movement that allowed ordinary Germans to take a proper holiday for the first time. Germans went to the Baltic coast, even abroad, as part of a large holiday organization. These "package holidays" gave Germans a leisure interest previously denied to them. Instead of a short cycling holiday, under the Nazis Germans were able to take a proper one- or two-week holiday. The *KdF* was originally established in imitation of an Italian fascist organization run along similar lines, and the aim was to stimulate workers' morale. The *KdF* was there to spur German

Below: For some life was hell: inmates of Dachau carrying out forced labour in the 1930s. During this period conditions in the concentration camps as experienced by the inmates varied from harsh to brutal in the extreme.

workers to greater productivity. *KdF* holidaymakers cruised on luxury liners and travelled by train to the Alps, Venice, Naples and Lisbon. Norway was also a favourite destination for *KdF* trips.

Workers welcomed these trips, which also brought large profits to rural hotel owners as well as to the *Reichsbahn*, the state railway system. The *KdF* programme also subsidized theatre performances, concerts, exhibitions, sporting events, hiking, folk dancing and adult education courses. The Nazis pumped money into it as a means of gaining mass support. The *KdF* received 24 million marks in 1933–34, 17 million in 1935 and 15 million in 1936. In the process it became a national business itself (rather like the *SS*). Within two years of gaining power, the Nazis had created a huge holiday organization so large that two ocean

Left: The Nazis placated the masses by offering them material advantages such as regular holidays. The "Strength Through Joy" holiday movement ran cruises and excursions.

Above: How the Nazis liked to portray life for the ordinary German in the 1930s to their own people and the outside world: happy families on holiday by the poolside.

liners with first-class accommodation were built specially for it. Even the famous *Volkswagen* (People's Car) was originally named the *KdF Wagen*, and large government subsidies went into its production. Until the *VW* came along, cars were symbols of bourgeois status. But with the *VW* (as with the Model-T Ford in America), a family car was within reach of the ordinary German family through a weekly installment plan (when war broke out, however, car production was halted in favour of military hardware and the ordinary German never got his vehicle).

The *KdF* was regarded by the Nazi élite as practical proof of the benefits of National Socialism. Robert Ley, in charge of *KdF* activities, summarized its goals: "The worker sees that we are serious about raising his social position. He

Above: Martin Bormann, one of Hitler's closest confidants. Called "the Machiavelli behind the office desk", like many Nazis he believed Nazism and Christianity were opposed.

sees that it is not the so-called 'educated classes' whom we show to the world." For Ley, the *KdF* was proof of the destructive potential of class conflict in Nazi Germany: "In the years to come the worker will lose the last traces of inferiority feelings he may have inherited from the past."

Most Germans did little to confront the regime. The experience of the communist Alois Pfaller, outlined at the beginning of Chapter Eight, was the exception rather than the rule. For Manfred Freiherr von Schröder, a banker's son from Hamburg, the Nazis were a force for stability and he joined the Nazi Party in 1933, the year Hitler came to power. "Everything was in order again, and clean. There was a feeling of national liberation, a new start," remembered von Schröder. Germans knew that opponents of the regime were

imprisoned in concentration camps, but these camps were dismissed as a necessity to restore order and German prestige. Von Schröder again: "You have never had anything of this kind since Cromwell in England. Closest is the French Revolution, isn't it? To be a French nobleman in the Bastille was not so agreeable, was it? So people said at that time, 'Oh, the English invented them [concentration camps] in South Africa with the Boers.'" In the 1930s, Germans could ignore the concentration camps that touched the lives of comparatively few of their countrymen. These were not the extermination camps of the 1940s, and released inmates were forced to sign a piece of paper saying they would never talk about their experiences inside the camps on pain of immediate re-arrest (and re-entry to a concentration camp).

PEOPLE AND RELIGION

The Nazis were forced to tolerate religion in Germany, but as Martin Bormann exclaimed: "National Socialism and Christianity are irreconcilable." Hitler supported this view, stating: "One day we want to be in a position where only complete idiots stand in the pulpit and preach to old women." The Nazis viewed Christianity as a faith tainted by the Jews. In response, the Nazis offered the German people a new religion based around blood, soil, Germanic folklore and the Thousand Year Reich. The Nazis were no different here to earlier revolutionaries who tried to offer the people a brave new secular world. It was no surprise that racial supremacy played a large part in the new "religion".

Nazis who still wanted a spiritual home were offered a faith called *Gottgläubig* (God believing) as an alternative to the established churches. The movement was heavily tainted with peculiar pagan practices. It was given official sanction by the Nazi authorities, and by 1939 the number of "God believers" exceeded three million. The Nazis stressed romantic notions of a pagan past, while simultaneously repressing the established churches. The Nazis were unwilling to tolerate (as with the family) an alternative power centre in the Christian religion. The rituals of life associated with the Church – birth, marriage and death –

were all criticized. As part of this attack, the Nazis also changed the calendar to downplay Christian celebrations and emphasize non-Christian ceremonies. Thus, in 1938 carols and the nativity play were forbidden in schools; at the same time, Christmas was replaced with the new term "Yuletide".

PROTESTANTISM AND *GLEICHSCHALTUNG*

The more extreme Nazis looked to extend the Nazi policy of *Gleichschaltung* (Coordination) to the churches. This policy of coordination aimed to fuse all areas of German life together into a supreme Nazi machine. Anything or anyone that opposed this process was suspect, and a collection of Nazi organizations tried to bring together all areas of German life under Nazi authority. A series of laws passed by the Nazis after 1933 was designed to destroy the traditions and privileges of the old German states and create a centralized one-party state. From the mass of new legislation new power groups developed: the party, Labour Front, *SS*, *SD* and *Gestapo*.

The churches were an obvious target, and in April 1933 hard-line Nazis demanded immediate *Gleichschaltung* of all Evangelical churches. The response of the two major denominations in Germany, Roman Catholic and Protestant, was mixed: some acquiesced to Nazi demands, others met the new threat with determined opposition. Nazi Protestants (often called "Positive Christians") believed that Jesus Christ had been sent to them in the form of Hitler, that God had sanctified the Aryan way of life and that racial mixing was wrong. With this in mind, "Positive Christians" attempted

to pass a motion that required Aryan origin as a basis for clerical office. Pastor Martin Niemöller took over leadership of the Confessional Church and formed a Pastors' Emergency League (*Pfarrenbund*) to oppose the hard-liners.

Niemöller was an ex-World War I submarine captain, awarded the *Pour le Mérite* decoration, who subsequently studied theology and was ordained in 1924. Some 7000 pastors joined Niemöller's opposition, but Nazi persecution decimated their ranks. Meanwhile, "Positive Christians" attacked the Old Testament and those parts of the New Testament considered tainted by

Right: Police units relax in a courtyard, 1932. The Nazi authorities brought great pressure on members of the police and armed forces to renounce their church membership.

Left: The splendour of Cologne's cathedral. The Nazis soon subdued most religious opposition, and it was left to a few brave churchmen to speak out against excesses.

record in 1935 to say that the entire Nazi racial-folk *Weltanschaung* was nonsense, 700 ministers were arrested, humiliated and their civil liberties restricted. Ultimately, while the Nazis failed to absorb these churches, by the late 1930s the policies of repression had effectively stifled open opposition within the Protestant movement.

THE CATHOLIC CHURCH

The Catholic Church represented more formidable opposition for the Nazis. The Catholics had two advantages over the Protestants: firstly, theirs was a truly international faith, under the central leadership of the Pope located in the Vatican; secondly, Catholics had a political party in Germany, the Centre Party, to represent their interests. The Catholic Church hoped to use its political influence to deflect Nazi interference in Church matters. Therefore, the Centre Party supported the Enabling Law of 1933 (a sweeping measure to enable the Nazi government to make laws without the approval of the Reichstag), that formed the constitutional basis of Nazi rule, in the hope this support would pay dividends in Nazi policy towards Catholics. Hitler was careful not to antagonize the Catholic Church, and his conciliatory phrases lulled it into a false sense of security. It was also the case that most German Catholics (and Protestants) were indifferent to the all-embracing Nazi ideology that made a complete claim on all Germans, and they failed to see its potential to threaten established religions.

By 1936, the Catholic Church was making official representations to Hitler about Nazi inference

Judaism. The policies of the "Positive Christians" were heavily criticized by many in the Protestant Churches, and were attacked by those such as Niemöller. In the end, the Nazis' attempts at *Gleichschaltung* for Protestantism failed. But this did not stop the Nazis persecuting religious opponents, including Niemöller, who was imprisoned in 1937 and subsequently sent to a concentration camp. When the Protestant Churches went on

in its affairs. When Cardinal Faulhaber, the Church's representative, complained about new laws for sterilization of those with genetic diseases, Hitler lost his temper and told the cardinal not to interfere. Five months after Faulhaber's encounter with the Führer, Pope Pius XI issued an extraordinary encyclical entitled *With Deep Anxiety* that condemned Nazi attacks on the Church. The Pope reminded Hitler that man as a human being possessed rights that must be preserved against every attempt by the community to deny, suppress or hinder them. This encyclical was read from the pulpit in all of Germany's Catholic churches. The Nazis responded by making attacks on priests, monks and nuns in the state-controlled press, and then arresting and charging a number of them on trumped-up accusations of financial and sexual impropriety. Göbbels, himself a former Catholic, orchestrated these attacks and sent hundreds of nuns and priests to the concentration camps.

In the end, both Christian Churches failed to understand the threat that the Nazis represented. While many individual clergy acted heroically, the Churches as organized bodies did little to impede the Nazi takeover of Germany; their response was to issue feeble objections rather than orchestrate mass protest. The Churches (and all Germans) would have done well to heed the famous comment of Pastor Niemöller: "First the Nazis went after the Jews, but I was not a Jew, so I did not object. Then they went after the Catholics, but I was not a Catholic, so I did not object. Then they went after the trade-unionists, but I was not a trade-unionist so I

Right: Pastor Martin Niemöller (left), one of the few Germans willing to speak out against the Nazis. Niemöller was a committed churchman and pacifist.

did not object. Then they came after me, and there was no one left to object."

What about everyday life in the countryside? Once the Nazis were in power, local mayors were replaced and opposition parties were banned. The Nazis also abolished any recreational clubs associated with the Left. This ideological reorganization and coordination (or *Gleichschaltung*, see above) was carried through in the countryside with little opposition from a traditionally conservative rural population. In case there was trouble, however, storm troopers from neighbouring villages were brought in as enforcers.

Not everyone went along with this regimentation of their lives. Some villagers avoided Nazi parades. When the Nazis came for the bicycles of the communist cycling club in the village of Körle in Hesse, the landlord of the inn where the club met refused to hand over the bicycles, claiming he was the owner of the machines. After the war was over he handed the bikes back to their rightful owners. When the Nazis held their first May Day parade in Körle, they were shocked to see themselves marching past a Weimar flag hoisted by a local woman.

VILLAGE LIFE

However, these acts of defiance were the exception rather than the rule. Soon in villages across Germany the Nazis were accepted and life changed. That the Nazis gained such support says much for their claims that they could cut unemployment and reduce poverty. The Nazis introduced a labour service programme (the *Arbeitsdienst*), they established organizations for women and children (see Chapters Four and Five), and offered cheap holidays for ordinary people via the "Strength through Joy" programme. In the countryside these measures appealed to the young, and only older people failed to accept them. The Nazis' appeal to youth led to generational problems as new Nazi structures replaced the old village life based around the family. Young men and women who had joined Nazi youth organizations carried their new confidence into the home and challenged traditional notions of parental control. For many villagers this resulted in mini wars within the household as loyalty to the Nazi state clashed with the more traditional set of structures of the older generation.

Under the Third Reich, the family in the countryside lost much of its role in the training and rearing of children. Distorted teaching in schools, coupled with the Hitler Youth, imparted to rural children a very different view of life than the one they had traditionally been used to. Time that youngsters would traditionally have spent helping in the fields was now taken up with exercise and paramilitary exercises associated with Nazi youth organizations. When they reached 18, young men (and women) were recruited into labour and military units, and this compounded the distance between the children of the village and their parents. It also made harvesting difficult, as young people who could help were away doing other things.

The Nazis justified these changes by saying that they were for the good of everyone; that the state was like a household and everyone was needed to feed the larger household. In this context, it was hard for villagers to object to the changes in their way of life. Once war broke out in 1939, men were drafted for frontline service and the villagers were forced to accept (as in Britain) evacuees from the Allied bombing of German cities. In villages across Germany, mayors were tasked with assessing each home in the village to see how much space could be made available for displaced Germans. As the war went against Germany on the Eastern Front, large numbers of German refugees moved west to escape the Red Army. These people all needed to be housed. These newcomers were accepted with passive resignation and silent anger. The course of the war convinced most villagers that the Third Reich had outlived its usefulness. As a consequence, by 1944 villagers began to openly defy the Nazi authorities and hoard foodstuffs. Villagers even hid deserters.

THE IRON GRIP

When the war ended in May 1945, life in villages such as Körle had changed irrevocably. The Nazis had destroyed the old order; the Allies then destroyed the Nazis. In Körle, virtually every household had suffered a loss at the front. The village was short of young men and had a disproportionate number of older people. The resettlement of refugees from the East had also changed the make-up of rural villages as newcomers temporarily housed took root and continued to live there after the war. Women had also been sucked into the war economy and were no longer willing to accept a traditional role in the village household. In the end, the Nazis' attempt to maintain a rural way of life based on Blut und Boden (Blood and Soil) failed as they unleashed a series of forces which effectively destroyed the old structure of village life.

The shadow cast across everyday life in Nazi Germany was Himmler's *SS* – the empire within

Above: German troops on manoeuvre in Hesse being watched by village folk. In rural areas new Nazi structures replaced the old system based around the family.

an empire. Starting out as a small bodyguard for the protection of Adolf Hitler, it grew into an immense organization. Its Reich Central Security Department (*RSHA*), under the command of *SS-Obergruppenführer* Reinhard Heydrich, had the most impact on life in the Third Reich. The most important sections within the *RSHA* were the *Geheime Staatspolizei* (*Gestapo*) under *SS-Gruppenführer* Heinrich Müller, the *Kriminal Polizei* (*Kripo*) under *SS-Gruppenführer* Arthur Nebe, the *Ausland* (External) *SD* (*Sicherheitsdienst*) – intelligence department – under *SS-Brigadeführer* Walter Schellenberg, and the *Inland* (Internal) *SD* under *SS-Brigadeführer* Otto Ohlendorf.

The *Gestapo*, the secret police tasked with tracking down subversives and maintaining the Nazis' iron grip, had no restrictions as to its powers of arrest. It had an army of informers to act as its eyes and ears. Each large department building, for example, had its own resident *Gestapo* informer who kept an eye on fellow tenants. By 1939 it had 20,000 functionaries, and by 1943 it had 100,000 informers. To be denounced by an informer meant being taken into custody, where officials had the right under the law to extract confessions by beating (which could go on for days at a time; the prisoner lapsing in and out of consciousness). The terrified prisoner could then be despatched to a concentration camp, never to be seen again. Small wonder that the *Gestapo*, through its use of intimidation and terror, kept a strict control on the state and its people.

CULTURE UNDER THE NAZIS

Hermann Göring summed up the Nazis' attitude to culture and art in his famous quip: "Whenever I hear the word 'culture', I reach for my revolver." Göring's attitude was echoed by most senior Nazis. As has been seen, Hitler hated the intelligentsia and all things intellectual, and seriously toyed with the idea of doing away with them once he was in power. After 1933, many German intellectuals saw the writing on the wall, especially those of Jewish descent, and emigrated. The list of those who fled says much for the strength of opposition to Nazism among German intellectuals, and this wave of emigration was a great loss for German culture: writers such as Thomas and Heinrich Mann, Arnold and Stefan Zweig, Franz Werfel and Jakob Wassermann; masters of the Bauhaus school such as Walter Gropius, Mies van der Rohe and Marcel Breuer; painters such as Max Beckmann, Oskar Kokoschka and Kurt Schwitters; film directors Fritz Sternberg and Fritz Lang; and actress Marlene Dietrich. The loss of talented musicians and composers was particularly pronounced: Paul Hindemith, Otto Klemperer, Kurt Weill, Hanns

Above left: German professors of Heidelburg University celebrate the founding of their historic institution.
Left: Books that did not conform to Nazi standards and were deemed to be "un-German" were liable to be burnt.

Above: Göbbels with his Führer at the opening of the Great German Art Exhibition in 1938. Nazi art followed predictable styles and emphasized military virtues.

Jelinek, Ernst Toch, Arnold Schönberg and Richard Tauber. Academics also left in their droves: Max Wertheimer, William Stern, Sigmund Freud, Paul Tillich, Ernst Bloch, Theodor Adorno, Ernst Cassirer, Kurt Goldstein, Erich Fromm, Fritz Reiche, Hans Bethe, Richard Courant, James Frank and Albert Einstein. Einstein's loss would be sorely felt when Germany embarked on its atomic weapons programme: it was Einstein's Theory of Relativity that was the basis of America's atom bomb dropped on Japan in August 1945. In total, some 2500 writers left Germany once the Nazis took power.

While many intellectuals, writers, musicians and scientists left Germany, some chose to stay. Notable among those who stayed were Otto Hahn, Werner Heisenberg, Max Planck, Gerhart Hauptmann, Gottfried Benn and Martin Heidegger. These people chose to stay because many intellectuals in Germany had traditionally remained outside the world of politics. Others went along with the revolutionary ideas of the Nazis, often tempted by the promise of official recognition for their work. Still others naively believed that the Nazis would not attack German intellectual life. They were wrong: the Germans applied their policy of *Gleichschaltung* to culture and the arts so as to coordinate this area of German life fully into the Nazi state machine.

In March 1933, just two months after Hitler became chancellor, Göbbels announced that culture and politics would be united. In September 1933 he established a new Reich Cultural Chamber (*Reichskulturkammer*); German artists had to join the organization if they wanted to work, while non-Aryans were banned from joining.

Alongside Göbbels' new chamber, other branches of the state involved themselves in culture and the arts. Alfred Rosenberg, one of the Nazis' ideological thinkers, dabbled in cultural control through his Office for the Supervision of Ideological Training and Education of the *NSDAP*. This had grown out of the earlier League of Struggle for German Culture (*Kampfbund für Deutsche Kultur – KfDK*). The *KfDK* had been founded in 1929 to combat "Jewish" influence on German culture. In its new form after 1933, Rosenberg's office developed blacklists, burnt books and emptied museums of anything considered "decadent". Rosenberg was an early anti-semitic writer whose *The Myth of the Twentieth Century* (published in 1930) was required Nazi reading. Its premise was that liberalism had wrecked the ascendancy of the Nordic people, allowing "lesser" races to take power, and that Germany's duty was to rule them. In 1940, he set up a task force to loot art treasures from conquered Europe, and a year later he became minister for the occupied Eastern territories. He was hanged as a war criminal in 1946.

The Nazis soon silenced independent cultural organizations. For instance, when members of the Prussian Academy of Arts signed a petition that opposed the Nazis in forthcoming elections, the Nazi commissioner for culture in Prussia told the academy's president that his academy would be shut if the troublemakers were not silenced. The organizers of the petition promptly resigned under pressure from their president. The president then got a majority of members of the academy to sign a resolution forbidding members from further political activity, and devoting members to the cause of national unity. Some academy members resigned at this threat to their freedom; others were sacked by ministerial decree.

BOOK-BURNING

Perhaps nothing signified the Nazis' attitude to culture better than public book-burning. As the poet Heinrich Heine observed, "where you burn books you burn people". The German Student Union led the way with pyres of books considered "not German" or "tainted by Jewry". Göbbels marshalled these displays where students and academics vied in their loyalty to the new regime by suggesting new tomes to be thrown onto the fire. Göbbels rationalized the burnings by proclaiming: "Fellow students, German men and women! The age of extreme Jewish intellectualism has now ended, and the success of the German revolution has again given the German spirit the right of way ... You are doing the proper thing in committing the evil spirit of the past to the flames ... This is a strong, great, symbolic act, an act that is to bear witness before all the world to the fact that the November Republic has disappeared. From these ashes there will arise a phoenix of a new spirit ... The past is lying in flames. The future will rise from the flames within our hearts ... Brightened by these flames our vow shall be: The Reich and the Nation and our Führer Adolf Hitler."

Those pieces of art that failed to meet the Nazis' bland new standards were humiliated in public exhibitions. Visitors were shown displays of "degenerate" art in the most unfavourable light possible: poor lighting and pejorative captions were used to denigrate modern art (though such displays proved popular with the public). The Nazis preferred "heroic" style art that conformed closely to the pictorial, and they showed their artistic preferences in a new House of German Culture in Munich. The building itself was in a style that Hitler liked: neo-classical with columns arranged with military precision. Inside, the displays showed the Nazis' obsession with power and simple eroticism: muscular nudes sat alongside alluring Aryan maidens. Hitler, the failed Austrian painter and architect manqué, was finally able to dictate German culture.

Hitler's architect, Albert Speer, produced designs that appealed to the Führer. A huge new capital city was planned with a domed building near the Reichstag that dwarfed St Peter's in Rome. The dome was to be 250m (825ft) in diameter and large enough to hold 125,000 spectators. Alongside this would be a huge triumphal arch that would dwarf Paris's Arc de Triomphe, an Adolf Hitler Square able to hold one million people, broad boulevards, a private palace for Hitler and a new Reichstag building. As was so often the way with the Nazis, this was the triumph of style over substance: only the Reichstag building was ever built.

Below: Gleeful storm troopers and youthful enthusiasts gather together books and pamphlets for burning. On 11 May 1933, 200,000 books were destroyed alone.

Josef Göbbels –
PROPAGANDA CHIEF

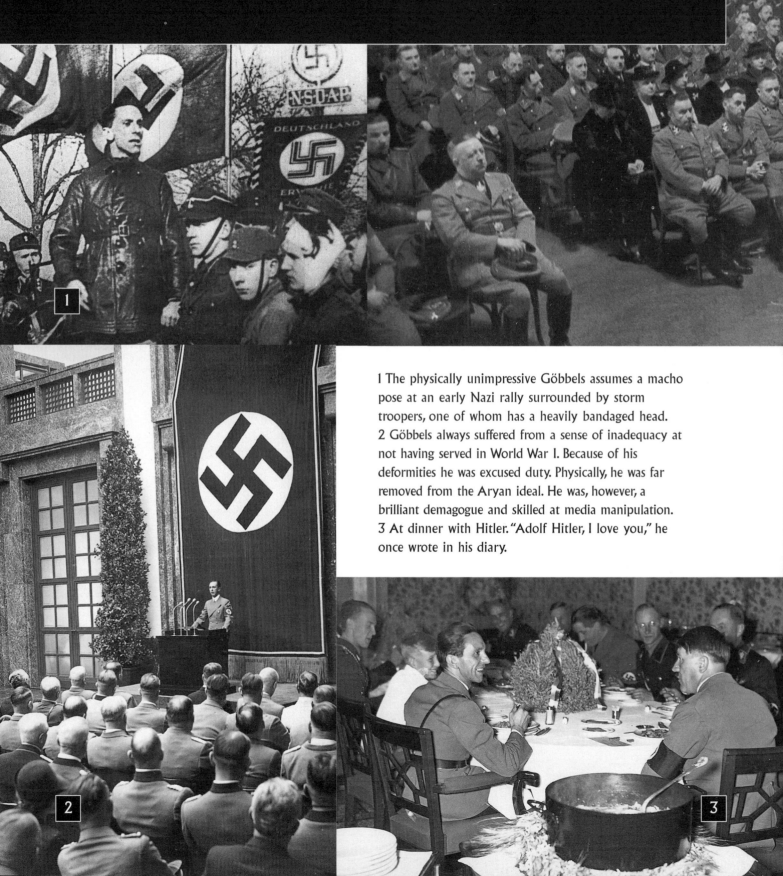

1 The physically unimpressive Göbbels assumes a macho pose at an early Nazi rally surrounded by storm troopers, one of whom has a heavily bandaged head.
2 Göbbels always suffered from a sense of inadequacy at not having served in World War I. Because of his deformities he was excused duty. Physically, he was far removed from the Aryan ideal. He was, however, a brilliant demagogue and skilled at media manipulation.
3 At dinner with Hitler. "Adolf Hitler, I love you," he once wrote in his diary.

4 Addressing the serried ranks of the party faithful.
5. The propaganda chief haranguing an audience. As head of the Reich Ministry of Information and Propaganda, Gőbbels controlled all writing, theatre, dance, painting, sculpture, film and radio.
6. Gőbbels and Hitler in Italy at the Milan Scala, 1937.
7. During World War II, Gőbbels was tasked with keeping up morale on the home front, visiting bombed cities and organizing relief. In this shot he is visiting bombed buildings in Berlin in 1944.

The rallies held by the Nazis at Nuremberg came to symbolize German culture in the 1930s. They proved that as far as the Nazis were concerned, people never counted as individuals: 400,000 Party faithful met at Nuremberg in a huge concrete stadium to be harangued by Nazi leaders. The 1936 Olympics in Berlin were held in a stadium designed to stress big open spaces for large groups of people. The community was all, individuality was nothing. Nazi art was propaganda that emphasized the impersonal eternal truths as the Nazis saw them.

Music also came under the Nazis' hammer. Hitler loved Wagnerian operas and anything that went beyond Wagner was considered suspect. Most musicians with any skill departed for more liberal societies. Any music that was considered at all "Jewish" was proscribed; musicians, conductors and directors across Germany who opposed the new trend found themselves out of a job. All music was sanitized: a scene from Paul Hindemith's opera *Mathis der Maler* drew condemnation as it purportedly showed Nazi book-burning. Not surprisingly, Hindemith emigrated and Germany's loss was America's gain. Jazz music was also a target for the Nazis, who considered it degenerate, American and "Negro" (see Chapter Four).

NAZI ART: A LOVE OF WAR

Most of what was written, composed, painted and built from 1933 to 1945 was worthless. The Nazis permitted the arts to flourish in four carefully controlled subjects: soil, race, war and the Nazi Party. The actions of German soldiers in World War I were a particularly popular topic. The war became a spiritual experience, and this approach was best exemplified in the books of Ernst Jünger (most famously in his book *The Storm of Steel*). The Nazis stressed military service and sacrifice. Militarism was stressed over the *avant garde*; conservative pagan ideologies triumphed over decadent modernism. These new art forms also sought to pursue particular themes in German history that appealed to the Nazis. Writers stressed the mission of the German people to save Europe from hordes of racially inferior Jews and Slavs. In his 1929 novel *Michael*, Göbbels laid out all the key fascist ideas:

Above: Hitler's architect: Albert Speer. For his part in the Nazi war effort, he was sentenced to 20 years in prison. He was one of the few senior Nazis to admit his guilt.

the comradeship of life in the trenches during World War I (Göbbels never fought in the war as he was a cripple), the post-war dislocation of the 1920s, the importance of iron will, the superiority of blood over brain, the mystical connection between *Volk* and Führer, the ideal of motherhood, and the need to fight decadent Western liberalism and communism.

Under Göbbels' leadership, the Nazis seized on new means of disseminating their message. It was here that the radio was particularly important. The Nazis subordinated all independent regional stations under a central authority, the Reich Broadcasting Company (*Reichsrundfunk Gesellschaft – RRG*). Cheap radio sets were produced that all

Germans could afford. Costing 76 marks, the People's Receiver took the Nazi message into factories and the workplace. A cheaper, smaller machine at 35 marks (called "Göbbels' Mouth") was designed for the home. Using these radio sets, the Nazis beamed their propaganda into every German home. Government broadcasts became an occasion to down tools in factories and offices. People gathered at set times to listen to the latest pronouncements. There was even a programme to build 6000 loudspeaker pillars in public squares across Germany. The actual broadcasts were pure propaganda about Nazi triumphs and were finished off with a thanksgiving hymn and marching music. After 1942, the broadcasts sometimes ended with a funeral march as the war went against Germany.

Below: Music was strictly controlled in the Third Reich and there was an emphasis on "Germanic" composers, such as the nineteenth-century composer Richard Wagner.

With their dominance of the radio waves, the Nazis resented the fact that Germans could still listen to foreign radio stations. Therefore, in 1939 listening to them was made illegal. Germans who obeyed the law (and punishments for breaking the law were harsh) received a daily fare of "news", military reports and music. At the same time, foreign broadcasts were jammed, preventing Germans from listening to the real truth about what was happening during the war. The jamming stations were codenamed "Concordia" and included the New British Broadcasting Station that sent messages from the renegade William Joyce back to Britain. (Joyce was given the sobriquet "Lord Haw-Haw", although the term was first used for another renegade, Englishman Norman Baillie-Stewart. Joyce was hanged after the war.)

Film was another key medium for Nazi propaganda. Göbbels established a Nazi film office in 1933 that advanced funds to film-makers who were willing to push the cause of National

Above: On the occasion of Hitler's birthday, guests gather to look at another grand Nazi building project – the Olympic stadium in Berlin.

Socialism. In total, the Nazis produced almost 1500 films. These films were either propaganda or entertainment pictures, and all of them were accompanied by a weekly newsreel. With controlled radio stations and the cinema newsreel, ordinary Germans had little way of finding out what was really happening in Germany and the outside world.

As film-makers had to stay away from any political subjects for their entertainment films, the result was a series of bland romance and adventure movies. As for the propaganda films, these were box-office flops. Films extolled the virtues of the Nazi Party and glorified the battles of the 1920s between Left and Right. Storm troopers who had

been beaten to death by communists in the 1920s became the subject of major Nazi films such as *SA-Mann Brand*, *Hitlerjunge Quex* and *Hans Westmar*. In addition, there was a batch of films designed to push the poisoned message of anti-semitism. Films such as *Robert und Bertram* (1939), *Die Rotschilds* (1940), *Jud Süss* (1940) and *Der Ewige Jude* (1940) were so extreme that film-makers had to be coerced into making them. They even caused anti-Jewish pogroms by crowds leaving the cinema. These films portrayed Jews as rats coming out of a sewer to take over the world. The message was simple: Jews needed to be wiped out before they, like rodents, took over the world.

At their best, Nazi films could capture the essence of the new mood of Nazism. This was nowhere more so than with the films of Leni Riefenstahl. In particular, her films *Triumph des Willens* (*Triumph of the Will*, 1935) and *Olympia*

Above: The Berlin Olympic Stadium in 1936, the backdrop for Leni Riefenstahl's film pro-fascist *Olympia*, a record of the 1936 Olympic Games.

(1938) were spectacular productions showing the mass rallies of the Nazis (*Olympia* was released in two parts: *Festival of the Nations* and *Festival of Beauty*). Riefenstahl was opposed by Göbbels, who felt his position as cultural and propaganda supremo being usurped, but as she had Hitler's personal approval she was able to go ahead with her films (the difficulties of working with Göbbels caused her to suffer a nervous breakdown while making the film *Victory of Faith*). Her work did much to show Hitler's charisma and the electrifying effect of the mass rallies of the 1930s, with their serried rows of marching storm troopers. Riefenstahl applied the same techniques in her film of the 1936 Olympics (after World War II Riefenstahl was imprisoned briefly by the French for her role in the Nazi propaganda machine).

The Nazis applied their policies of coordination to all areas of German life, and culture and art in the 1930s suffered accordingly. Conformity and control replaced creativity. Under the leadership of Josef Göbbels, Germans were fed a carefully planned cultural diet designed to make Nazism more acceptable and to prepare the German population for war. Instead of being an expression of individual freedom, art was indistinguishable from propaganda, and ironically came close to the official art of the Soviet Union in style and format. The German population could believe this propaganda in the 1930s, but after 1942 with German casualties mounting, Allied bombing attacks being launched on German cities and German armies in retreat on all fronts, not even Göbbels could hide the truth.

Above: "Whoever wears this symbol is an enemy of our people." Anti-semitic poster in pre-war Germany.
Below: Jewish businesses were targets. Those not destroyed were "appropriated" and passed on to "Aryans".

THE TERROR BEGINS

Once in power, Hitler was ruthless with all those who opposed him, even erstwhile comrades. One of the Nazis' most dramatic coups on coming to power was a purge of fellow Nazis considered a threat to the new regime. This perceived threat centred on Ernst Röhm, a hard, stocky man who had been a close friend of Hitler since the early 1920s. Röhm had been wounded three times in World War I and bore the scars: half his nose was missing and his cheek was rutted by a bullet wound. As has been seen, Röhm had established the *Sturmabteilung* (Storm Troopers or *SA*) in the 1920s to fight for the Nazis. It was Röhm's brown-shirted *SA* who won the street battles with the communists, and Hitler was grateful to Röhm for his help prior to 1933. He proclaimed that he wanted "to thank Heaven for having given me the right to call a man like you my friend and comrade-in-arms". However, once in power, Hitler increasingly found Röhm an embarrassment and an alternative centre of power. Röhm, along with other Nazis such as Gregor Strasser, formed a "left-wing" branch of Nazism that stressed the "socialism" side to the National Socialist German Workers' Party, and called for a second workers' revolution; for Röhm, the Nazi movement was a working class movement and revolution was a permanent state. Hitler, on the other hand, had come to power in 1933 with the help of Germany's reactionary élite of businessmen, politicians and army officers.

The German armed forces and senior industrialists who had helped Hitler to power viewed

Above: Storm troopers pass notices with stereotypical Jewish images. *Der Stürmer*, a weekly Nazi newspaper, used such images as part of its anti-semitic crusade. It was the only newspaper that Hitler read from cover to cover.

Röhm with trepidation. Hitler knew that he had to assuage his new backers. The German armed forces suspected Röhm of having greater ambitions. One professional officer recalled how his comrades disliked the upstart *SA*: "One rejected the Storm Troopers because of their behaviour, the way they looked, the way they were … they were hated by most soldiers." Hitler tried to talk Röhm around to his way of thinking. On 4 June 1934, he spent five hours with Röhm in an attempt to curb his wish for continued revolution. After several of these fruitless meetings, Hitler concluded that only force would work. In June 1934, therefore, Hitler personally led loyal *SS* troops in a bloody purge of the *SA*. More than 150 senior *SA* figures were shot by firing squads. Many shouted "Heil Hitler!" prior to being executed for they had no idea why they were being shot. Röhm himself

refused the revolver left in his cell and two *SS* guards were forced to shoot him dead. As Alan Bullock recounts in his *Hitler: A Study in Tyranny*: "Hitler ordered a revolver to be left in his [Röhm's] cell, but Röhm refused to use it: 'If I am to be killed, let Adolf Hitler do it himself.' According to an eyewitness at the 1957 Munich trial of those involved, he was then shot by two *SS* officers who emptied their revolvers into him at point-blank range: 'Röhm wanted to say something, but the *SS* officers told him to shut up. Then Röhm stood at attention – he was stripped to the waist – with his face full of contempt.'"

Above: Brownshirts parade through a German town. These same brownshirts were used to attack Jews, wreck Jewish shops and prevent shoppers entering Jewish businesses.

Many Nazis and non-Nazis with no connection to Röhm were also shot in the days following the "Night of the Long Knives" (or *Nacht der langen Messer*) as Nazis close to Hitler took the opportunity to settle old scores. For instance, Hermann Göring, jealous of the rank and influence of General Kurt von Schleicher, had the retired general shot. The men sent to do the job also shot his wife dead and threatened his 14-year-old stepdaughter that she would suffer the same fate if she informed on them. In Munich the 75-year-old Gustav Ritter von Kahr, who had crushed Hitler's "Beer Hall Putsch" in 1923, was dragged from his home, beaten to death and his dismembered body left in a swamp. There were many mistakes in the confusion. Willi Schmid, a respected music critic,

was confused with a Willi Schmidt and died as a consequence. Hitler's number two, Rudolf Hess, subsequently visited Frau Schmid to express his condolences, to give her a pension and tell her to think of her husband's death as a "great sacrifice".

After all the killing had died down, Hitler concluded with the chilling words: "In this hour I was responsible for the fate of the German people, and therefore I became the Supreme Justice of the German people ... Everyone must know that in all future time if he raises his hand to strike at the state, then certain death will be his lot." Wilhelm Frick, the Reich Minister of the Interior, then framed an extraordinary law that declared all Hitler's actions during the purges to be legal. A compliant Reichstag passed the law without comment. The "Night of the Long Knives", conducted against erstwhile comrades, proved the ruthlessness of the new regime and was a foretaste of the terror to come. For those who were on the

Left, those considered racially inferior or those deemed in some way socially unacceptable, an equally severe fate awaited.

As has been seen, Alois Pfaller was a communist, a member of the *KPD*. While most communists kept their heads below the parapet once the Nazis achieved power, in 1934 Pfaller restarted his old communist youth group. This was an heroic act, but one doomed to failure against a regime as ruthless as that of the Nazis. Pfaller was betrayed by a female double-agent – someone working for both the Nazis and the communists – and Pfaller was taken in by the *Gestapo*. In prison Pfaller was severely beaten and badly maltreated. His nose was broken and he was beaten unconscious with leather belts: "And when I came-to again, they did it a second time, again unconscious, the fourth time, again unconscious, then they stopped because I hadn't said anything." The *Gestapo* then changed their interrogation techniques. One man took his confession down while another repeatedly hit Pfaller in the face every time he failed to answer a question correctly. The policeman doing the hitting sprained his right hand and began using his left. In the process he split Pfaller's ear drum: "Then I heard an incredible racket ... It was roaring as if your head was on the seabed, an incredible roaring." Pfaller then haemorrhaged and was given a bucket and mop and ordered to clean up his blood off the floor. Subsequently he was placed in a cell and then a concentration camp where he languished until 1945.

ANTI-SEMITISM

The Jews became a prime target as racial doctrines in Nazi Germany were codified in a series of laws and spurious theories. However, Nazi policies towards the Jews varied through the 1930s. There were a series of uncoordinated attacks after the election of 1933. In Würzburg, a Jewish man was publicly humiliated and imprisoned for having an affair with a non-Jew. Jews were beaten by *SA* thugs brought in to villages across Germany to attack Jewish families; Jews had their beards shorn or were forced to drink castor oil. Rudi Bamber's family was Jewish and lived in Nuremberg. In 1933 the *SA* arrived and "took my father away, and

together with many other Jews in Nuremberg, they were taken to a sports stadium where there was a lot of grass and they were made to cut the grass with their teeth by sort of eating it ... It was to humiliate them that they were the lowest of the low and simply to make a gesture."

Soon the Nazis organized boycotts of Jewish shops. Premises were daubed with paint and storm troopers would stand outside to intimidate any shoppers still willing to give them their custom. In

Below: Hitler and Röhm. The latter, a paedophile homosexual, was seen by Hitler as being a threat by 1934, and was assassinated by *SS* men loyal to the Führer.

1935 the Nuremberg Laws codified Nazi anti-semitism. Jews were stripped of German citizenship and forbidden to marry "Aryans". Pressure on Jews eased up temporarily in 1936 and 1937 after protests from Schacht, Minister of Economics, worried about the economic consequences of persecuting Jews, and because of the Olympic games being held in Berlin in 1936. But the underlying racial hatred remained.

Throughout the 1930s, Jews were forced from businesses and subjected to boycotts. Arnon Tamir's father ran a cigarette factory; soon he was having problems because the town's cigarette dealers, with whom he had always had good relations, were unable to sell his cigarettes. Within two months of this boycott, his factory was forced to close down. In professions like the civil service, legislation was passed that prohibited Jews from employment.

Arnon Tamir grew up in a fearful atmosphere of anti-semitism. This tainted his attitude to non-Jewish German girls: "The mere idea of becoming friendly, or more, with a German girl was poisoned right from the start by those horrible cartoons and headlines which claimed that the Jews were contaminating them." Nazi cartoons in the popular press played on the salacious dimension by portraying Jewish men as lecherous fiends intent on seducing innocent German girls. When Tamir worked on a building site, he overheard one Nazi Party member claim that a Jewish woman in his village was a sorceress. She was able, it was claimed, to turn herself into a foal. Such crude anti-semitism had been a thread running through European society for centuries. However, it was now actively encouraged by the government of a well-organized modern state.

Below: Once in power, the Nazis were ruthless with all real or imagined opponents. This is a photograph from the "Night of the Long Knives".

In 1938, the Nazis' persecution of the Jews exploded in *Kristallnacht* (Night of Broken Glass). Following the assassination of a German diplomat in Paris by a Polish Jew, Josef Göbbels asked Hitler if he could release his storm troopers against Germany's Jewish population. Hitler agreed to the request, and on 9 November the attacks began. Across Germany the homes of Jews were raided. For the Bamber family, the first they knew of *Kristallnacht* was when Nazi thugs broke down their door. Storm troopers proceeded to smash up their flat. The police did nothing: after all, the men doing the damage were themselves in uniform. "We had three elderly ladies who were living on the first floor with us," recalled Rudi Bamber, a boy at the time. "One was dragged out and beaten up, for no reason except she got in the way or something. And I was knocked about and finally ended up in the cellar … A great many people were arrested that night and it was obviously their intention to arrest me as well. But after a while they found that the leader of the group had gone home. He had obviously had enough and they were very irritated by this. They weren't going to waste any more time, so they gave me a swift kick and said 'Push off' … and they walked out and left me to it." When Rudi re-entered his parents' flat he discovered his father dying from the beating administered by the Nazis: "I was absolutely in shock. I couldn't understand how this situation had arisen … uncalled-for violence against a people they didn't know."

Ordinary people went along with this appalling violence against fellow Germans. One remembered that while *Kristallnacht* was a shock, "When the masses were shouting 'Heil' what could the individual person do? You went along. We went along. That's how it was. We were the followers." This line of argument does not, however, explain away the behaviour of those in Nuremberg who went to the Bamber's house the morning after *Kristallnacht* and threw stones at the windows. At the end of *Kristallnacht*, more than 1000 synagogues were destroyed and anything up to 400 German Jews had been killed. The broken glass littering the pavements of German cities on the morning of 10 November gave this bout of violence its title. World opinion was shocked by the

Above: Wilhelm Frick, Reich Minister of the Interior after 1933. Frick was responsible for the Nuremberg Laws of 1935 that made Jews second-class citizens.

night's events. The Americans withdrew their ambassador and a boycott of German goods intensified. But world opinion could do little for Germany's isolated Jewish community.

After this pogrom, the position for Germany's Jews went from bad to worse. Discriminatory laws were passed with the objective of creating a "Jewish-free" economy. Jews were now forbidden to practise trades or to own shops, market stalls or businesses. Jewish businesses were "Aryanized" – that is they were compulsorily sold to German non-Jews. Subsequently, Jews were banned from schools, universities, cinemas, theatres and sports facilities. Specific areas of cities were designated "Aryan" and forbidden to Jews. Local Germans zealously enforced these laws, and by the time war broke out in 1939 the Jews were well on their way to becoming pariahs in German society.

Above: One of the slogans of Julius Streicher, owner of *Der Stürmer* and *Gauleiter* of Franconia: "The Jews are our Ruin". It was typical of Nazi anti-semitism.

These harsher policies coincided with Schacht's dismissal as Minister for Economics. Schacht had done something to temper the worst excesses of the Nazis, if only on the grounds that anti-semitic policies harmed the German economy. Once Göring was in charge he aimed to create a "Jew-free" economy as quickly as possible. This coincided with events such as *Kristallnacht*. Anti-Jewish policies were also a result of intrigues at the highest levels of the Nazi decision-making process. For instance, Göbbels was keen to ingratiate himself with Hitler after news leaked of his various extra-marital affairs: *Kristallnacht* was a means of currying favour with the Führer.

Hitler never swerved from his anti-semitism. As war clouds gathered in Europe in 1939 he told an enthusiastic Reichstag: "[If] International Jewish finance inside and outside of Europe succeeds in involving the nations in another war, the result will not be the Bolshevization of the earth and the victory of Judaism but the annihilation of the Jewish race in Europe." At the same time, Hitler told the

Czech foreign minister: "We are going to destroy the Jews. They are not going to get away with what they did on November 9th, 1918." This was a reference to the myth that Jews and Marxists forced Germany's surrender in November 1918.

In addition to persecution, the Nazis embarked on a policy to encourage Jewish emigration. As early as 1934, a sub-section of the *SS* proposed to solve the "Jewish question" by pursuing an orderly and systematic policy of mass emigration. This was, however, not very successful: only 120,000 of Germany's 503,000 Jews had left by 1937. When Austria was annexed in 1938, 190,00 Austrian Jews were added to the Third Reich. This increase appalled the Nazis, who forced 45,000 to leave within six months by a policy of forced confiscation of Jewish property. This campaign was led by Adolf Eichmann, who fled to South America after the war, but was taken by Israeli agents in 1960, put on trial in Israel in 1961 and subsequently executed. In 1937, Eichmann had actually visited Palestine to meet Arab leaders as a means of expediting Jewish settlement. In 1939, a further 78,000 Jews were forced out of Germany and 30,000 from recently annexed territory in Czechoslovakia. In an effort to find countries willing to accept these

Jewish migrants, the Nazis even worked with Zionist organizations keen to establish a Jewish state outside Europe.

It was during the 1930s that the Nazis established concentration camps. The term "concentration camp" was first used in the context of the 1899–1902 South African War (or "Boer War"), where British troops "concentrated" *Afrikaaner* women and children to stop them helping Boer fighters. Some 20,000 women and children died as a result of neglect by the British authorities in the camps. When Hitler came to power, he looked with interest at a different type of concentration camp for Germany. In a talk with a confidant before he became chancellor, Hitler stated: "We must be ruthless! We must regain our clear conscience as to ruthlessness. Only thus shall we purge our people of their softness and sentimental philistinism … and their degenerate delight in beer-swilling. We have no time for fine senti-

ments. I don't want the concentration camps transferred into penitentiary institutions. Terror is the most effective instrument. I shall not permit myself to be robbed of it simply because a lot of stupid bourgeois mollycoddlers choose to be offended by it."

With this in mind, concentration camps were quickly established once the Nazis were in power. The avowed goal was to "reform" political opponents and turn anti-social elements into useful members of society. This was a nonsense. On 28 February 1933, a law was passed suspending those clauses of the German constitution that guaranteed personal liberties. Three concentration camps were then established: Dachau in the south near Munich, Buchenwald in central Germany and

Below: Once the war began, German anti-semitism expanded into occupied Europe. This is a picture from an anti-Jewish exhibition in Paris held in 1941.

Heinrich Himmler –
SS OVERLORD

1 Himmler visiting some of his *Waffen-SS* troops .
2 Himmler with his wife Margarete, seven years his senior. She awakened in him an interest in homeopathy, mesmerism and herbalism.
3 Like many Nazis, Heinrich joined the army during World War I. Himmler served as a cadet-clerk in the 11th Bavarian Infantry Regiment.
4. Himmler with Ernst Kaltenbrunner (on the right with scar), the head of the Reich Central Security Office.

5 Himmler at Auschwitz in 1942. For his part in the Holocaust, Himmler would have been hanged. However, he escaped trial by taking poison in May 1945 while in British custody.

6 Himmler visiting *Waffen-SS* troops in the icy wastes of Finland. German troops served with the Finns against the Soviets until 1944.

7 Himmler with fellow *SS* officers in 1944. By 1945 the *Waffen-SS* numbered one million men, while the business enterprises of his empire controlled 20 concentration and 165 labour camps.

Sachsenhausen near Berlin. The first inmates were Jews and communists, but soon socialists, democrats, Catholics, Protestants, pacifists, Jehovah's Witnesses, clergymen and even dissident Nazis filled the camps. To meet the demand, other camps were established: Ravensbrück, Belsen, Gross-Rosen and Papenburg. Once Austria was annexed, Mauthausen was built, and then Theresienstadt in Bohemian Czechoslovakia in 1939. With the conquest of Poland, extermination camps in the East were then constructed to carry through the "Final Solution".

Conditions in the concentration camps in the 1930s were brutal in the extreme. *SS* guards, selected from the worst elements of the Nazi movement, worked the starved and beaten inmates beyond their limits of physical endurance. Torture was commonplace. Inmates were divided into four groups: political opponents of Nazism;

Below: Following the *Anschluss* with Germany, Viennese Jews are forced to clean the streets of the city. The Nazis tapped into a rich vein of anti-semitism in Austria.

Right: The official boycott of Jewish shops began in April 1933. In 1937, Jewish businesses could be confiscated without legal justification.

those deemed to be racially inferior; criminals; and "shiftless" elements believed to be anti-social. The second group (of those deemed racially inferior) was marked out for special treatment. Criminals were divided into two groups: the *Befristete Vorbeugungshäflinge* – or *BV* – (Prisoners in Limited-Term Preventive Custody) represented those who had already been in prison; the *Sicherungsverwahrte* – or *SV* – (Prisoners in Security Custody) consisted of convicts actually serving sentences. The political opponents were a spectrum of German society: from listeners of illegal radio stations to those actively opposed to the Third Reich. The "shiftless" element included homosexuals, who were singled out for ghastly castration experiments to "correct" their sexual orientation (see below).

All the inmates wore a coloured patch on the left breast and right leg of their clothing. In addi-

tion, at many camps a serial number was tattooed on the left forearm. All political prisoners had a red patch; criminals, green; the "shiftless", black; homosexuals, pink; Gypsies, brown; and for Jews there were two yellow triangles which together formed a six-pointed Star of David. Foreigners in the camps were identified by letters: "F" for France, "P" for Poland. The letter "A" marked out a labour disciplinary prisoner (from the German word *Arbeit* for "work"). Those deemed "feeble-minded" were marked with *Blöd* ("stupid"). Inmates deemed an escape risk had to wear a red-and-white target sewn on the chest and back of their clothing.

Few groups within Germany, with the exception of the Jews, were treated with more brutality than the Gypsies. Two major groups of Gypsies, the Sinti and Roma, had migrated to Germany in the fifteenth century. While many had converted to Christianity, this did not protect them from persecution. Everything about them seemed wrong to the Nazi-sympathizing German: they were unkempt, they were nomadic and their customs and language singled them out from the surrounding German population. According to the Nazis' new racial science, they were seen as habitual thieves and criminals. For all of these reasons, Gypsies were quickly rounded up and sent to the

Below: Rudolf Hess, deputy leader of the party until his bizarre flight to Britain in 1941 when he tried to negotiate a peace with Britain. He died in Spandau prison in 1987.

concentration camps. In September 1939, at a conference in Berlin chaired by Heydrich, a genocide programme for the Gypsies was agreed upon, and they began to be murdered in the camps.

Paragraph 175 of the Reich Criminal Code, dating back to 1871, specified that sexual relations between men was a criminal act punishable by prison. This law was not as harshly enforced during the period of the Weimar Republic, and in the 1920s Hitler had turned a blind eye to the homosexuality of some of his followers; most famously, Röhm was an active homosexual. However, once Röhm's name was blackened following the "Night of the Long Knives", Hitler gave his support to the harshest treatment for homosexuals. Himmler, the head of the *SS*, proclaimed that any *SS* man found to be a homosexual would be "sent on my instruction to a concentration camp and shot while attempting to escape". Himmler was also responsible for establishing a central registry of all known homosexuals and an office to combat homosexuality. In the late 1930s, persecution speeded up and some 15,000 homosexuals were sent to concentration camps where many of them were humiliated, tortured, castrated and killed.

"ASOCIALS"

In an effort to criminalize certain behaviour, in 1938 the Reich Criminal Office defined "asocial" in the most general way as anyone who did not fit into the so-called people's community (the *Volksgemeinschaft*). This included vagabonds, Gypsies, beggars, prostitutes, alcoholics and anyone who was "work-shy" (*arbeitscheu*), a drifter or eccentric. With this catch-all classification, the Nazis could label someone "asocial" and send them off to the camps. With the Law for Prevention of Progeny with Hereditary Diseases, the hapless "asocial" could even be sterilized. There was little chance of rehabilitation, only imprisonment and death.

The mentally ill were also singled out for "special" treatment. The Nazis had long wanted to eradicate them, but public opinion was sufficiently strongly against it to prevent any "euthanasia" programme (Christians and the various German Churches were particularly prominent in this opposition). In 1935 Hitler told the Reich's leader of physicians, Dr Wagner, that large-scale killing of the mentally ill would have to wait until wartime, when it would be easier to administer. But then, in 1938, a petition reached Hitler from a father who requested that the life of his deformed son be ended. Officials in the Chancellery of the Führer, headed by Philip Bouhler, had decided that this petition should be passed on to Hitler rather than be dealt with by a ministry official. Hitler then handed the decision to one of his personal doctors, Karl Brandt, who created a Reich Committee for the Scientific Registration of Serious Hereditary and Congenital Illness. This body served as an organizing force for reports sent in by doctors, nurses and midwives across Germany wanting to know what to do with deformed children. These reports were scored by three doctors with a red plus sign (for death), a blue minus sign (for survival) or a question mark (for further assessment). The children marked with red were then killed with a lethal injection.

THE MENTALLY ILL

Gerda Bernhardt's family was one of the thousands to suffer from this "euthanasia" policy. Gerda's younger brother, Manfred, was retarded. When he was 10 he could say little beyond "Mum" and "Dad", and "Heil Hitler" – something he was proud to be able to pronounce. Neighbours suggested that it would be best if Manfred was "put away", but Manfred's mother resisted. Eventually, under pressure from her husband, Manfred's mother agreed to send Manfred to a children's hospital in Dortmund called Aplerback. Herr Bernhardt consoled his wife with the thought that Manfred would be put to work with animals on the hospital farm. Manfred's family visited every fortnight, all that was allowed, but soon discovered that their son was becoming weak and apathetic. Soon after he died. The hospital authorities said that Manfred had died from natural causes, but when Gerda went to see the body she discovered many other small bodies covered in white sheets in the hospital morgue.

What was happening at Aplerback? Paul Eggert was the son of a violent, drunken father and, after being sterilized at the age of 11, was sent to the hospital at Aplerback as a "delinquent". He was there at about the same time that Manfred died. As he was not mentally ill, he carried out odd jobs around the hospital. Eggert recalled pushing children's bodies around the hospital and how Dr Weiner Sengenhof, one of the hospital's senior doctors, would "select" children at mealtimes for an immunization injection. The children knew that those selected for "immunization" were never seen again. One child clung on to Eggert outside the consultation room screaming for help as a nurse pulled him into the room. Later in life, Eggert recalled how: "These pictures would swim in front of my eyes when I lay in bed at night and

they are still before my eyes today." Dr Theo Niebel, the doctor in charge of the Special Children's Unit at Aplerback, remained in his post until his retirement in the 1960s.

Similar programmes were instituted for mentally ill adults. At six selected asylums, specially trained teams of *SS* doctors and nurses prepared the way for the actual exterminations from late 1939. Adult patients were killed in gas chambers disguised as shower rooms or in mobile vans with carbon monoxide (often by the simple expedient of redirecting the exhaust fumes back into the locked van). Specially constructed crematoria then disposed of the corpses. News soon spread about these actions, and ugly scenes ensued as staff in some asylums sought to protect their patients from the *SS*. Relatives notified clergymen and judicial authorities. One judge who initiated criminal proceedings against Bouhler was promptly retired. These protests had some effect. Pressure from the upper echelons of the Catholic Church resulted in Hitler cancelling the killings in August 1941, but not before 70,273 people had been killed. The methods of gassing for the mentally ill would be refined and extended when the Germans looked for a "Final Solution" to the "Jewish problem".

What was the view of ordinary Germans on the use of terror against specific groups? It is a sad fact that there existed much popular approval when it came to the use of terror to deal with non-standard behaviour or non-standard categories of person (and the excuse of ignorance is not credible, as Nazi terror was highly visible, documented in the press and given legitimacy in the speeches of the Reich's leaders). Even some of those who criticized

Left: A German Jew forced to wear the yellow Star of David. The wearing of yellow stars became compulsory for Jews living in Germany in September 1941.

the regime for the detention and torture of political opponents approved of long prison sentences given to groups such as professional criminals, Gypsies and homosexuals.

For most Germans, however, dissent was not an option. Their only response to what they must have guessed was happening was to shut their eyes to it. For the Nazis had taken measures to crush dissent soon after coming to power. Following the Reichstag Fire in February 1933 (the Reichstag building burnt to the ground in an arson attack; it was a Godsend to the Nazis, who used it to consolidate power), a decree was issued which suspended all civil liberties. This decree became constitutional law in March. In the same month, the Communist Party was banned. Slowly but surely the Nazis consolidated their iron grip. Hitler declared May Day a "Day of National Labour", and made it a paid holiday, something that German workers had long desired. On May 2, however, the Nazis occupied union offices all over Germany using storm troopers in a well-planned and military like operation; all workers' organizations were merged into the German Labour Front.

Above: Roll call for the female inmates at Auschwitz-Birkenau. These women have had their heads shaved and would have been tattooed with a prison number.

Seizing and maintaining control was not just a matter of passing laws and decrees, of course; behind these measures was the use of terror. In the spring of 1933, units of the *SA*, *SS*, *Gestapo* and police sealed off whole areas of towns and cities and combed them house by house (these operations were well planned, and often involved hundreds of personnel), searching for anything and anyone considered anti-Nazi, leaving no stone unturned. The raids were accompanied by threats, beatings and arbitrary arrests. They created an atmosphere of fear and helplessness, and the subsequent build-up of the *Gestapo* surveillance system made resistance very difficult and dangerous. "After the Nazi terror of the spring of 1933, and with the increasingly systematic build-up of the *Gestapo*'s surveillance apparatus, resistance could be pursued only by determined minorities. The structural preconditions for 'mass resistance' did not exist." (Detlev Peukert)

WHIRLWIND VICTORIES

Germany under Nazi rule became a highly militarized society. Hitler reintroduced universal male conscription in an effort to meet his desire for a large army. From the 100,000 professional soldiers in 1933, the German Army

Left: German troops rush past a burning train in Russia during Operation Barbarossa. The *Wehrmacht* swept all before it in the first years of the war.
Below: Victorious German troops parade in Athens, 1941.

had grown to almost four million men when it was mobilized for war in 1939. As the war went on, military commitments increased, casualties grew and the *Wehrmacht* increasingly had to reduce exemptions to comb out men for combat duty – the age of enlistment was eventually reduced and the net cast ever wider. By 1943 there were nine and half million men under arms. Although the actual numbers declined thereafter due to ever-increasing losses and ever-shallower pools of replacement manpower, by the last months of the war virtually any male, and even some women, who could carry a rifle or even merely a Panzerfaust antitank weapon was pressed into service. This being the case, the majority of adult German males would have spent some time in a branch of the *Wehrmacht*

between 1939 and 1945. Thus their experience is central to any understanding of Germany in this period.

Hitler did not expect the British and French to go to war over Poland. He expected them to back down in the face of his demands, just as they had done so many times before. He confidently predicted: "The English will leave the Poles in the lurch as they did the Czechs." Therefore, at 12:30 hours on the afternoon of 31 August 1939, certain of victory, he issued Directive No.1 for the Conduct of the War:

Below: A *Waffen-SS* machine-gun crew in the West in 1940. Superior leadership, training and doctrine enabled the Germans to defeat the British and French Armies.

"1. Now that all the political possibilities of disposing by peaceful means of a situation which is intolerable for Germany are exhausted, I have determined on a solution by force.

2. The attack on Poland is to be carried out.
Date of attack: 1 September 1939
Time of attack: 4.45 am."

As the the evening lengthened, a million and half German troops moved up to their jumping-off points on the border with Poland. Hitler needed an excuse for his actions, and so a number of "Polish attacks" on German territory were staged. The principal incident was a supposed raid on the radio station at Gleiwitz. *SS* men in Polish uni-

Below: Polish prisoners under guard, September 1939. In the month-long Polish Campaign vast numbers of Polish troops were encircled by rapid panzer advances.

forms undertook the action, killing a number of drugged concentration camp inmates – code-named "Canned Goods" – to provide suitably realistic casualties. The *SS* commander, Alfred Naujocks, described the incident at the Nuremberg Trials: "At noon on 3 August I received from Heydrich [the head of *Sicherheitspolitzei* – Security Police] the codeword for the attack which was to take place at 8 o'clock that evening. Heydrich said: 'In order to carry out this attack report to Müller [of the *Gestapo*] for "Canned Goods". I did this and gave Müller instructions to deliver the man [actually in this case not a concentration camp inmate but a local known for his pro-Polish views] near the radio station. I received the man and had him laid down at the entrance of the station. He was alive but completely unconscious. I tried to open his eyes. I could not recognize by his eyes that he was alive, only by his breathing. I did not see the gun

Above: German horse-drawn artillery moves through Warsaw in 1939. The city had been heavily bombed by the German *Luftwaffe*, as can be seen in this photograph.

wounds but a lot of blood was smeared across his face. He was in civilian clothes. We seized the radio station, as ordered, broadcast a speech of three to four minutes over an emergency transmitter, fired some pistol shots and left."

Photographs were taken and Hitler could announce to the Reichstag on 1 September 1939: "Polish troops of the regular army have been firing on our territory during the night. Since 05:45 hours we have been returning fire." World War II had begun and the conflict soon spread. True to their guarantee to Poland, Britain and France declared war on Germany on 3 September.

For Germany a period of almost uninterrupted triumph followed as victory came upon victory. Yet very few Germans were happy to hear the news on 1 September 1939. American journalist William Shirer wrote in his diary that morning: "Everybody against the war. People talking open-

ly. How can a country go into war with a population so dead against it." Paul Stresemann, a young soldier, was perturbed: "I was very alarmed and said goodbye to my parents and girlfriend" before returning to his unit on the Polish border. Housewife Heidi Brendler, although a long-time supporter of Hitler, felt: "The whole business came as a terrible shock, for we all thought right to the last that the politicians would see sense and war would be avoided. I know I suddenly realized that both my husband and brother would be in danger and I grew very worried." There were no cheering crowds such as had characterized the outbreak of World War I – the reaction to Hitler's speech announcing war was given to a handpicked

Above: German troops advance through Norway in April 1940. The British and French, as well as the ill-prepared Norwegians, were no match for the *Blitzkrieg*.

audience at the Kroll Opera House, and was received in a more muted manner than might have been expected.

Such feelings were not limited to ordinary Germans; even at the highest levels of the Nazi Party and the military many were very concerned. Hermann Göring, head of the *Luftwaffe* and one of the highest-ranking Nazis, was beside himself with anger and shouted down the telephone at Joachim von Ribbentrop, the Foreign Minister: "You've got your damned war! It's all your doing!", before slamming down the receiver. Grand Admiral Erich Raeder, commander of the *Kriegsmarine*, the Germany Navy, viewed the prospect of naval war with Britain with gloomy foreboding. Indeed, he felt somewhat betrayed and noted on 3 September that: "Today the war

against France and England broke out, the war which according to the Führer's previous assertions, we had no need to expect before about 1944." Germany's navy was far below its projected 1944 level and Raeder lamented that "it was no way adequately equipped for the great struggle with Great Britain", and that the "surface forces … are so inferior in number and strength to those of the British Fleet … that they can do no more than show that they know how to die gallantly."

Similar feelings were being expressed in the army. General Heinz Guderian, commander of XIX Corps poised to invade Poland, recalled: "It is not with the knowledge of hindsight that I can declare that the attitude of the Army was very grave indeed and that had it not been for the Russian pact [a non-aggression treaty signed on 23 August 1939], there is no telling what the Army's reaction might have been. We did not go light-heartedly to war and there was not one general who would not have advocated peace. The older,

and many thousands of men, had been through World War I. They knew what war would mean if it were not simply confined to a campaign against the Poles … Each of us thought of the mothers and wives of our German soldiers and of the heavy sacrifices they must be called on to bear even if the outcome of the war were a successful one."

Special pleading aside, Guderian cannot be accused of being disingenuous on his last point. As he noted: "Our own sons were on active service. My elder boy, Heinz Günther, was regimental adjutant of Panzer Regiment 35: my younger son, Kurt, had been commissioned second lieutenant in the 3rd Armoured Reconnaissance Battalion of the 3rd Panzer Division and so was in my Army Corps." It is hardly surprising that Guderian's responsibility sat heavily upon him. Indeed, Heinz Günther was to be seriously wounded in France.

Germany needed a quick victory in Poland to avoid the perils of a two-front war should Britain and France attack in the West. Five German armies invaded Poland on 1 September and the *Luftwaffe* bombed Warsaw that morning. Poland's small air force was destroyed on the ground, as pilot Norbert Limmiker recalled – "in fact we saw

no combats at all in the air". The panzers drove deep into Poland under the *Luftwaffe*-controlled skies according to the *Blitzkrieg* (Lightning War) doctrine. Yet despite this the Poles fought with determination and heroism. They proved dauntless opponents. Combat engineer officer Paul Streseman described a river crossing made under fire early in the campaign and there can be no doubt that he respected his opponent. "The Poles fought hard," he recalled, "even though we had great superiority in all arms." Although "sick and frightened", he and his men moved up to the river: "'We ran forward with our rubber boats and timbers with all kinds of shellfire coming at us. It was absolutely terrifying … The dust from explosions was flying over us as we ran straight into the river … as soon as we floated into deeper water we came under terrible fire from a machine gun and the man nearest me was killed. I saw him fall off into the water and float away. I think our Stukas [Ju 87 dive-bombers] must have dealt with the

Below: The *Blitzkrieg* turns west. Motorcycle reconnaissance troops were the eyes and ears of the panzers, which burst through the French defences in the Ardennes in May 1940.

Above: The first setback. RAF pilots race to their Hurricanes during the Battle of Britain. The *Luftwaffe* was unable to establish air superiority over Britain in 1940.

opposition because the enemy fire became much less, and at last we were able to make some progress and get a bridge across. The infantry were splendid and rushed across almost as soon as we had our last timber in place. It was then that I was able to look around and found that our commander had vanished along with several more men."

Despite Polish bravery the German Army advanced remorselessly, followed by *SS Einsatzgruppen* which systematically murdered professional Poles such as teachers, doctors, officers, government officials, and also the clergy, aristocracy and Jews. General Franz Halder noted cryptically in his diary: "Housekeeping: Jews,

intelligentsia, clergy, nobility." The Poles finally surrendered on 4 October 1939. For Streseman it was not soon enough: "I personally had seen enough of war, but my fate was not in my hands." Indeed it was not, and he would see combat soon enough when Germany invaded France the following year. Nonetheless, he acknowledged in the short term that the Polish victory was greeted with "great celebrations at home".

Hitler's first major campaign in western Europe was the invasion of Norway launched on 9 April 1940. In an audacious combined operation the Germans seized Norway's major ports and two key airfields at Stavanger and Oslo. However, General von Falkenhorst, who planned and commanded the operation, prepared it in a rather unorthodox manner: "I went to town and bought a Baedeker, a tourist guide, in order to find out what Norway was like … I had no idea; I wanted to know where

Above: A Heinkel He III bomber shot down over Scotland, one of the 1293 *Luftwaffe* aircraft lost during the Battle of Britain. These aircraft were sorely missed later in the East.

the ports were, how many inhabitants Norway had, and what kind of country this was … I absolutely did not know what to expect." Nor did his men who saw some fierce fighting, particularly at Narvik where the Allies scored one of their few major successes of the campaign. A German sailor, ashore with his army colleagues, described being underneath the British preparatory naval bombardment: "All the cannons spewed out a devastating fire. Hundreds of shells crashed without interruption on the railway, exploded with a tremendous roar in front of the tunnel entrances, rained down with a terrific whine on the cliffs on Framnes, detonated among the houses of Vassvik, as huge boulders came hurtling down the slopes of Fagersnesfjell with an earth-shaking roar. In the town, as in the harbour, at Fagernes and on the shores of Ankenes, wooden houses burned like torches. Each detonation … sent thousands of

fragments whistling in all directions … The whole coastline … was blotted out by a thick cloud of powder and dust, which was pierced by the flashes of new explosions."

The Germans at Narvik seriously considered retreating across the border into Sweden. However, they were saved from this fate by the sudden British and French withdrawal on 8 June 1940, due to the serious crisis facing the Allies in France.

In France and Belgium, the Germans faced the well-equipped British Expeditionary Force, while the French Army was considered the best in the world at the time, and sat behind strong defences. Yet the Germans succeeded spectacularly in May

Indeed, throughout the whole campaign casualties were fairly light, about 10,000 less than in the war of 1870–71. France surrendered on 22 June. This was not merely victory but conquest. The Germans were soon given the opportunity of trying out their schoolboy French in the cafes and on the French girls. Two accounts of the period provide good examples of the prevailing German sense that, given the defeat of the French, the war was all but won. They were soon disabused.

Reinhardt Fuschler, a *Luftwaffe* technician, was aware that "overall it was a very great victory, and when at last peace came we were able to relax on the grass of the French countryside for a while." He continued: "Everybody thought the war was over. The English Army had fled back to England and lost all its equipment and we could not see how the war could continue. Hitler visited the troops, though we did not see him ourselves, then he returned to Berlin for the great victory parade so we wondered when we too would be home again. Meantime life was very good to us. I borrowed a bike and travelled all around the countryside, and found a farmer happy to let us have eggs and vegetables in barter, so all was well with us."

Luftwaffe pilot Werner Bartles, wing-man to famous ace Adolf Galland, recalled: "[Galland] and I were the first pilots to walk down the Champs Elysées after France capitulated. We made plans to be the first ones to walk down Bond Street in London as well. In fact, it didn't take long for me to get to London after all – only I wasn't a victor, I was a prisoner."

The campaign to achieve air superiority prior to an invasion of Britain was Germany's first setback. The brunt of what was known to the British

and June 1940, the panzer divisions tearing a hole through those defences and racing westwards towards the Channel coast. Those breakthroughs were achieved by a mixture of careful preparation and extraordinary *élan*.

Guderian recalled an attack on the French forts around Belfort: "The tactics employed were very simple; first a short bombardment by the artillery … then Eckinger's battalion (part of the 1st Panzer Division), in armoured troop-carrying vehicles, and an 88mm AA gun drove right up to the fort, the latter taking up position immediately in front of the gorge; the riflemen thus reached the glacis without suffering any casualties and climbed up it, clambered over the entrenchments and scaled the wall while the 88mm … fired into the gorge at point-blank range. The fort was then summoned to surrender, which under the impact of the rapid attack, it did … our assault troops turned to their next task. Our casualties were very light."

as the Battle of Britain was borne inevitably by the *Luftwaffe*. Fuschler described the period thus: "Those summer days of 1940 are a hazy memory; they were all very much the same … We would rise at dawn to begin work to ensure that every valuable machine was in flying condition, and they mostly were. I remember the young faces of the pilots: they were brimming with confidence and eager to get into the fight with the RAF [Royal Air Force]. Day after day we watched anxiously for their return. On the first day of combat there were strained faces on the ground as we counted them back – there were two missing."

As losses mounted and summer turned to autumn, "it became obvious that the battle could not be won" – and as the Battle of Britain dragged on Fuschler and his comrades "knew that we had reached a stalemate". Leave began to be offered more frequently as the campaign slackened: "But as the winter came we wondered what would happen next as the invasion of England was not on. I had more leaves to my home and a really grand Christmas, the last good celebration of the war, a good festive time with many friends calling but with much uncertainty for the future."

The immediate future saw more, rapid victories in the Balkans as German forces poured south on 6 April 1941: Yugoslavia fell in 11 days and Greece

Below: A Soviet captive emerges from his bunker. The Germans captured more than three million Soviet prisoners during the first months of the war in the East.

Left: German troops on the outskirts of Smolensk, July 1941. The encircled Red Army troops burnt the city to ground, in accordance with the Soviet "scorched earth" policy.

in about 17. Although impressive, this merely delayed Hitler's real ambition – his war to crush the Soviet Union. As the possibility of defeating Britain in 1940 receded, in December Hitler decided: "In view of these considerations Russia must be liquidated. Spring '41. The sooner we smash Russia the better. The operation only makes sense if we smash the state to its core in one blow. Mere conquest will not suffice." The offensive, he said, needed to be carried out as a single, unbroken operation. Hitler did not intend to make Napoleon's mistake and be defeated by the Russian winter. He would launch the operation in May 1941.

The decision to invade Yugoslavia and Greece pushed this date back to June. Nonetheless Hitler felt he had little need to worry, after all he had quickly defeated the armies of France, Britain, Belgium and the Netherlands. All of these he considered better organized and equipped than the Red Army which had performed poorly against the Finns in the winter of 1939–40. Given the size of the Soviet forces, he would need merely a bigger army and a little more time due to the vast distances involved. Hitler told his generals that the Russians "will think a hurricane has hit them". They were convinced because he had been right so many times before. But Germany was in no position to beat the Soviet Union in five months,

yet, in a remarkable act of collective self-delusion – particularly among a group of such inherently cautious men – the general staff simply changed their estimates to prove that they could win in four months. To quote General Heinz Guderian again: "Our successes to date ... and in particular the surprising speed of our victory in the West, had so befuddled the minds of our supreme commanders that they had eliminated the word 'impossible' from their vocabulary. All the men of the *OKW* [*Oberkommando der Wehrmacht* – High Command of the Armed Forces] and the *OKH* [*Oberkommando des Heeres* – High Command of the Army] with whom I spoke evinced unshakable optimism and were quite impervious to criticism or objections."

Army divisions and the *Luftwaffe* were shifted to the East in preparation. Like Guderian, many of the ordinary soldiers were somewhat dubious about the merit of the great undertaking. Paul Streseman recalled of 22 June 1941 (the opening day of Operation Barbarossa, as the invasion of the Soviet Union was codenamed): "On that quiet and terrible day when the Führer's proclamation [announcing Barbarossa] was read to us before dawn ... I just wanted to curl up somewhere and escape it all. I can tell you that not one among us showed any bravado or 'get up and go' spirit. They did their job but with no joy, even when the victories came."

Another junior officer, Hans Herwarth von Bittenfeld, remembered that: "We soldiers already had an eerie feeling when we first marched into

Opposite top: General Winter. The harsh Russian winter took its toll on German soldiers and horses alike.
Opposite bottom: In an image reminiscent of Napoleon's retreat from Moscow, Germans trudge through the snow.

the Soviet Union. I was with a regiment that was half East Prussian and half Bavarian. Prussians and Bavarians alike were in awe of the size of Russia; it reached all the way to the Pacific Ocean. The troops were not at all enthusiastic about the prospects of fighting in the Soviet Union."

He also described the ideological preparations: "Once, a representative from the Propaganda Ministry visited us and gave a speech that was, in fact, quite excellent. In an attempt to prepare us for what lay ahead, he reminded us that in the Middle Ages German knights had also ridden east. We listened silently, and there was no applause. Afterwards we stood around and the speaker said to my divisional commander: 'I am actually rather disappointed. I don't see any enthusiasm here.' A captain responded: 'Sir, enthusiasm is not the point. But when we are ordered to fight, we do it extremely well.' In a sense, this explains the tragic situation of the German front officer. We did our

damned duty, but we never believed in ultimate victory over the Soviet Union."

Indeed, the *Wehrmacht* did fight "extremely well". Operation Barbarossa did hit the Russians like a "hurricane" much as Hitler predicted. The German Army made astonishing advances through the summer and autumn of 1941. It had surrounded and defeated Soviet forces in numbers running into millions by the time it had reached the outskirts of Moscow in late November. It had covered 960km (600 miles) and captured three million Soviet prisoners. This was unprecedented – it had advanced faster and farther than any other army in modern history and was now poised outside the Soviet capital. Walter Schaefer-Kehnert, a signals officer in 11th Panzer Division, was drawing maps for his artillery battalion in preparation for the attack: "I measured the distance to the Kremlin and said 'What the hell, if we had long-range cannon we could shoot at the Kremlin.'" His remark soon spread throughout the battalion, and that night as the batteries fired "the guys were ... saying 'We're shooting at the Kremlin.'" Reconnaissance units reached the outskirts of the

Below: The Soviet counterattack outside Moscow in 1941 halted the German advance. As this photograph shows, many Soviet troops were fully equipped for winter warfare.

Right: Soviet infantry in a recaptured town during Zhukov's December 1941 offensive. The warmly dressed Soviet troops are in stark contrast to the German dead in the foreground.

city, yet the German supply lines were stretched to breaking point and their army was ill-prepared to fight in winter, for the campaign was already supposed to have been won.

On 4 December, after heavy snowfall, the temperature dropped to -34 degrees Celsius, immobilizing much German equipment. Josef Hühnerbach, an infantry NCO recalled: "I was on the Russian front in 1941, when the great cold came. We were fighting near the town of Klin, forty-odd kilometres [30 miles] from Moscow. The cold was terrible, and we got our winter uniforms in the spring. I'll never forget it … Up to then we had regular clothing: an overcoat, a pair of gloves, and headgear. And Hitler said – I'll never forget this – 'The Russians will lay down their arms within the next eight weeks. I'm sure of it.' After that he didn't say anything. After that came the end, and we were the ones laying down the arms."

ZHUKOV'S COUNTERATTACK

On 5 December, as the temperature sunk still lower to -40 degrees, Soviet commander Georgi Zhukov ordered a counterattack with the nine armies he had conserved for the defence of Moscow. At this time the Red Army had 718,000 men, 7985 guns and mortars, and 721 tanks, mostly T-34s, on their central front. Karl Krupp, a tank man explained: "That was when I became familiar with the crack Siberian troops who'd been thrown into action on the Moscow front … These troops were excellently equipped: fur coats, fur caps, fur-lined boots and gloves. Our *Landser* [infantry] were a pitiful sight in comparison: light coats, rags wrapped around feet or shoes. I myself had managed to get some Russian felt boots; I'd taken them off a dead Russian. You had to do this right

away, because rigor mortis set in very quickly in that cold."

Although Zhukov's offensive was not totally successful, the Germans were pushed back to the positions they had held in November and Moscow was saved. The German offensive would restart the following spring and massive advances would again be made, but the checking of the *Wehrmacht* outside Moscow was a turning point in the war. There would be no more "whirlwind victories" after that. Losses had been enormous. To give one example, at the beginning of Barbarossa the Germany Army had 500,000 trucks; by December 150,000 had been lost and another 275,000 were in need of urgent repair.

Perhaps the last word should lie with an ordinary soldier, Karl Krupp: "The first time I got the idea that things might go wrong was during my leave from the front, after the battle of Moscow. The German people were being told that only the cold winter was to blame for the disaster, and not the Russian Army. Well, it was just as cold on the other side. The Russians were better and more thoroughly prepared to deal with the severe conditions. They knew what was at stake: their homeland. We, on the other hand, had not only heard so many lies, but we also saw the rear-echelon and home troops taking it easy. We felt like we'd been already written off."

PORTENTS OF DOOM, 1941–44

Above: A haggard German machine-gunner at Stalingrad. This German defeat marked a turning point in the war. Below: Bomb-damaged Panther tank turrets in the railway yards at Anchaffenburg in Germany, November 1944.

Chief-of-Staff General Halder noted that up to Moscow the *Wehrmacht* had lost 743,112 men killed, wounded or captured in the campaign. This was over 23 percent of the army's strength. He reckoned this was half the fighting strength of the infantry since the vast majority of casualties are not inflicted on clerks, cooks and drivers, but frontline troops. German replacements in this period were less than 100,000. This stretched and weakened army was hit by Zhukov's massive counteroffensive in December 1941. Although Army Group Centre, responsible for the assault on Moscow, rallied and held firm, the battle for Moscow marked a turning point in the war. There would be no more *Blitzkrieg*-style victories, the war in the East had turned into a remorseless and attritional slogging match in which weight of numbers in both men and matériel would count for as much if not more than tactical *élan*.

The Russian winter had come early and would be unusually long and cold. Dr Henrich Haape in the 106th Infantry Division recalled: "In this unearthly cold, in which the breath froze and icicles hung from nostrils and eyelashes all day long, where thinking was an effort, the German soldiers fought … Habit and discipline kept them going; that and the flicker of instinct to stay alive. And when a soldier's mind had become numb, when his strength, his discipline and his will had been used up, he sank into the snow. If he was noticed, he was kicked and slapped into a vague awareness that his business in this world was not finished, and he staggered to his feet and groped on. But if

he lay where he had collapsed until it was too late, as if forgotten he was left lying at the side of the road and the wind blew over him and everything was levelled indistinguishably."

The winter clothing finally began to arrive in March: far too late. The terrible winter had caused heavy attrition of men, vehicles and weapons. Yet the lull in the fighting allowed the re-equipment and preparation of German forces for a renewed offensive in 1942. In April Hitler decided to concentrate the advance in the south, merely holding the line in other sectors of the front. This plan, codenamed Plan Blue, was intended to lead to the capture of the vital oil fields in the Caucasus. Forces were shifted southwards, and on 28 June 1942 the great offensive opened. For a while it was like Barbarossa again as the German armoured spearheads made massive advances. Paul Streseman returned to his unit in the midst of the offensive "which seemed to achieve all its objectives". However, as Streseman pointed out: "No matter how much territory we took or how many 'Russkis' we killed or captured, or the booty gained, there was always more." The steppes stretched on and on, as Field Marshal von Rundstedt said in the summer of 1942: "The vastness of Russia devours us." Streseman concurred and could at least count small mercies: "Those Russian summer days were very, very hot, but far

Above: An RAF Mosquito sinks *U–251* in the Kattegat. By late 1942, Allied technological advances and the increased deployment of aircraft led to mounting U-boat losses.

preferable to the cursed cold of winter."

The Germans drove south at a rapid rate, and the city of Stalingrad sat on the left of the German axis of advance. Thus Hitler gave the capture of the city priority in July and gave the task to General Fredrich Paulus's Sixth Army, supported by Hermann Hoth's Fourth Panzer Army. By early September Paulus's men had reached Stalingrad, yet Stalin's determination to hold the city that bore his name meant they would have to take the city street by street. Unlike Streseman, many German troops thought victory was in their grasp. A soldier in the 389th Infantry Division wrote home: "You can't imagine the speed of our dear motorized comrades and with it the rolling attacks of our *Luftwaffe*. What a feeling of security we get when our pilots are above us, because you never see any Russian aircraft. I would like to share with you a little glimmer of hope. Our division will have fulfilled its duty as soon as Stalingrad falls. We should then, God willing, see each other again this year. If Stalingrad falls, the Russian army in the south is destroyed."

Stalingrad did not fall. Street-fighting is particularly costly, and casualties mounted as the Sixth

Above: General Franz Halder, Chief of the Army's General Staff. His was dismissed in September 1942 after a disagreement with Hitler on strategic issues.

Army was sucked deeper into the city. Antony Beevor, in his study of the battle, *Stalingrad*, described the conditions facing the German troops as the battle dragged on: "German soldiers, red-eyed with exhaustion from the hard fighting, and mourning more comrades than they ever imagined, had lost the triumphalist mood of just a week before. Everything seemed disturbingly different. They found artillery far more frightening in a city. The shell burst itself was not the only danger. Whenever a tall building was hit, shrapnel and masonry showered from above. The *Landser* had already started to lose track of time in this alien world, with its destroyed landscape of ruins and rubble. Even the midday light had a strange, ghostly quality from the constant haze of dust."

This was very different from battle in the open countryside. A panzer officer wrote: "The air is filled with the infernal howling of diving Stukas, the thunder of flak and artillery, the roar of engines, the rattle of tank tracks, the shriek of launcher and 'Stalin organ' [the German nickname for Soviet rocket artillery], the chatter of sub-machine guns back and forth, and all the time one feels the heat of a city burning at every point."

THE SIXTH ARMY GRINDS TO A HALT

Hitler's frustration with the slow progress in Stalingrad led to his dismal of Chief-of-Staff Halder, whom he regarded as an overly cautious pessimist. Halder, in turn, regarded Hitler as a dangerous amateur when it came to military strategy. Hitler told Halder on 24 September: "You and I have been suffering from nerves. Half my exhaustion is due to you. It is not worth while going on. We need National Socialist ardour now, not professional ability. I cannot expect this of an officer of the old school such as you." Halder's dismissal and Hitler replacing him with the more compliant Kurt von Zeitzler thus removed one of the few checks on the Führer's increasingly inept military interventions.

National Socialist ardour, however, could not save the Sixth Army. By the end of September, Paulus' and Hoth's men had taken two-thirds of the city and Hitler announced to the German people and the world that the city would fall. However, in November Zhukov sprung his trap. He had been secretly assembling Soviet reserves to the east of the city, and on 19 November he launched his forces at the two Romanian armies flanking Germany's Sixth Army. The Romanians fought hard but soon collapsed, and the Red Army was able to complete the encirclement of German forces in the city by 23 November. Paulus, who had 20 divisions – some 250,000 men – asked for permission to break out but Hitler refused. He assured Paulus that contact would be re-established soon, and in the meantime the Sixth Army would be supplied by air. Göring assured Hitler his air force could deliver 305 tonnes (300 tons) a day to the encircled troops in the the pocket. The

Right: A German soldier captures two Soviets during the siege of Sevastopol, June 1942. The German offensive in the south led to the capture of the Crimean port.

Luftwaffe managed barely 91.44 tonnes (90 tons) a day. Conditions deteriorated for the troops in Stalingrad. Heinz Pfennig, a young lieutenant, recalled: "Our real trouble began as soon as we were encircled. We were placed on short rations some time in December … Our potatoes were just dried potato flakes." As the weather further hampered air supply things became worse. Pfennig continued: "At Christmas, each of us got a tablespoon of peas, two tablespoons of a soup made of dried potatoes, two squares of chocolate. We had no winter clothes, and the only thing we could do was bundle up in the snow and wait for the enemy to come and get us."

Tank man Count Friedrich Ernst von Solms's Christmas diet was even grimmer. "Christmas was miserable," he recalled. "We ate cats and dogs, we had only a little bread. Even the horse meat had run out." Pfennig also vividly described life in the frontline: "We developed a system at the barricades. It was a little warmer in the basements of these houses, and, while one or two soldiers sat watching upstairs, all the rest huddled downstairs with their weapons. The guys on watch … gave us a signal if anything was up. They put me up there on guard duty. Since I had pieces of cloth wrapped around my hands and wrists [he was suffering from frostbite] and couldn't hold on to anything, they hung a bag of nails from the ceiling. If I shook that bag it was the signal that the Russians were coming, and my comrades would charge up the basement stairs and open fire."

The Soviets gradually strangled the encircled army. Jesco von Puttkamer, a Sixth Army staff officer, described the fatalism that set in among the beleaguered Germans in the pocket: "Although we were resigned, we kept on fighting. There wasn't any other alternative. I was in the isolated northern pocket. There was nothing left – ammu-

Right: Colonel-General Hermann Hoth, commander of the Fourth Panzer Army, which spearheaded the drive towards the Caucasus and took part in the battle for Stalingrad.

Left: A Type VII U-boat in the Atlantic. The failure of the U-boats to cut the Atlantic supply lines allowed the United States to deliver massive aid to Britain.

field marshal. That day the slogan went around the pocket: "We will not surrender on the tenth anniversary of the national revolution (30 January 1933)". As Heinz Pfennig eloquently put it: "Big words in a shitty situation." The inference to be drawn from Paulus's promotion was clear – Hitler expected his subordinate to kill himself as no German field marshal had ever been captured. The following day Paulus surrendered. The Germans slowly emerged from the bunkers and cellars to be marched into captivity. Those who were too badly wounded to move were often finished off on the spot. A number of survivors from the 297th Infantry Division were confronted by a Russian officer, who pointed at the ruins that surrounded them and shouted: "That is how Berlin is going to look!" The German Red Cross estimated that Germany lost 200,000 troops in Stalingrad. About 130,000 of these had been captured. Their fate was not pleasant. Food was in short supply, but as Puttkamer remembered "The initial months were the worst; our men died like flies. But the Russians themselves in the Stalingrad sector had nothing to eat either." The provisional holding camps were exceedingly grim; typhoid, diphtheria and dysentery were rife. An Austrian doctor noted his first impression of the prison camp at Beketova: "Nothing to eat, nothing to drink, filthy snow and urine-yellow ice offered the only relief for an unbearable thirst ... Every morning more corpses."

nition, no rations, nothing at all. We walked into total annihilation with our eyes wide open. There was a division commander who, wearing his trousers with the general's stripes on the sides, stepped on a railway embankment and just stood there until a bullet hit him. That was General von Hartman [commander of the 71st Infantry Division]. Others, like Paulus, just waited in their bunkers until the Russians walked through the door. There was no more heroism, there was hardly even suffering, there was just the inferno."

On 30 January 1943 Hitler promoted Paulus to

The setback greatly shocked Hitler. Guderian found him changed: "His left hand trembled, his back was bent, his gaze was fixed, his eyes protruded but lacked their former lustre, his cheeks were flecked with red." The defeat marked a considerable change in Hitler's life. The luck which had taken him through victory after victory finally seemed to elude him now. He withdrew further into his inner circle; indeed, he only made two more public appearances after the defeat.

Stalingrad was just the most serious among a number of a defeats from late 1942 to early 1943. The German Army in the Western Desert was beaten by the British at the Battle of El Alamein and was in steady retreat. The Americans and British had also landed in North Africa, further threatening the Axis position on the continent. The British were finally gaining the upper hand in the battle against German U-boats in the Atlantic. As U-boat ace Erich Topp noted: "Submarine warfare reached a critical stage towards the end of 1942. The chart curves representing U-boats destroyed and those built began to intersect. By the end of that year, we had more submarines being sunk than manufactured. Allied technical developments had advanced rapidly." Topp listed the British measures which had tipped the balance, such as the convoy system, long-range aircraft and particularly radar equipment. "Allied technology had developed so much that we had nothing in comparison." The British had also cracked the German enigma code, which meant that "all of our transmissions were intercepted … Not only did the Allies know that enemy submarines were in the area; they also knew the exact position and direction each boat was heading." The result of this was, Topp pointed out, "the relation of freighters sunk to U-boats was one to one!"

Horst Elfe, a U-boat commander, described the fate of many a U-boat in these circumstances: "The destroyer turned and at high speed headed towards my *U-93*. Its searchlights were on. Its guns bracketed us but made no direct hits … Both engines running full speed, I turned hard to starboard to avoid being rammed … The British

Below: *Africa Korps* soldiers after the Battle of El Alamein, one in number of serious German setbacks that marked a turning point in the war in late 1942 and early 1943.

Turning point of the war – STALINGRAD

1 Stalingrad burns. The *Luftwaffe* attempted to "soften up" the Soviet defences by heavy bombing in August 1942, but Stalin was determined to defend Stalingrad, the city which bore his name, regardless of the cost.

2 Two Germans in the "Stalingrad Academy of Street-Fighting". City combat was very different from the mobile war in open country at which the *Wehrmacht* excelled.

3 German troops move ever deeper into the city.

4 Despite the efforts of the Sixth Army, the Red Army clung on to its precarious toehold in the city.

5 Zhukov's offensive had encircled the Sixth Army by 23 November 1942 – it could only be supplied by air.

6 Russian POWs unload a Ju-52. Göring promised 300 tons of supplies a day – the *Luftwaffe* managed barely 90.

7 Field Marshal Friedrich Paulus, whose Sixth Army lost 200,000 troops in the Stalingrad battles.

Above: Panzergrenadiers of the élite *Grossdeutschland* Division at the Battle of Kursk, July 1943. The massive clash of armour was a strategic defeat for the Germans.

destroyer, HMS *Hesperus*, was faster and rammed us at high speed ... I gave the order to abandon ship ... the crewmen standing on the conning tower, including myself, were thrown overboard as the boat sank. We lost six men ... The *Hesperus* turned around, switched on her searchlights, threw out nets aft and moved slowly through the swimmers ... The British commander's orderly took me aboard, wrapped me in a woollen blanket, poured me a strong rum, lit me a Players Navy Cut and stuck it between my lips. He tried to console me by saying, 'You take it easy, sir' instead of something like, 'You bloody German Nazi!'" Elfe was considerably luckier than most German submariners: of the 40,000 sailors sent out by the *Kriegsmarine*, less than 10,000 came back.

Stalingrad may have shaken Hitler somewhat, but he remained convinced of his military genius and continued to direct the German war in the East. He expected 1943 to be a period of retrenchment. The Germans had extricated themselves pretty successfully from the Caucasus. The bulge in the lines around the town of Kursk left by the Soviet counteroffensive provided the Germans with the opportunity to inflict a heavy defeat upon the enemy. However, the Red Army had prior knowledge of the German intention and set about turning the salient into a huge fortress, building up belt after belt of mine-fields, entrenchments and bunkers. The confrontation that followed involved 900,000 German and Axis troops and 2700 armoured vehicles facing 1,337,000 Russians with 3330 tanks, making it the largest tank battle in history. The German attack, codenamed Citadel, began on 5 July 1943. The battle soon became a brutal contest of attrition as the

Germans struggled to make any headway against the well-prepared Soviet defenders.

STEEL INFERNO AT KURSK

The official history of the *Grossdeutschland* Division vividly described the scene: "The Panzer Regiment GD [*Grossdeutschland*] and Panther [the new German tank] brigade were supposed to attack … however they had the misfortune to drive into a minefield that had escaped notice until then – and this even before reaching the Bolshevik trenches! It was enough to make one sick. Soldiers and officers alike feared that the entire affair was going to pot. The tanks were stuck fast, some bogged down on the tops of their tracks, and to make matters worse the enemy was firing at them with antitank rifles, antitank guns and artillery. Tremendous confusion breaks out. The fusiliers advance without tanks – what can they do? The tanks do not follow. Scarcely does the enemy notice the precarious situation of the fusiliers when he launches a counter-attack supported by numerous close-support aircraft. The infantry companies of III Panzer-Fusilier Regiment *GD* … walked straight into ruin. Even the heavy company suffered 50 killed and wounded in a few hours. The Pioneers were moved up immediately and they began to clear a path through the mine-infested terrain. Ten more hours had to pass before the first tanks and self-propelled guns got through and reached the infantry."

The battle climaxed on 12 July, when Hoth's Fourth Panzer Army with 700 tanks clashed with the 800 tanks of General Rotmistrov's Fifth Guards Tank Army around the town of Prokhorovka. Waves of Soviet T-34

tanks closed to point-blank range and the battle degenerated into a gigantic mêlée. Soviet General Kirill Moskalenko described the tank battle: "It was hard to tell who was attacking and who was defending … There was no place for manoeuvre. The tank men were forced to fire point-blank. Villages and heights changed hands repeatedly. The enemy lost heavily … [and] were compelled to go over to the defensive … the Nazis had dreamed of reaching Kursk in four days but in the first 11 days of fighting failed to penetrate deep into half our defensive line…"

After Prokhorovka there was little likelihood that Citadel would succeed. The rebuilt German armoured force had been squandered, its reserves eaten up in a massive attritional battle in which lit-

Right: Soviet T-34s in the Kursk salient, July 1943. The Red Army's antitank defences and armoured reserves defeated the Germans' Tiger and Panther tanks.

Above: Field Marshal Erwin Rommel, commander of Army Group B, inspects part of the "Atlantic Wall" in France in 1944 prior to the D-Day landings.

tle if anything had been gained. Hitler cancelled the assault on 17 July, his attention distracted by the Anglo-American invasion of Sicily. Guderian summed up the implications of Kursk thus: "By the failure of Citadel we had suffered a decisive defeat. The armoured formations, reformed and re-equipped with so much effort, had lost heavily both in men and equipment and would now be unemployable for a long time to come. It was problematical whether they could be rehabilitated in time to defend the Eastern Front; as to being able to use them in defence of the Western Front against the Allied landings that threatened for next spring, this was even more questionable. Needless to say the Russians exploited their victory to the full. There were to be no more periods of

quiet on the Eastern Front. From now on the enemy were in undisputed possession of the initiative." The Germans would never advance again in the East. From Kursk onwards the Germans were doomed to retreat.

The Soviets had long been advocating that the Western Allies – Britain and the United States – open a Second Front in France to relieve the pressure on the Soviet Union in the east. By summer 1944 they were finally in a position to do so. The long-awaited invasion of France – the largest amphibious operation in history – took place (codenamed Operation Overlord) on 6 June 1944. The Germans had expected that an invasion would come and had been preparing the defences in France for some time. Field Marshal Erwin Rommel, who commanded the army group which covered the expected invasion area, reckoned that the Allies had to be stopped on the beaches. He said: "The enemy's weakest moment is when he lands. The men are uncertain, possibly seasick. The terrain is unfamiliar. Sufficient heavy weapons are not yet available. I must defeat them at that moment." He constantly toured the coast, exhorting the men to greater efforts preparing the defences. He visited positions of the 709th Division on the Contentin Peninsula on 11 May 1944. The troops remembering his visit recalled his poor mood. His usual wit and charisma were absent – he "hadn't even handed out cigarettes". Lieutenant Arthur Jahnke, a veteran of the Eastern Front and Knight's Cross holder, showed the field marshal round the preparations. Rommel suddenly demanded: "Show me your hands, lieutenant." Jahnke took off his grey doe-skinned gloves and showed him his calloused hands. He

had soon learned to handle wire and his entrenching tool in Russia. Rommel nodded: "Well done, lieutenant; the blood of officers from entrenching is just as valuable as that shed in battle." Nonetheless Jahnke, like his commander, remained concerned about the state of the defences.

THE SECOND FRONT

They had to endure weeks of preparatory bombing, the effects of which Jahnke examined at the battery St Martin de Varreville. Paul Carrel noted in his account of the German experience of Normandy, *Invasion! They're Coming!*: "Not one stone was left on top of another. The position and its guns had been atomized." Janhke's Corporal Hein summed the situation up: "Nice prospects indeed, if they can do that." At barely quarter-past midnight on 6 June 1944, the first American and British paratroops jumped out of their aircraft over Normandy. The Americans dropped 17,000 men on the Contentin Peninsula. By 01:50 hours the German coastal radar picked up what Signals Senior Lieutenant von Willisen described to Chief-of-Staff, Naval Group West, Admiral Hoffman as "very many targets on the cathode ray tube … That can only be the invasion fleet...the invasion has begun."

The Army Command, however, was disbelieving. Yet the opening of the massive Allied naval bombardment announced the invasion incontrovertibly. Robert Vogt, an infantryman stationed near Arromanches, recalled: "It must have been around 2:30am when I jumped out of bed at the sound of a

Left: US troops embark at a British port in preparation for the D-Day landings. The Allies deployed massive firepower to support their invasion of Normandy.

huge crash. At first I had absolutely no idea what was going on. Of course we had been expecting something, but we didn't have a clue as to where and when. We didn't know that this was the invasion. In the distance, we heard bomb carpets falling all along the coast and in the rear areas. There were intermittent pauses which lasted anywhere from half an hour to an hour, but the area we were in was a terrible mess."

By the time the landings took place Vogt was in position above the beach. The defenders had already opened fire: "Then a voice called, 'Enemy landing boats approaching!' I had a good view from the top of the cliffs and looked out at the ocean. What I saw scared the devil out of me. Even though the weather was so bad, we could see a huge number of ships. Ships as far as the eye could see, an entire fleet, and I thought, 'Oh God, we're finished! We're done for now!'"

A DELUGE OF FIREPOWER

This was a different war to that on the Eastern Front. The Red Army had been profligate in its use of men, launching massive yet determined attacks at heavy cost. The Soviets had also – particularly at Stalingrad – relished close-quarter combat. In the west the British and Americans relied heavily on their superior firepower. Vogt summed the Allied attitude up well: "The Allies could afford to spare their troops, what with their superiority in equipment. They said 'Why should we sacrifice a single GI against German infantry fire; the Germans outdo us there anyway. No, we'll just carpet bomb them. We'll just use our flyers to drop the sky on their heads. We'll just make use of our superior artillery.'"

The fate of the Panzer Lehr Division provides ample evidence of the overwhelming nature of Allied firepower. After fighting for 49 days solidly the division was reduced to a mere 2200 men and 45 serviceable tanks. By 25 July 1944, it sat squarely in front of the proposed site for the US offensive, Operation Cobra, which broke the German posi-

Left: German self-propelled antiaircraft guns in action in Normandy. The Western Allies held almost total supremacy in the air during the battle for France in 1944.

tion in France. That morning, waves of American P-47 Thunderbolt fighter-bombers swept over the division, 50 fighters at a time every two minutes. They dropped high-explosives and napalm. They were followed by 400 medium bombers carrying 500lb (227kg) bombs. Finally, 1500 B-17 Flying Fortress and B-24 Liberator heavy bombers carrying a total of 3300 tons of bombs attacked. They obliterated everything; tanks were picked up and hurled into the air by the blasts. This was followed by 300 P-38 Lightning fighter-bombers carrying

Below: British troops pour ashore in Normandy on 6 June 1944. The Allies soon established a strong bridgehead in Normandy – Hitler now faced a war on two fronts.

fragmentation and napalm bombs. Nearly half the Panzer Lehr died in the air attack. Many hundreds more were killed by the 10,000 guns that opened up from the moment the aircraft left. The divisional commander, General Fritz Bayerlein, veteran of North Africa, later told his captors that that morning was his worst experience in battle. When ordered to hold the position, he replied: "Everyone is holding up front … everyone. My grenadiers and pioneers, my antitank gunners, they're holding. None of them have left their positions, none. They're lying in their foxholes, still and mute, because they are dead. Dead, do you understand? Tell the field marshal [Von Kluge, Rommel's replacement] that the Panzer Lehr is

destroyed. Only the dead can still hold." As if to emphasize the point a nearby ammunition dump was hit by a fighter-bomber, blowing in the windows of the building in which he was standing. Bayerlein was not exaggerating by much.

The course of the war had turned decisively against Germany on all fronts. In June 1944, the Soviets launched a massive offensive (codenamed Bagration) in support of Operation Overlord which took them to the gates of Warsaw and into East Prussia by January 1945. The Western Allies – though checked temporarily by the disastrous failure to seize the bridge over the Rhine by an airborne operation at Arnhem – continued to push steadily towards the borders of the Reich. Siegfried Kügler, a German paratrooper, was captured in early 1945; he recalled American material strength: "The Americans were marching towards the Rhine. When we saw everything that was

Above: Knocked-out Tiger tanks in France, 1944. Even the Germans' heaviest armour could do little more than slow the inexorable advance of the Western Allies.

going past, all the artillery, tanks and trucks, well I've got to say I just flipped. I thought: 'how do you declare war on such a country?' We asked ourselves, 'Didn't that guy Hitler learn any geography, or what?' No matter how good or bad the Americans were as soldiers, their equipment alone was enough to win the war."

Nevertheless, these battles proved that the German soldier was a skillful opponent who had been taught to use his initiative to exploit tactical situations, and this was especially true of junior commanders, who were allowed to display personal initiative and freedom of action. In this way the German Army was able to resist Allied numerical superiority and therefore prolong the war.

HOME FRONT: INDUSTRY & PRODUCTION

Above: A foreign worker in Germany. Industry was increasingly forced to rely on imported labour in the war. Below: German men conscripted to dig defensive earthworks – such work detracted from industry's needs.

Germany was the industrial centre of the Axis powers and the economic powerhouse of continental Europe, the only Axis nation that could come anywhere near to matching the prodigious output of the Soviet and American economies. After the stunning military successes of 1939–41, Nazi Germany also controlled the resources and manufacturing facilities of occupied Europe – the raw materials and factories of Belgium, the Netherlands, France, Luxembourg, Denmark and Norway all lay under German rule. Yet the Allies continued to out-produce the Germans in almost all spheres of military equipment, and by late 1942 they were building three times as many aircraft and tanks. There can be little doubt that throughout the war, Hitler's Germany produced far fewer weapons than its resources in materials, manpower, technical and scientific skill and manufacturing capability could have made possible. Admittedly, Britain, the Soviet Union and the United States had access to a massive weight of resources, but it is not just a question of a balance of raw material and manufacturing capability, there were other factors as well. Up until 1943 Britain out-produced Germany and its empire in almost all major weapon systems, despite Britain's smaller economy. In 1942, the Soviet Union had lost a third of its rail network and had its supply of iron ore, coal and steel cut by three-quarters due to the rapid German advance across her territory. The Soviet industrial base had been reduced to a size even smaller than that of Britain, yet it produced half as much again as Germany between 1942 and 1945. As historian Richard Overy notes, "however much the statistics may mask differences in policy and circumstances, this is still a significant contrast. Had the situation been otherwise German fighting power might well have avoided the remorseless attrition which set in in 1944."

Yet before the war broke out the German economy was probably better prepared for conflict than any other in Europe. Rearmament had begun in 1933 and accelerated from 1936 onwards. Nonetheless, as far as the levels of armaments were concerned, the war in Europe began three or four years prematurely for the *Wehrmacht*. While Hitler mobilized the armament factories and civilian industries after the outbreak of war, in an

Below: The U-boat Atlas Works at Bremen. Despite considerable priority given to the building of submarines, losses in the Battle of the Atlantic outstripped supply.

attempt to make up the difference, there was no total economic mobilization in preparation for a long war. To quote the *Oxford Companion to the Second World War*, "the peacetime war economy (from August 1936) was followed … by peace-like wartime economy. By and large business as usual prevailed."

Nonetheless, by the summer of 1941 more than half of the German workforce was engaged in military construction. This was a higher level of commitment than Britain in 1941 and higher than that of the United States throughout the war. On top of this, Germany had access to the resources of conquered Europe, as stated above, including almost the entire European coal and steel industry, as well as the workers and manufacturing capability of the

conquered continent. However, the output of armaments was little higher two years after the outbreak of war than it had been at the start. Yet by mid-1941 Hitler was about to launch Operation Barbarossa, which would draw him into a terrible war of attrition against the Soviet Union where manufacturing capabilities and economic output would be as important, if not more so, than skill on the battlefield.

There are various reasons for the failure to increase production levels in the first years in an economy as advanced as that of mid-twentieth century Germany. German bureaucracy was confused and stultifying, and Germany did not possess a single central administrative authority to coordinate the war effort. The Council of Ministers for Reich Defence, which was the responsibility of Hermann Göring, had been formed in August 1939 and might have played a useful role in coordinating civilian and military and industrial needs. However, it had been dis-

Below: German women collect glass bottles for the war economy. All the belligerent nations used recycled household goods for use in vital military production.

Above: Despite this image, one of the great flaws of the German war economy was its inability to mobilize women, whose place was seen as being in the home.

banded after six meetings because Göring did not want to come into conflict with Hitler, who had concentrated much of the power over industry in his hands. Although Hitler could order the types of weapons he thought necessary, without a centrally planned economy the implementation of his proposals was somewhat erratic. To quote Overy once more,:"there was no straight line of command between Führer and factory. In between lay a web of ministries, plenipotentiaries and Party commissars, each with their own apparatus, interests and rubber stamps, producing more than the usual weight of bureaucratic inertia. At the end of the line was a business community most of whom remained wedded to entrepreneurial independence, and who resented the jumbled administration, the corrupt Nazi Party hacks, the endless

form-filling, which stifled what voluntary efforts they might have made to transform the war economy."

The Germans never really mastered the modern concept of mass production. The German armed forces had traditionally worked with smaller firms and skilled craftsmen who could produce sophisticated weaponry. Indeed, German industry had always been strong in terms of quality skilled workmanship and advanced technology. However, these virtues were demanding in time and material. Sophistication was preferred to high-quantity production. The technically brilliant German

Above: Forced labour at work in 1944. Given the Nazi Government's reluctance to harness much of its own workforce, it looked to occupied Europe to fulfill its needs.

tank, the Mark V Panther, was a superlative weapon system but it took time to produce. This was illustrated by the production methods of, for example, the Maschinenfabrik Niedersachsen Hanover plant, which ignored the mass production methods that had been pioneered in the United States. The Panthers were not built on a Henry Ford-style production line as was preferred in the West and the Soviet Union (though German workers still undertook repetitive tasks). At the Hanover plant, however, the tanks were moved from station to station where a specific task was performed. It ensured excellent workmanship but did not speed production.

For the workers, the tightly controlled Nazi state meant that industrial disputes were not an option. This did ensure that production was not interrupted by industrial action. Willi Erbach, a metalworker recalled: "You couldn't say anything; the shop steward was always standing behind you. Now it all wouldn't have been so bad, we would have been able to come to terms even with all of that – if you resigned, what were you going to do then? You thought about your enjoyments in life … There were no conflicts in the firm at that time, everyone was in the *DAF* [*Deutsche Arbeitsfront*, German Labour Front], since you couldn't risk anything … When you did your work – there weren't any conflicts, you just had to get on with your piecework – [there were] strict controls. You know German craftsmanship, which used to be good and is just as good today – I hope that it's just as good today, and, after all, you wanted to earn money."

Erbach's attitude was understandable given that early attempts at industrial action had been brutally suppressed by the police. Recalcitrant cases often had to endure a spell of "education of the work-shy" in Dachau concentration camp. Nonetheless, slightly more subtle forms of resistance could be undertaken in response to the longer hours, wage-freezes and worsening conditions in Germany's factories as the drive to increase production continued. The great strain imposed by the long hours led to a staggering rise in illness (real or feigned) among employees and into the growth in the number of accidents at work. In some key industries, there was a fall

rather than a rise in productivity. Absenteeism and indiscipline were common. The police and *Gestapo* were increasingly used to combat such behaviour. Resentment could grow; the *Sicherheitsdienst* (*SD* – Security Service) in Würzburg in the spring of 1941 painted a rather bleak picture of worker opinion: "In some sections of the working class there is unrest. There the word 'swindle' can again be heard: the people will have nothing to laugh about even if we win the war; we are being lied to at every turn; what is pointed out as a weakness for England is supposed to be a good thing for us; some are getting fat while others starve; workers' wives are conscripted for service, the wives of high civil servants and especially of officers continue their comfortable life of idleness (*drohnenleben*)

Below: German workers toil in an armaments factory. The German armaments industry was generally ill-equipped to deal with the massive requirements of Total War.

Left: German workers in a heavy industrial plant rest in the air-raid shelter. Such shelters became increasingly necessary as Allied bombing of Germany intensified.

just as before; the 'rubbish' (*krampf*) is worse than during the world war [World War I]; most people are sick from pure anger in their belly; it's time the swindle stopped."

LABOUR SHORTAGES

The need for more and more men to fill the ranks of the *Wehrmacht* led to chronic labour shortages. The Nazi regime saw two possibilities: increasing hours and holding down wages, which, as mentioned above, met with little success; or make use of new labour resources. There were two sources of labour that Nazi Germany could tap: women and foreign workers. The extensive mobilization of women that proved so successful in the United States, Britain and the Soviet Union did not occur in Germany. Nazi ideology emphasized the woman's role as wife and mother rather than worker. Half-hearted efforts to encourage women into the factories were largely unsuccessful. By the eve of the Russian campaign in 1941, the numbers of women employed in German industry was scarcely higher than at the start of the war. In Germany, the number of economically active women did not rise above the level of May 1939 until 1943, when Hitler's deputies finally overrode his opposition to

drafting women into war work. All citizens had to register for employment, but women found it easy to evade employment because officials were often reluctant to enforce the measure. Many female Nazis despaired because, having supported a powerful leader who had placed strong families at the centre of Nazi ideology, they imagined this was being undermined. After all, Nazi policy maintained that women's major function was to breed children for the Reich. As Auguste Reber-Gruber, a high-ranking female Nazi in the Education Ministry confided: "Oh, how our old rivals would rejoice if they could see how badly the Party treats its women."

Far more than the employment of women,

Right: A foreign worker in a German factory. Imported workers provided a useful source of additional labour, but were no real substitute for skilled German workers.

German war production relied heavily on foreign labour. By 1944 foreign workers amounted to 21 percent of the industrial workforce. However, foreign labour was no real substitute for skilled German workers. The Germans also drew on concentration camp labour; in 1944 their number rose from 30,000 to over 300,000. The conditions for foreign workers were by no means identical. The concentration camp inmates were worked to death in appalling conditions. The post-war Nuremberg Trials described this as a policy of "extermination through work". The eastern workers, the Russians and the Poles, were poorly treated, even if they were not worked to death; almost universally their physical health was ruined. Workers from countries such as Denmark and France were not so horrendously treated, yet even they lived in squalid conditions on low pay and were bullied and victimized by German workers, whose conditions in the industrial regions of Germany were also growing worse.

Above: The concentration camps also provided a source of forced labour. Inmates were deliberately worked to death in appalling conditions as a matter of policy.

Hitler had recognized the problem of the military interfering in industry and he berated it for burdening production with unnecessarily complex demands. Hitler wanted "more primitive, robust construction" and the introduction of "crude mass production" methods. However, it took the appointment of Albert Speer as Minister of Armaments to bring German industrial production to something like its proper potential. He established a centralized planning board and rationalized arms production. He closed down small firms and redistributed the released skilled labour. He decided upon the allocation of raw materials and resources at a national level. He set up an interlocking system of production for major weapon systems and planned and supervised all military production. Speer's reforms resulted in large improvements in efficiency, coordination and control. He also managed to reduce the role of the military in the war economy. The military had interfered in the development and manufacturing of weapons and largely slowed down the production of goods. Hitler noted that this interference meant that his industrialists "were always complaining about this niggardly procedure – today an order for 10 howitzers, tomorrow for two mortars and so on." Military interference meant that German industry lost a sense of priority due to conflicting and complicated demands. As a group of German engineers from Rechlin complained in 1944, "nobody would seriously believe that so much inadequacy, bungling, confusion, misplaced power, failure to recognize the truth and deviation from the reasonable to really exist." Speer successfully pushed the military out of the war economy and allowed production to be run by industrial engineers. This paid considerable dividends in production, which rose markedly in 1943–44.

THE ALLIED BOMBING CAMPAIGN

Only the success of the Allied bombing campaign in the summer of 1944 slowed down and finally collapsed German production. The effects of Allied bombing were twofold. It directly halted and reduced production. Hits on factories slowed the output of goods. The American daylight bombing and British night-time raids also had an effect on the city around the industrial area or factory that was nominally the target. Water, gas and electricity supplies were disrupted or cut, as were railway lines and roads. Many smaller component-producing factories might also be hit. Much of that damage could be rapidly repaired and production might restart within months, weeks or even days. However, on top of all this, bombing produced indirect problems such as sapping the morale of the workforce. The population was under constant strain and this produced exhaustion and listlessness. One German civilian said: "One can't get used to the raids. I wished for an end. We all got nerves. We did not get enough sleep and were very tense. People fainted when they heard the first bomb drop." The Ford Plant in Cologne in the Ruhr, which suffered some of the heaviest

Allied bombing, suffered absenteeism of 25 percent of the workforce throughout 1944. Even in Munich, which suffered far less, the BMW works had rates of up to 20 percent in the summer of 1944. The government recognized the problem and pressured the factory managements to enforce discipline. On 4 May 1944, the plant leader at the Daimler-Benz Untertürckheim factory outlined some of the penalties that could be imposed: "All available measures must be taken to combat absenteeism. I refer you in particular to relevant decrees of the Reich Minister for Food and Agriculture of 7 April 1942 and 20 October 1943 according to which, in cases of unexcused absence from work (absenteeism) and irresponsible reduction in work performance, the plant leader is not only entitled but is even duty bound to withdraw the offenders' bonus food ration cards, since in such cases the preconditions which are necessary for the provision of bonus food ration cards are no longer fulfilled."

There were harsher penalties, too, and occasionally the *Gestapo* would make an example of an employee. Another example from Untertürckheim is illustrative: "The typist Maria S.... had to be reported to the Reich Trustee of Labour for frequent absence from work without leave ... He ordered her imprisonment where she remained until the prison was destroyed by fire. Subsequently she was transferred to the Rudersberg Work Re-education Camp from where she was released after seven weeks."

BOMBING AND PRODUCTION

Bombing also disrupted mass production. Speer's deputy, von Heydekampf, who was responsible for tank production, explained that the bombing forced him to modify production by "the breaking down and dispersal of plants, starting up factories on account of their geographical position instead of their technical capacity". It is of interest to note, however, that the Allies often had poor intelligence about the effects of raids on German industry. At the beginning of April 1944, for example, air attacks on German ball-bearing factories stopped – Allied air staffs had assumed that they had totally destroyed German ball-bearing capability. As

Above: The result of Allied bombing on a marshalling yard in 1944. Allied bombing both disrupted production and hampered the delivery of military hardware.

Speer commented: "Thus, the Allies threw away success when it was already in their hands."

German production facilities were forced into smaller and camouflaged premises. Much German work moved underground, which made expansion of production considerably more difficult. In January 1945, Speer reckoned that bombing had reduced tank production by 35 percent, aircraft production by 31 percent and lorry production by 42 percent. Though German industry and its workers made fantastic efforts and sacrifices to fill orders – in early 1945, for example, the average monthly production figures for armoured vehicles numbered 1258 – Speer concluded that the victory of the bombers was "the greatest lost battle of the war".

Above: Surveying the aftermath of an Allied raid in 1943. Below: "We greet the first worker of Germany: Adolf Hitler", reads the message on a bombed-out building on the Führer's 55th birthday on 20 April 1944.

Wir grüßen den ersten Arbeiter Deutschlands: Adolf Hitler!

HOME FRONT: LIFE IN GERMANY

In 1949, the Public Opinion Institute in Germany summarized some of the positive aspects of life under National Socialism: "The guaranteed pay packet, *KdF* and the smooth running of the political machinery ... thus National Socialism makes them think merely of work, adequate nourishment, *KdF* and the absence of disarray in political life." If one were not Jewish, a communist or various other undesirables, and one kept one's head down, domestic life in Hitler's Germany was tolerable. Indeed, as noted above, it had its positive aspects. However, war changed much of this. While the early victories were largely greeted with much enthusiasm, as the conflict dragged on things changed.

As far as public opinion was concerned, while the German Army seemed unbeatable, the regime's popularity remained high. Heidi Brendler, a member of the German Nazi Welfare Service, recalled her family's reaction to the fall of France: "After the great victory in France the atmosphere was unbelievable in Germany. Everyone was delirious with joy. I know my father got quite drunk

Above: Civilians and soldiers enjoy the sun on the terrace of Kranzker's café on the Unter den Linden in Berlin, in the days before rationing and bombing were the norm.

when the end of the fighting was announced. It seemed impossible to believe that France had collapsed and England was beaten back across the Channel; I know we were terribly relieved when our men came home safely. Ludwig [her husband] had been in some fighting but had not, he claimed, been in any great danger. He was of course delighted to be back with his wife and daughter and we had a good time celebrating." The German population had begun the war with little enthusiasm. They were delighted, however, by the rapid and relatively painless successes that Hitler brought them.

As the war dragged on, however, and Germany failed to defeat Britain, and subsequently invaded the Soviet Union in 1941, concerns began to grow. An *SD* report from Stuttgart dated 29 July 1941 noted a mood of disgruntlement: "In domestic politics, the mood and bearing of the population is still depressed, worried, full of mistrust, annoyance and frustration, although the food situation has improved somewhat." Another *SD* report from Leipzig on 6 August of that year had more fundamental concerns: "The events in the East are causing people a great deal of concern. Whilst nobody doubts that the Soviets will be defeated, they had not reckoned with such a tough opponent. People are anticipating heavy losses, including on our side, and expecting the exhaustion of our reserves of human material, which for months will make it impossible to achieve our real war aim of finishing off England. There is concern about a new wartime winter involving very hard work with minimum food …"

A German ration card (Ausweiskarte) with grid entries including: Kartoffeln, Hülsenfrüchte, Fleisch oder Fleischwaren, Brot oder Mehl, Milcherzeugnisse Öle und Fette, Zucker und Marmelade, Nährmittel, Kaffee Tee oder Kaffee-Ersatz, Milch, Eier, Kohle, Seife.

Center card text:

Ausweiskarte

Herrn für Frau Fräulein: *Brunhilde Brandt*
Lebensalter: *26 Jahre*
Beruf: *Ehefrau*
Wohnort: *Berlin-Schwargwart*
Straße (Platz): *Linkstr.* Nr. *9*
Gebäudeteil: *von I Treppe*

Rückseite beachten!

Left: A German ration card. Although initially food rations were kept high, the Nazi Government was forced to reduce them in the spring of 1942.

one who does not have time to wait and queue, anyone who is too decent to push himself forward everywhere has to put up with getting the worst that's on offer. One should not be surprised that, in these circumstances, hoarding and uncontrolled purchasing – under the counter, round the back, on the black market and through barter, inevitably with excessive prices – is continually on the increase as is, at the same time, the bitterness of all those groups who lack 'connections' or time and opportunity for illegal purchases, or whose conscience forbids them to break the law."

REALITIES OF DAILY LIFE

Mathilde Wolff-Mönckeberg wrote to her children about how she conducted her domestic life: "Believe it or not, even I have taken to bartering, as everybody else does, and it really has its fascination … in the cellar is our large dining room table … It is getting damp and warped, poor old thing. For many years the Wolff family gathered round it to eat big wholesome meals … I am quite upset about this table, but we cannot afford sentimentality now. I have exchanged the table for fat and meat and quite a number of delicatessen that the new owner will bring from her canteen. But what else can one do these days? The stomach demands its due and money does not buy a thing."

Betti Brockhaus, a civilian working for the *Luftwaffe*, recalled that the authorities did their best to prevent such activities: "Things became very scarce as the quantity and quality of supplies became worse; all we seemed to get was potatoes, bread, sausage and cabbage … we did not do too well. The inspections became a lot more rigorous as there was a constant drive to prevent black marketeering and the siphoning off of military sup-

This report illustrates two of the most important concerns of the German civilian population in World War II; the losses of their loved ones as the fighting became more costly, and the imposition of rationing. As for the latter, to quote Heidi Brendler again: "When the war started everyone was issued with ration cards and at first everything seemed well organized: there were no shortages. We heard tales from the Allied side that Germany was in all sorts of difficulties as a result of the English and French blockade; I know our papers under Dr Göbbels used to make fun of such things. It is a fact that no real shortages occurred for some time, though there were people who missed luxuries such as we never had. The basic foodstuffs were never in short supply until about 1943."

The combination of shortages and also a sense that there was some unfairness in the distribution of commodities, with the rich and those with connections being favoured, created a climate conducive to illicit trading and the black market. One Nazi district leader noted that the population demanded "above all absolute fairness" and resented the fact that, for example, horsemeat was rationed whereas poultry was not and could be had at exorbitant prices.

"Anyone who is not a regular customer of long standing with a grocer or with market stalls, any-

plies for civilian use. We even had the Cologne *Gestapo* visit us one day concerning some profiteering scandal."

Gesa Hachmann, a child at the time, recalled a conversion with her mother: "One time I asked my mother, 'What is peace?' 'When people like each other again,' she said. 'And could we,' I asked, 'could we go to the grocer and say, "I'd like two eggs, please?"' 'No,' my mother answered, 'in peacetime you can ask for seven or eight eggs, or one for however many of us there are.' 'And butter,' I asked, 'could we buy a whole half-pound of butter?' And my mother said, 'You could buy two

pounds of butter, or as much as you like.' And I said, 'So peace is when I can spread butter on both sides of a slice of bread.'"

A joke from 1943 is worth telling:

Customer: What kind of dogs have you got for sale?

Salesman: Pekinese, Dwarf Poodles, Yorkshire Terriers…

Customer: Stop, stop – haven't you got a dog big enough for a family of five?

DISTRACTIONS

Yet despite the hardships, people sought diversions to keep up their morale. In the same letter by Mathilde Wolff-Mönckeberg she explained: "Yet our life is not completely materialistic, concentrated solely on business deals. Never before have I listened to such beautiful music as during this fifth war winter. We treated ourselves to season tickets for various music cycles and trudged through rain and storm, and even when it snowed during the 4pm concerts at the Musikhalle … More than ever people need to restore themselves with spiritual and artistic gratifications … public lectures on Shakespeare are packed. The biggest auditorium is stuffed to capacity with all sorts of people who, in the old days, would never have dreamed of coming."

Greater Germany contained over 7000 cinemas; Berlin alone had 400. Göbbels went to great lengths to keep them open, even as Allied bombing turned the major cities to rubble, so aware was he of their importance to civilian morale. He viewed the wireless as similarly vital,

Front und Heimat die Garanten des Sieges

Left: Propaganda for Total War. This poster equates the sacrifices of those who remain at home with those endured by the soldiers at the front.

Above: Female harmonica players give a street concert, while a colleague makes a collection for the war effort. Music was a distraction from the hardships of war.

given that the average person spent four and half hours a day listening to the radio. Music was constantly broadcast to keep the nation cheerful. However, given the extreme situation faced by the population, particularly as the air raids became worse, a desire to cast inhibitions aside and let the future take care of itself took hold of some. Young Prussian noblewoman Ursula von Kardoff captured this mood in her diary entry for 13 December 1943: "Life is strange. Up and down, bad and then once again good. But always colourful. Yesterday, an evening in Zehlendorf [expensive Berlin suburb] at which people drank in an uninhibited almost dogged fashion. Everyone flirted with everyone else, and succumbed to the general dissolution. A shimmering swamp."

She recorded four days later: "After every air raid I get the same feeling of irrepressible vitality. One could embrace the world that has been given back to one. Presumably that's the reason why we so greedily grab every opportunity to have a party."

The air raids became a major part of the urban German's existence, particularly after the British improved their bombing techniques from late 1942 onwards. However, the first attack on a German city came on 26 August 1940. With Britain's expulsion from the continent, bombing was the only means available to conduct offensive operations. Indeed, the destruction of the morale of the German people became a professed aim of the British air campaign. As the RAF began to operate more effectively, acquiring bigger and better aircraft, radar guidance systems, target-marking and introducing the method of area bombing – that is "carpet bombing" a city rather than attacking a specific factory – so its impact on the German population increased. In 1942 the RAF was joined by the Americans, who attacked in the daytime in contrast to the night-time raids of the British.

This combined bomber force struck Hamburg on 24–25 July 1943. In the unfortunately named Operation Gomorrah, more than 30,000 people died in the raid and subsequent firestorm: the heat was so intense that it created a tornado effect, oxygen was sucked into the fire with such force that people were dragged into the flames. Ines Lyss experienced the raid: "You could already hear the whistling of the bombs. Naturally we all ran as fast as we could. I remember first sitting on a small wooden bench in the basement. Then everybody jumped up when the first bombs hit. Dust and limestone whistled through the air, the walls cracked. When it didn't seem it was going to stop, people began to pray; some started to scream. The fear that prevailed as the bombs continued to fall

was incredible. We were totally paralysed. I started to pray too: 'Oh dear God… ' We were all a little religious, that's why the 'Oh dear God.' I kept saying, 'I'll never see Jupp again, I'll never see Jupp again.' He was my fiancé at that time."

Klaus Kühn, a Hitler Youth flak auxiliary, described the air raid shelters in Hamburg: "Underground bunkers were built 90–183cm [three to six feet] below the surface of the earth, and consisted of two to four large tubes about 46m [150ft] in length. The tubes, which were situated pretty far apart from one another, were connected by fireproof doors. You got into the bunker by using stairs – like in an underground garage. Once you got down the stairs, you had to walk down a long hallway. Depending on the size of the

Below: The Berlin Philharmonic, conducted by Wilhelm Furtwangler, gives a performance of Beethoven to workers at an armaments factory in 1944.

The Reich Under Attack – THE RAID ON DRESDEN

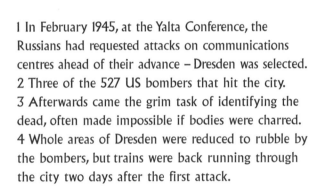

1 In February 1945, at the Yalta Conference, the Russians had requested attacks on communications centres ahead of their advance – Dresden was selected.
2 Three of the 527 US bombers that hit the city.
3 Afterwards came the grim task of identifying the dead, often made impossible if bodies were charred.
4 Whole areas of Dresden were reduced to rubble by the bombers, but trains were back running through the city two days after the first attack.

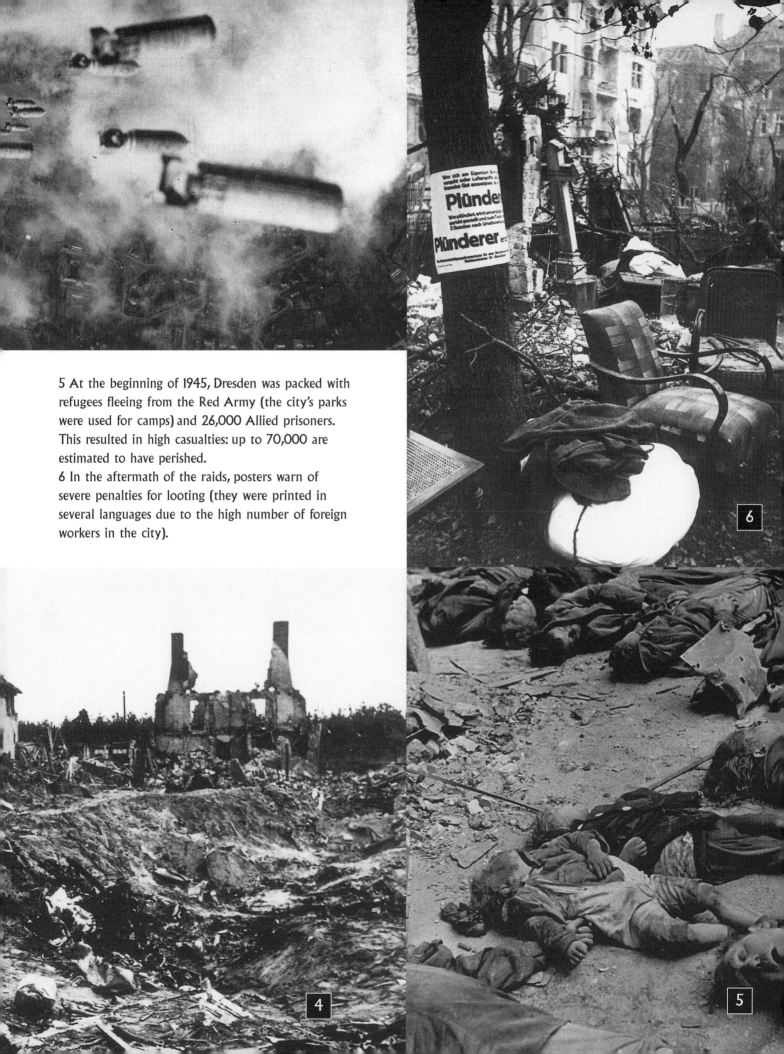

5 At the beginning of 1945, Dresden was packed with refugees fleeing from the Red Army (the city's parks were used for camps) and 26,000 Allied prisoners. This resulted in high casualties: up to 70,000 are estimated to have perished.

6 In the aftermath of the raids, posters warn of severe penalties for looting (they were printed in several languages due to the high number of foreign workers in the city).

Above: A US daylight raid on Kiel in May 1943. Though air raids failed to break civilian morale, they added to the overall strain experienced on the Home Front.

bunker, two or three tubes were connected to this main entrance. These tubes were nothing more than long, narrow hallways. Benches sat on either side of the hall. And each tube was separated from the other by thick concrete walls so that in case one tube got a direct hit, it would be the only one destroyed."

In a firestorm, however, direct hits were not the only danger, as the following account shows. Erich Andres was visiting his wife in Hamburg. Fortunately they were away from home but he witnessed the aftermath: "Not one house was standing. The entire place was one huge pile of bricks. They had been bombed Monday night, and I didn't get there until Saturday but the heat was still intense, the walls of houses still burning hot. I finally reached my house. There it was in a terrible condition – black, scorched holes in place of the windows. Once inside the house, I was able to make my way through the wreckage … to the basement stairs. The heat coming from downstairs was so intense … The beds hadn't been burned, and there were people lying on all of them. I couldn't stand the heat and the awful smell any longer and went back upstairs."

Thirty or 40 people had died there. The basements were full of the dead who had suffocated as the air was sucked into the firestorm: "I passed a number of dead bodies lying close together, mostly only half dressed. It looked like the women had ripped their clothes off, either because they were on fire or they couldn't stand the heat. Perhaps their clothes had caught fire after they'd become unconscious, which would explain why they were half or totally naked. In the middle of the group, I noticed a 10-year-old boy lying there, clinging to one of the air raid wardens. The boy must have crawled along the floor with the last bit of life left in him, over to the warden who had probably already suffocated and was dead."

Uwe Köster, Hitler Youth member, was involved in the clearing up: "We stacked the bodies in 30–35 layers on top of each other. We stacked them all, and if you went past two or three days later you could only go with cellophane over your eyes because everything was smoky. The air was absolutely still. We didn't have any sun at all for three or four days; it was completely dark. We saw only a blood red ball in the distance, which didn't penetrate the dark cloud that hovered over Hamburg for days: smoke, cinders and ashes. The dead were piled in the entrances of houses. And when you went by you just saw a heap of feet, some barefoot, some with burned soles. The corpses were beyond identification. We would dig entire families out of their basements, sometimes two or three weeks later; they'd fit into a bathtub. Even adults were very small. They were completely mummified, burned and melted by the heat. Yes, stacking the dead near the house entrances was actually the fastest and best way of getting them off the streets. After a while they were taken away to a mass grave."

Below: The destruction wrought by Operation Gomorrah on Hamburg in July 1943. On 24–25 July, both the RAF and USAAF attacked the city, killing 30,000 people.

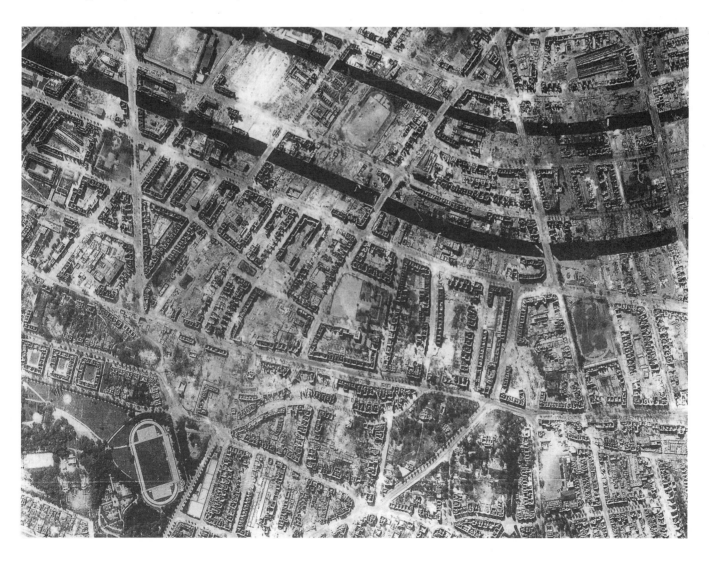

As for the living, they had to be cared for in the aftermath. Teenager Wolf Sohège remembered what happened after the Hamburg raid: "After the air raids, everything was really well organized. It was very surprising; all of a sudden everything was there, food and so on ... Food was also made available from mobile kitchens, the Red Cross and so on. Hot meals were distributed in the fields outside the city ... Care for the wounded was also well organized. They had to be carried; some were so badly burned that we had to put them on stretchers. When the phosphorus canisters hit the houses, this phosphorus stuff ran down the stairs and out into the street ... The people ran out the houses like living torches and the flames on their bodies were put out by whoever could help them. The badly burned had to be taken away in trucks or ambulances. Sometimes people carried them short distances to a place where they could be picked up by ambulances. But the drivers had to be careful that the phosphorus didn't get under their tyres – the rubber burned immediately ... the hospitals were already overcrowded in the central areas ... the local hospitals were, of course, quickly filled with burns victims. These people had second- and third-degree burns. There were no special wards for burns victims back then."

THE POPULATION'S MORALE

The Allied bombing continued, and by the end of 1944 most major German cities had been bombed both heavily and regularly. Quite apart from the physical dangers, the air raids had a psychological effect on the population. Some could not endure it. Kaethe Breuer recalled of her neighbour who refused to go down into the shelter during a raid: "My husband went up to their apartment and saw he had been shot through the temple and the pistol was lying on the ground. He had shot himself; he couldn't bear it any longer." His suicide had implications for his wife, so Breuer's husband took the pistol away with him. The suicide victim's wife later said, after the doctor had determined the cause of death, "Thank you, Mr Breuer, for taking the pistol away. The doctor said it was a bomb fragment – otherwise I would have had no claim to supplementary insurance."

Even experienced soldiers struggled to endure the bombing when home on leave. Inge Meyn-Kommeyer came downstairs to find her brother marching up and down in the kitchen in his boots:

Left: Two women carry an injured child out of the ruins after an Allied attack. Air raids became an integral part of life in most German cities.

Right: In July 1945, "Trümmerfrau" (literally ruin or rubble women) clear the debris caused by three years of heavy and constant British and American air raids on Berlin.

"I said 'Edi, what on earth are you doing? Are you crazy, and get rid of those boots.' He looked at me and said, 'Why?' I said, 'It's six o'clock in the morning and we all want to get some sleep! If you can't sleep then get dressed and go out into the yard or go for a walk in the park. Do whatever you want. Just don't keep us awake marching around in those ridiculous noisy boots!' He looked at me with a dazed expression on his face and said, 'That's it I'm going back!' I asked, 'Where to? The front?' 'Yes!' he replied. He couldn't stand the air raids because he didn't feel he could defend himself as well as at the front."

What was the attitude of Hitler to air raids against Germany, and its effects on the population? Albert Speer gives a telling insight into the Führer's mind regarding Allied raids. When informed of one particularly heavy raid: "Hitler was obviously shaken by these [bombing] reports, although less by the casualties among the populace or the bombing of residential areas than by the destruction of valuable buildings, especially theatres ... Consequently, he was likely to demand that burned-out theatres be rebuilt immediately."

When it came to visiting bombed towns and cities to raise morale, Hitler was uninterested. Speer again: "I tried a few times to persuade Hitler to travel to the bombed cities and let himself be seen there. Göbbels, too, had tried to put over the same idea, but in vain." Indeed, such was his lack interest in seeing bomb damage that when being driven through Munich or Berlin, he ordered his chauffeur to take the shortest route. Shattered German cities did not sit comfortably with his dream of a Thousand-Year Reich.

Most ordinary people, however, just endured – they had little choice (and, strange to say, never blamed Hitler directly for their plight – subordinates came in for criticism). Despite the terrible toll in human lives and damage to German cities that the RAF and US Army Air Force (USAAF) wreaked upon Germany, civilian morale never really cracked. German civilians had to carry on with their lives and counted the psychological cost later. Hugo Stehkämper provides a suitable example: "You learned to live from one air raid to the next; it became routine ... Naturally you knew you risked your life every day staying in the big city. You simply continued to live from day to day with a certain degree of indifference. During the actual bombings, this feeling of indifference was replaced by a deathly fear, fear for life, a fear that still haunts me today. Even after over forty years, I cannot bring myself to watch a film about the bombings; it would rob me of at least three nights' sleep. Those memories are still very real. It would be like rubbing salt into the wound."

THE FINAL CAMPAIGN

Above: Red Army troops on the advance. By the end of 1944 they were poised on the border of Greater Germany. Below: Lying in the ruins, a German MG42 machine-gun team tries to halt the relentless Soviet advance.

"Soldiers of the Western Front! Your hour of greatness has come. Powerful assault forces today moved against the Anglo-Americans. Nothing else needs to be said. All of you feel it. It's do or die. Uphold the solemn pledge to do your utmost and perform super-human deeds for our Fatherland and our Führer."

On 16 December 1944, Field Marshal von Rundstedt launched the German offensive in the

Ardennes with this order. Its language was familiar – Hitler and his senior commanders had been making similar exhortations since the reversals in the Soviet Union in 1942–43, and for while it met with some success. This and the halt of the Soviet advance on the River Vistula led to an increase in civilian morale – salvation for the Third Reich seemed to be at hand. The Reich Propaganda Ministry reports of the time note that "Yuletide" was "generally observed in good spirits and full confidence in the future." The report continued: "The German western offensive has made a profound impression even on those citizens who are outright pessimists and who have believed the leadership remained silent because it has a great unpleasantness to hide; in general trust in the *Wehrmacht*, in the political leadership and especially in the *NSDAP* has greatly increased."

Above: Two cheerful members of the *Volkssturm*, which was formed on 25 September 1944. This image conveys the age and poor clothing of many of its members.

Such optimism was ill placed, though. By 23 December the Ardennes Offensive had petered out, and on 12 January 1945 the Soviets launched the largest single offensive of the war. German resistance had been weakened by the drain of manpower for the offensive in the West (the total cost to the Germans in manpower for their Ardennes Offensive was 100,000 killed, wounded and captured, 800 tanks and 1000 aircraft; the Americans lost 81,000 killed, wounded or captured, the British 1400). Despite the undoubtedly "superhuman" efforts of the members of the *Wehrmacht*, the true reality of war was brought onto German soil by the mass divisions of the Red

Army in the East and the Western Allies advancing from France.

The Red Army offensive against Greater Germany was preceded by a five-hour artillery barrage. The Soviets had committed 180 divisions, a high proportion of them armoured, in East Prussia and Poland alone. The Germans had only 75 divisions in the East, stretching from the Baltic to the Carpathian Mountains, and all of those were below strength. The *OKH* calculated that the Soviets held a superiority in infantry of 11 to one and in tanks of seven to one. There was little the *Wehrmacht* could do to stop them. Guderian noted: "By 27 January the Russian tidal wave was assuming for us the proportions of a complete disaster." Indeed, East and West Prussia were cut off from the Reich and that day Zhukov's forces crossed the Oder after a rapid 350km (220-mile) advance in a fortnight, and were firmly established on German soil only 160km (100 miles) from Berlin itself.

Very few Germans wished to stay in their homes and meet the invading Red Army. Almost the entire East Prussian population decided to flee the fighting. The evacuation was badly organized, if organized is the right word for the chaos that ensued, and catastrophic transport conditions aggravated the situation. The population trudged westwards through appalling winter conditions. A teenage girl gave a moving account of the trek. Attempting to cross the frozen *Frische Haff* was perilous: "The ice was brittle and in places we had to wade through water 25cm [10in] deep. We kept testing the surface in front of us with sticks … Often one slipped and thought one had had it. Our clothes, which were soaked through, only allowed us to move clumsily. But fear of death made us forget the shivering which shook our bodies. I saw women performing superhuman feats. As leaders of the treks they instinctively found the safest paths for their wagons. Household goods were strewn all over the ice; wounded people crept up to us with pleading gestures, hobbling on sticks; others were carried on small sledges by their comrades."

HELLISH JOURNEY

Food and clean water were in short supply. Anne Seddig, carrying her one-year-old son Siegfried, recounted this terrible journey: "[there was] Nothing to eat. Siegfried was very thirsty and although I was pregnant again I still breast-fed him. I also let snow melt in my mouth so he could drink it. We had snow after all."

To return to the teenage girl's account, conditions steadily deteriorated: "On the next day we walked in the direction of Danzig. On the way we saw gruesome scenes. Mothers in a fit of madness threw their children into the sea. People hanged themselves; others fell upon dead horses, cutting

Right: German troops pause beside a knocked-out US halftrack during the Ardennes Offensive in December 1944. The attack initially caught the Americans by surprise.

Above: German paratroopers on board a King Tiger tank in the Ardennes. The campaign destroyed much of the *Wehrmacht's* precious reserves of men and material.

out bits of flesh and roasting them on open fires. Women gave birth in the wagons. Everyone thought only of himself – no one could help the sick or weak." This girl and her sister and mother made it to the relative safety of Gera in Thuringia. Many were not so lucky. An estimated one million Germans died in the huge migration westwards.

Those who chose not to flee or were caught by the rapid advance of the Soviet forces often met an equally grim fate. The Red Army had been relatively well behaved as it advanced across occupied Europe. However, once Soviet soldiers reached German territory they indulged in a terrifying orgy of murder, rape, looting and destruction. Given the barbarous nature of the German occupation of areas of the Soviet Union, the first-hand evidence of which they encountered as they liberated occupied territory (including the concentration camps), and the constant diet of anti-German propaganda they were fed, the behaviour of the Red Army soldiers is at least understandable. That does not detract from the horrific nature of their actions. Anne Seddig eventually ran into Russian troops: "The Russians came and shone their torches on me and one said 'Now woman you will get a place to stay.' The place was an air raid shelter. There was a table in it and that night one Russian after another raped me there on the table. It's like being dead. Your whole body is gripped by cramp. You feel repulsion … They considered us fair game. I can't tell how many men there were – 10, 15. It just went on and on. There were so many one after the other. One of them I remember also wanted me, but then he said, 'How many comrades have already been here? Put your clothes on.'"

The Russians were indiscriminate. Renate Hoffman was raped: "They put guns to our heads. Any attempt to defend ourselves meant certain death. The only thing you could do was to pretend you were a rock or dead. I don't want to talk about what happened next." Her older relatives also suffered: "My aunt and my mother were both over 50 years old, and both had been raped by young Russian soldiers." Attempts to avoid this fate met with mixed success. Hedwig Sass was in Berlin when the Soviets arrived: "Most of us tried to make ourselves look a lot older than we really were. We wore old rags on purpose. But the Russians always said, 'You not old. You young.' They laughed at us because of the old clothes and eye-glasses we were wearing. They knew what we were up to!" An estimated two million German women were raped by the soldiers of the Red Army in 1945.

THE *VOLKSSTURM*

Most of this behaviour took place after the fighting had moved on, or even after the end of the war. The combat itself continued as ferociously as ever, although German resources were heavily overstretched. Almost any man or boy capable of holding a rifle, or more commonly a *Panzerfaust* antitank weapon, was pressed into service. The desperate shortage of manpower and the dire situation facing

Below: An increasingly common sight as the Allies drove into Germany: prisoners (these are *Luftwaffe* personnel) being marched into captivity by US Military Police.

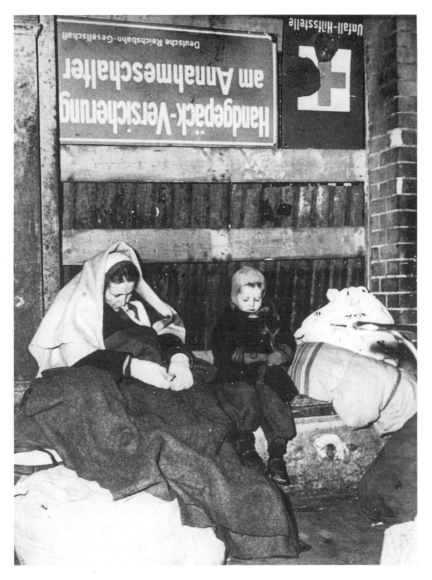

Left: A woman and child slump exhausted near a Berlin railway station. As the Red Army advanced, many Germans fled rather than wait for the vengeful Soviet troops.

The *Volkssturm* was never a serious fighting force. Its members often lacked experience, were poorly trained, minimally equipped and morale was understandably low. A member from the rural district of Fürth in northern Bavaria provides a suitable example of the quality and morale of these units: "I was never a soldier and so hadn't a clue about anything, and when they gave out the 'uniforms' [there was, in contrast to the October order, an incomplete attempt to provide some sort of military clothing, if only an armband] in Neustadt they wanted to give me an *SA* coat as well as a Labour Service uniform. I didn't accept the coat, with the excuse that it was too big. In reality I didn't like the lots of Party badges on it. I wasn't a Party member. Then they gave me another coat, this time a Labour Service one; but this was too small. But I took it anyway and cut all the buttons off. I got ticked off for that at our first parade. A mate of mine who was also involved sewed the buttons back on the outside edges, otherwise I couldn't have worn the coat. If I held my breath I could even button it up. After three hours' instruction from a holder of the Knight's Cross, we were 'ready for action' to use a bazooka. Our platoon had twenty-three members and for these twenty-three we even got given twelve weapons. I didn't get one and didn't make any effort to. I didn't understand how they worked in any case."

It is not difficult to imagine what happened when units such as these came up against the battle-hardened Red Army and well-equipped British and Americans. Rolf Pauls, a tank officer defending the area around Düsseldorf, recounted a conversation between the *gauleiter* (responsible for all

Germany led to the creation of the *Volkssturm*, a kind of German "home guard". Hitler decreed that it would contain "all Germen men aged between 16 and 60 who are capable of bearing arms. It will defend the homeland with all weapons and all means that seem appropriate." While Martin Bormann, Hitler's secretary, insisted that: "the members of the German *Volkssturm* count as combatants within the definition of the Hague Convention on land warfare." The fact that the October Decree establishing the organization read "All *Volkssturm* soldiers irrespective of rank will provide their own uniforms and equipment", sometimes meant they could be shot out of hand when they were captured if in civilian clothes and carrying a weapon.

economic and political activities in their respective districts) of Cologne telling Pauls' divisional commander he would send some 35,000 *Volkssturm* men to help the defence who, the *gauleiter* maintained, could hardly wait for the opportunity to defend their home town: "Hearing that, my boss blew up into the air. He yelled back, 'I'll tell you what the *Volkssturm* can hardly wait to do – they can hardly wait to get out of here! The last 24 hours have proved that – they are taking off in all directions. And to tell you the truth, I can't blame them.'"

The exception to the poor morale among *Volkssturm* units were some youngsters, the well-indoctrinated members of the Hitler Youth. Walter Knappe, a disabled *Luftwaffe* officer who had been seriously wounded early in the war, was sent to Berlin in April 1945 and assigned command of a Hitler Youth unit: "We fought tanks with bazookas. There was a great danger that my eager Hitler Youth would run into Russian fire without even being able to fire their bazookas properly. I was so glad when our mission was called off and I could release them all. Only too well could I

Below: US infantry crawl forward in the town of Julien in Germany, February 1945. German resistance in the West could still be tenacious and well planned.

understand their crazy enthusiasm; they went to their doom in their belief that they were fighting for Germany."

Similarly, 24-year-old Gustav Schütz, who had lost his left arm in 1942 and led 14- and 15-year-olds into combat at the end of the war, could see: "The kids were thrilled with the idea of fighting as 'soldiers' for the final victory. We could hope to bring them back safely, only if the war would end soon."

Enthusiasm could hardly make up for lack of training and equipment. In a recollection similar to that of the more mature Bavarian *Volkssturm* member, Hugo Stehkämper recalled: "In February 1945, two months before my 16th birthday, I was drafted into the *Volkssturm*. They stuck us in old black *SS* uniforms which you didn't see anymore during the war, brown Organization Todt coats and blue air force auxiliary caps. We thought we looked like scarecrows. And we were ashamed of the French steel helmets they slapped on us. This didn't fit the picture of a German soldier for us. As boys of 15, well, if we were going to be called up, we wanted to be real German soldiers, not imitation French."

Nonetheless, such units saw considerable combat in the final month of the war. Zhukov launched the final assault on Berlin on 16 April 1945. First he had to break through the German defensive line on the Seelow Heights, east of Berlin. Hitler had ordered that the city should be defended "to the last man and the last shot". It took him three attempts before he could advance on Berlin proper. Despite the hopelessness of their position, the German defenders put up fanatical resistance. Among them were many Hitler Youth members of the *Volkssturm*. Lothar Loewe, a 16-year-old, explained the motivation of his fellow defenders: "It was the courage of desperation which motivated the soldiers. Berlin was defended so bitterly because so many of the soldiers, so many of the civilians, were afraid of Soviet imprisonment. They wanted to save themselves, to keep the Russians out of Berlin for as long as they could. Everything possible was done to stop them, to gain a little more time … To me Bolshevism meant the end of life. And in my opinion, that's the reason for the terribly bitter fight in Berlin, which wasn't only street to street, but house to house, room to room and floor to floor. The Russians and the Germans suffered such horrible casualties because every single brick was bitterly fought over for days on end."

FIGHTING IN BERLIN

Karl Damm, another Hitler Youth member, also looked back to the fighting in Berlin: "The end of the grisly game was clear. We had only restricted movement and defence possibilities. We were like pinpricks – able to delay the Russian penetration here and there, only to increase the city's suffering. It was clear to every participant that there would be no escape. The older soldiers, which meant the 22- and 23-year-olds, may have recognized the uselessness and irresponsibility of this street battle. But we youngsters, who had had our baptism of fire only a week before, were still naive."

Left: A battery of Soviet artillery opens fire. On 12 January 1945, the Red Army launched 2.2 million troops against Army Group Centre and 1.6 million against East Prussia.

Above: Red Army infantry, supported by a tank, rush forward. By 1945, Red Army soldiers were formidable, well-equipped and implacable opponents, and unstoppable.

Loewe, with his "Belgian pistol and Italian tommy gun with no safety catch", refused to wear a helmet because "the things were so big they slipped down on my nose, and besides, I couldn't hear when I wore one". He soon lost his naivety: "It was a bad war. The nights, when the women in the occupied side streets were raped by Russian soldiers, were awful; the screams were horrible. There were terrible scenes. But these, on the other hand, only encouraged us all the more. We were genuinely afraid the Russians would slaughter us."

Fear of the Russians was not the only motivation for fighting on; in the increasingly desperate last weeks military discipline was enforced with particularly arbitrary brutality and an alarming degree of randomness. Severely wounded, Rudolf Vilter was evacuated from Berlin at the last moment: "A major, along with two officers and a few MPs [military policemen], stood by the side of the road. These were also people we were very

afraid of – an important reason why we didn't desert. We saw what happened to deserters who were caught; they were hanged from trees."

Similarly, Lothar Rühl, who had been involved in the last-ditch fighting in Berlin, recalled: "I was picked up by the *SS* on 29 or 30 April. An *SS* patrol stopped me and asked me what I was doing. Was I a deserter? ... I saw an officer, stripped of his insignia, hanging from a streetcar underpass. A large sign hung around his neck read, 'I am hanging here because I was too much of a coward to face the enemy.' The *SS* man said 'Do you see that? There's a deserter hanging already.' I told him I was no deserter ... I wound up at an assembly point. One of our platoon leaders sat there. He saw me and yelled, 'Hey, what are doing with one of our men?' The answer was, 'We picked him up.'

Left: A Soviet flamethrower team advances. Fear of the "Bolshevik Menace" meant the Germans continued fighting despite a hopeless strategic position.

The platoon leader asked, 'What do you mean "picked him up"? This man is our messenger and I know him very well. Let him go so he can get back to his duties.' They finally let me go."

Few were as lucky as Rühl when confronted by the *SS* or police in these circumstances. For Lothar Loewe, also fighting in Berlin, "anywhere you went, you saw military police. Even when the Russians were already in sight, you could see police 100 metres further on, still trying to check people. Whoever didn't have the right papers or the correct pass was strung up as a deserter, and hung with a sign saying, 'I am a traitor.' or 'I am a coward.'"

NAZI VENGEANCE

Such discipline was not only applied to military personnel. Civilians who tried to surrender faced the same treatment. Loewe witnessed an incident in Berlin: "This had all happened on one of the side streets of the Kürfürstendamm. People who lived there had put out white flags of surrender. There was this one apartment house with white sheets waving from the windows. And the *SS* came – I'll never forget this – went into the house and dragged all the men out. I don't know whether these were soldiers dressed in civilian clothing, old men or what. Anyway, they took them into the middle of the street and shot them."

Although the Germans put up fierce resistance in the West, once the Rhine was crossed and it became increasingly obvious that the war was lost, there was a very different attitude evident. The contrast between the bitterness of fighting in the East and West in the last month or so of the war is striking. The attitude of Rudolf Escherich, a young fighter pilot, is illustrative. He and 12 men of Fighter Squadron *Udet* agreed to undertake a suicide mission against a bridge captured by the Red Army across the River Oder. They signed a document stating: "We sacrifice ourselves voluntarily for our Führer, our homeland and for Germany." He explained he and his comrades' motivation: "We were all young enthusiastic pilots and were burning to do something to fight for the salvation of our Fatherland, even if it was practically hopeless." The first missions failed and the operation was subsequently cancelled.

When asked if he would have undertaken such a mission in the West, Escherich replied, "no, no, no, certainly not." He explained: "The conditions were completely different in the West, they were civilized. They treated their Prisoners of War in a halfway humane fashion and you could expect them to treat the defeated German population more or less decently. But the Russians were not like this."

The comparatively better treatment of German civilians in areas captured by the British and American armies meant that few were as determined to fight to the last, especially as word of the correct behaviour of the Western Allied troops spread. This, coupled with Allied propaganda and an increasing belief that the war was lost, meant many were content to let, as an *SS* report noted, "the war sweep over them". Indeed a *Gestapo* report concerning the rare recapture of a town noted the deep impression made by the American troops, who freely distributed food to the starving indigenous population: "After the liberation of Geislautern by German troops ... officials observed that the homes in which the Americans had stayed had neither been damaged nor had anything been stolen. The general assertion here was also that they conducted themselves better 'than our German troops.'" The report then concluded: "Based on these experiences with the Americans, the populace remaining behind has the highest opinion of them. They will therefore no longer leave their homes and cellars even though, for military reasons, a renewed order for the evacuation of the Saar was issued long ago by military authorities."

The whole of the western population of Germany could not be forcibly evacuated, hanged or dragged in front of a court martial. Nazi propaganda claimed that the Americans the population had come into contact with "were combat troops whose only function was to fight; but after them come rearguard service troops, and especially the Jews, who have in all other cases acted ruthlessly against the population."

Few were convinced, as some of these examples prove. An account by the mayor of the village of Frankenbach in northern Württemberg is telling. The *Volkssturm* considered mounting a defence of the village, but: "People had made sure that the *Volkssturm*'s bazookas had no detonators. That may have saved our village from disaster ... A *Volkssturm* leader, who the day before had been full of how he was going to destroy every American tank, had suddenly lost his heroic heart and stayed at home ... before one knew it there

Below: As the end neared, the authorities imposed increasingly harsh discipline on their troops. Here, SS men prepare to shoot suspected deserters in April 1945.

Into Hitler's Citadel – THE BATTLE OF BERLIN

1 Josef Stalin II heavy tanks roll through Berlin. Zhukov's forces reached the outer defences of Berlin on 21 April.
2 Soviet troops observe the burning Reichstag in the aftermath of the battle for the strongpoint.
3 The spearhead of the Red Army takes the opportunity to clean up in a Berlin street. Their tanks and self-propelled guns sit in the background.
4 The final stages of the fighting. Soviet troops, supported by a T-34 and antitank guns, sprint from the basement of Himmler's palace towards the Reichstag. On the whole the frontline Soviet troops did not treat the civilian inhabitants of Berlin particularly badly, in contrast to the second-echelon soldiers (many newly liberated from prison camps) who followed.
5 Victory! The Soviet flag is hoisted over the Reichstag on 1 May 1945. Its defenders fought to the last when the Red Army stormed it on 30 April 1945. Hitler shot himself that day, while Berlin itself surrendered on 2 May.
6 The Red Army also suffered heavy losses in the city – a stretcher team rushes a wounded comrade to safety.

was tank after tank on the Frankfurter and Neckargartacher Strasse. But a huge white flag was waving from the church tower … It was a great piece of luck for our village that the Hipperg was not occupied by German troops. Otherwise our nice village would presumably within a short time have become a heap of ruins."

Many soldiers felt similarly. Gustav Schütz, a commander of a group of teenagers, recounted a conversation with his lieutenant who said: "Shültz, you're the only one I've known for a while and believe I can trust. There's already been one Children's Crusade, and none of those chil-

dren came back. I don't want to be responsible for being involved in this one. We've got to prevent a blood bath when we meet American tanks. What do you think?' I told him that I considered it suicide to take these inexperienced boys into battle against well-trained troops."

Paul Stresemen, who had seen so much and been invalided home from the East, made considerable efforts to escape to the West, and he perhaps provides a typical example of most Germans' attitude: "I will never forget my immense relief when we saw the first American tanks. I don't think those Yanks realized how relieved we were to see them."

In Berlin the fighting was almost over. On 30 April the city commandant, Lieutenant-General Karl Weidling, reported that ammunition would

Below: Admiral Friedeberg meets British Field Marshal Bernard Law Montgomery on Lüneberg Heath on 3 May 1945 to surrender to him all German forces in the West.

Right: A German civilian reads of the war's end in a British or American newspaper. All German forces finally surrendered to General Dwight Eisenhower on 7 May.

probably run out the following day. There was no hope of relief from outside the city, despite the continued exhortations and promises of the propaganda ministry. That afternoon, while the Red Army stormed the Reichstag building, where the German defenders stayed true to the demands of their leader and fought pretty much to the last man and last bullet, Hitler killed himself. During an impromptu ceasefire the following day, the Germans tried to negotiate for less than unconditional surrender. However, Weidling decided that resistance had to cease. Brunhilde Pomsel, who worked at the propaganda ministry, was called to her boss, Hans Fritzsche. She recalled that he "personally dictated to me the declaration of surrender of the city of Berlin. This declaration was to be handed over to the Russian commander, General Zhukov. Next, we spent hours sewing white flags out of flour sacks. A White Russian woman who was with us translated the declaration of surrender into Russian. Then Fritzsche and a couple of others left the shelter carrying the declaration and a huge white flag." Zhukov accepted the surrender on 2 May.

THE GENERAL SURRENDER

Meanwhile, on the morning of 3 May, Hitler's successor, Grand Admiral Dönitz, sent a delegation headed by Admiral Friedeberg to British Field Marshal Montgomery's headquarters at Lüneberg Heath in northern Germany, where they signed an instrument of surrender for the German armed forces in the Netherlands, northwest Germany and Denmark. However, all German forces were finally surrendered to the supreme commander, General Eisenhower, on 7 May. The terms came into effect at midnight on 8/9 May 1945. The main clause of the document read: "We the undersigned, acting by authority of the German High

Command, hereby render unconditionally to the Supreme Commander, Allied Expeditionary Force and simultaneously to the Soviet High Command, all forces on the land, sea and in the air which are at this date under German control. This act of surrender is without prejudice to, and will be superseded by, any general instrument of surrender imposed by, or on behalf of, the United Nations and applicable to Germany and the German armed forces as a whole."

Dönitz then sent a despatch to the officer corps: "Comrades, we have been set back a thousand years in our history. Land that was German for a thousand years has now fallen into Russian hands [the obsession with the 'Bolshevik horde' continued even after the end of hostilities] ... despite today's military breakdown, our people are unlike the Germany of 1918. They have not been split asunder. Whether we want to create another form of National Socialism or whether we conform to the life imposed upon us by the enemy, we should make sure that the unity given to us by National Socialism is maintained under all circumstances." Two weeks later, he and the rest of the German High Command were taken into captivity.

Hitler's war was over. His cites lay in ruins and his armed forces were shattered. For those who were still alive in May 1945, the immediate task was to stay alive. Then would come rebuilding their country and their lives.

RESISTANCE

Although brave opponents of Hitler's regime emerged from all walks of life, resistance during the war was very limited in size. It became more difficult to differentiate between Germany and Nazism, or to decide whether to struggle against the regime or comply and fight for the nation. Moreover, resistance also had to take place in considerable secrecy because criticism of the German conduct of war became a capital crime after 1 September 1939. Given the pervasive nature of the *Gestapo* and its informers, organized political opposition on any scale was almost impossible. Indeed, the great majority of German society remained compliant to the regime even through the worsening situation of the later war years. A Berlin joke from 1944 reflects the attitude of the public: "I'd rather believe in victory than run around with my head cut off."

Resistance can be broadly categorized into four groups: the communists, the students, the Church and the conservative élite. The major problem for resistors after the outbreak of war was that resistance to the Nazi regime was overwhelmingly seen as not just unpatriotic but treasonable. This was not such a problem for the communist resistance, because ideologically their primary loyalty was not to the nation but to the international working class. They had no sympathy whatsoever for Nazism, its goals and its values. The communists had borne the full brunt of Nazi repression since 1933. The outbreak of war had disrupted what remained of the *KPD* organization. The leadership had been based in Paris, and was soon either interned or forced to flee. Things became even worse after the German occupation of France in 1940. Communists within Germany largely lim-

Above left: Major-General Ludwig von Beck, a leading opponent of the Nazi regime.

Left: Major-General Henning von Tresckow, who initiated several attempts on Hitler's life, including Plan Valkyerie.

Right: Paster Martin Niemöller, head of the Confessing Church. An outspoken critic of the Nazi regime, he was arrested on Hitler's personal order in 1937.

ited their activities to maintaining contacts with their comrades. Thus, the output of communist propaganda leaflets fell from 1000 in 1938 to 82 in April 1940. Similarly, the number of communists arrested fell from over 950 in January 1937 to 70 in April 1940, and remained around that level. The German invasion of the Soviet Union in June 1941 had a galvanizing effect on communist resistance. Propaganda leaflets found by police in the first half of 1941 remained at low levels, but they rose to 3787 in July of that year, and peaked at 10,227 in October. The following is an example from Robert Uhrig's communist cell in Berlin: "Middle class citizens [*Bürger*], Peasants, Workers – in a word Patriots! Germany is in peril! It is in peril from within. If a ship is in distress, people throw everything overboard which can threaten them. So everything which can harm the nation must now be removed from its midst ... Hitler is not the state, we are the state, we the people! The people must now form themselves into battalions. On this side, the workers – peasants, on the other the middle class. But they must march together as a national front for a free and independent Germany. And this Germany must be fought for."

THE LEFT

The communists' organizations were highly vulnerable to the *Gestapo*. In the spring of 1942 the Uhrig organization was destroyed, and by the following year virtually all the major communist networks had been broken up. By the end of the war, more or less half the *KPD*'s 300,000-strong membership of 1933 had been persecuted in some way. In addition, 25,000–30,000 communists were either murdered, executed or found dead in concentration camps. For a communist, arrest invariably meant a death sentence, or at best a long period of imprisonment. The farewell letter of communist Walter Husemann, written to his father prior to his execution on 13 May 1943, gives an example of the determination that sustained them.

"Be strong! I am dying as I lived, as a fighter in the class war! It is easy to call yourself a communist as long as you don't have to shed blood for it. You only show whether you really are one when the hour comes when you have to prove yourself. I am one, father . . .

"The war won't last much longer and then your hour will have come!

"Think of all those who have already travelled down this road that I must go down today, and will still have to travel down it and learn one thing

Above: The atrium library of the University of Munich, where students Hans and Sophie Scholl of the White Rose Group scattered hundreds of anti-Nazi leaflets in 1943.

from the Nazis: every weakness will have to be paid for with hecatombs of blood. So be merciless! Remain hard!

"I would have gladly experienced the new era. The fact that I will never now experience it has sometimes made me bitter. But Lenin, Liebknecht [murdered leader of the Spartakus League, the forerunner of the German Communist Party], Luxemburg [Rosa Luxemburg, murdered Spartakist] weren't able to harvest the fruits of their labours, and they deserved to a thousand times more than I do. We are merely the fertilizer, which has to be in the earth for a new and finer seed to grow for the sake of humanity . . .

"Oh father, father you dear and good man! If only I did not have to fear that you will collapse under the shock of my death.

"Be tough, tough, tough!

"Prove that you have been a whole-hearted life-long fighter in the class struggle!

"Help him, Frieda, raise his spirits. He must not be allowed to succumb. His life does not belong to him but to the movement! Now, a thousand times more than before!"

THE RED ORCHESTRA

Perhaps more dramatic were the efforts of the Red Orchestra, a wartime organization of German communists. Its Berlin section was made up of senior civil servants, as opposed to the ordinary workers discussed above, and it provided intelligence for the Soviet Union and aid to Russian agents. It was broken up by the police in 1942 and its members were executed. In 1948 a lawyer who had been involved in the prosecution of the Red Orchestra, described the group's activities to American authorities. "The information which was sent to Russia concerned events from the military and economic life of Germany. It included quite secret things which those concerned managed to find out about by virtue of their ministerial connections ... the Soviet intelligence service was told about new aerial weapons, of planned German attacks in the east, of the prospective use of volunteer Russian units, of air support and so on in the Caucasus ... other information concerned industrial sites and industrial production. As far as I could gather, the actual extent of the treason was greater than what was actually discovered. The value of the information given to the Russians cannot be overestimated. Its effect on the train of military events must have been significant."

The White Rose Group grew up during 1942–43 at Munich University. At its centre were Hans and Sophie Scholl. In the autumn of 1942, together with friends Willi Graf, Christoph Probst, Alexander Schmorell and philosophy professor Kurt Huber, the Scholls wrote a series of leaflets criticizing the Nazi regime in an attempt to arouse a university movement against Hitler. This is an example from their first pamphlet:

"It is certain that today every honest German is ashamed of his government. Who among us has any conception of the dimensions of shame that will befall us and our children when one day the veil has fallen from our eyes and the most horrible of crimes – crimes that infinitely outdistance every human measure – reach the light of day? If the German people are already so corrupted and spiritually crushed that they do not raise a hand, frivolously trusting in a questionable faith in lawful order in history; if they surrender man's highest principle, that which raises him above all other of God's creatures, his free will; if they abandon the will to take decisive action and turn the wheel of history and thus subject it to their own rational decision; if they are so devoid of individuality, have already gone so far along the road toward turning into a spiritless and cowardly mass – then, yes, they deserve their downfall … Offer passive resistance – resistance – wherever you may be, forestall the spread of this atheistic war machine before it is too late. . . .Do not forget that every people deserves the regime it is willing to endure."

DEATH OF THE SCHOLLS

The Scholls' sister, Inger Aicher-Scholl, described what happened on 18 February 1943: "Hans and Sophie filled a suitcase with leaflets before they went to the university. They were both pleased and in good humour when they set off. But Sophie had a dream that she couldn't quite shake off: the *Gestapo* had arrested them both. They reached the university, and since the lecture rooms were due to open any minute, they hurriedly emptied the contents of the suitcase in the corridors and from the second floor into the entrance hall. But the janitor saw them. All the doors of the university were locked immediately, sealing their fate. The *Gestapo* was notified at once and arrested them."

The Scholls were tried by a people's court headed by Roland Freisler and sentenced to death. Hans and Sophie seemed sure that their action would be supported by their fellow students. On the morning of her execution on 22 November 1943, Sophie Scholl said to a fellow prisoner, "What does our death matter, if thousands will be stirred

and awakened by what we have done? The students are bound to revolt!" Unfortunately, the opposite was the case. That evening, a demonstration was held by the official students' union to express their support for the Nazi regime; 3000 students attended. One of the students present remembered: "That demonstration … is one of the most terrible memories I have of those days. Hundreds of students shouted and stamped their feet to greet the beadle of the university who had denounced [Hans

Below: General Carl-Heinrich von Stülpnagel, the military commander in France, 1942–44. A key member of the 20 July 1944 conspiracy, he was executed by the Nazis.

and Sophie Scholl]. He received their ovations standing and with open arms."

Inger Aicher-Scholl recounted the deaths of her brother and sister: "They were taken away, the girl first. She went without flinching. The executioner said he had never seen anyone die like that before, and Hans, before he laid his head down on the block, yelled loudly enough for his voice to resound throughout the prison 'long live freedom!'"

Hitler did not hold religion in high esteem. He reckoned that "all of the confessions [all the

Below: Keitel (far left), Göring and Hitler at Rastenburg after the attempt on the Führer's life. Keitel, nicknamed the "lackey", was hanged at Nuremberg in 1946.

Churches] are the same. Whichever one you choose, it will not have a future. Not for the Germans anyway. [Italian] Fascism may, in the name of God, make its peace with the Church. I will do that, too. Why not! It won't stop me eradicating Christianity from Germany root and branch. You are either a Christian or a German. You can't be both." However, although Hitler was fundamentally hostile to the Christian Church, it was difficult for him to proceed against institutions of which most Germans were members. Resistance within the Protestant and Catholic Churches was focused largely on the defence of Church autonomy. Nonetheless, the Churches avoided conflict with the regime whenever possible and had sympathy with its professed role as a bastion against

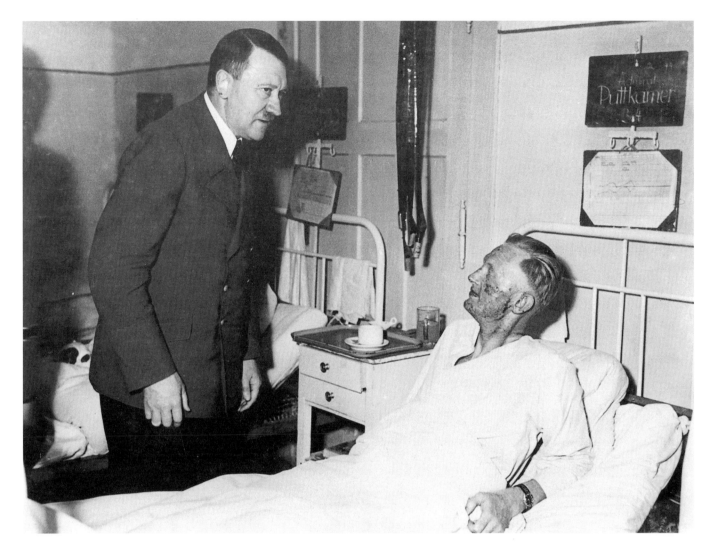

godless Bolshevism. Indeed, the Churches were largely supportive of the war effort, particularly after the attack on the Soviet Union in 1941. Hitler's attempt to Nazify Protestantism led to Martin Niemöller setting up his outspokenly anti-Nazi Confessing Church. He met Hitler in 1934 and was told: "You confine yourself to the Church. I'll take care of the German people." Niemöller replied, "Herr Chancellor, you said just now: 'I will take care of the German people.' But we too, as Christians and churchmen, have a responsibility towards the German people. That responsibility was entrusted to us by God, and neither you nor anyone in the world has the power to take it from us." When Niemöller was finally arrested in 1937, it was on Hitler's personal order. Niemöller admitted after World War II that the Confessing Church "neither in the Hitler Reich nor later placed value

Above: Hitler visits Admiral Puttkamer, who was badly injured when Stauffenberg's bomb exploded. Three other members of the Führer's staff were killed in the explosion.

on being a 'resistance movement'." It merely wanted "to testify to the word of God in our world and time."

Some individual churchmen spoke out against some of the grosser abuses of the Nazi regime. Bishop Hilfrich of Limburg wrote to Reich minister Gürtner on 13 August 1941, protesting against the policy of euthanasia against mentally ill and handicapped Germans. "All God-fearing people feel this extermination of the helpless is an almighty crime, and if this is the same as saying that Germany cannot win the war if there is still a just God, then these statements are not caused by a lack of love for the Fatherland. But rather from a

Left: Roland Freisler, President of the People's Court. An ardent Nazi, he presided over the trials of the Scholls and the 20 July 1944 conspirators, yelling insults at the defendants.

In the pre-war years, a number of senior army officers, diplomats and officials had become increasingly concerned at the shape the Nazi regime was taking. Their disillusionment came to a head in 1938. This reflected the split between the German conservative élites and the Nazi Party, and the growing concern that Hitler's increasingly aggressive foreign policy might lead to a war that Germany would lose.

EARLY ANTI-NAZI PLANS

There had been plans to overthrow Hitler in 1938, but his success at Munich had led to the cancellation of the plot. However, the outbreak of war and the barbarous actions of some elements of the military in Poland led to a revival of the conservative élite's alarm. Ulrich von Hassell noted in his diary in October 1939: "Among well-informed people in Berlin, I noticed a good deal of despair ... there is a growing awareness of our impending disaster. The principal sentiments are: the conviction that the war cannot be won militarily, a realization of the highly dangerous situation, the feeling of being led by criminal adventurers and the disgrace that has sullied the German name through the conduct of the war in Poland ... when people use their revolvers to shoot down a group of Jews herded into a synagogue, one is filled with shame ... and all this time a man like Niemöller has been sitting for years in a concentration camp! The situation of the majority of politically clear-headed and reasonably well-informed people today ... is truly tragic. They love their country, they think patriotically as well as socially, they cannot wish for victory ... and they see no feasible way out ... because there is no con-

deeply concerned frame of mind, about our *volk* ... the authority of the government as a moral concept is suffering a dreadful trauma because of these events." Ten days earlier, Bishop von Galen of Münster had preached a public sermon in which he identified specific victims of euthanasia and prophesized doom if the German people tolerated this transgression of the commandment "thou shalt not kill". For once, this act of resistance was successful and the euthanasia action was stopped on Hitler's personal command. However, in the final analysis the Churches in Germany failed to offer concerted and consistent opposition to the Nazi regime.

fidence that the military leadership possesses enough insight and willpower to assert itself at the decisive moment."

To treat the conservative resistance as if it were a single concept is largely inaccurate. As Joachim Fest, a German historian, has pointed out: "It was a loose assemblage of many groups objectively and personally united only in antipathy for the regime." He identifies three groups "with somewhat sharper contours".

The "Kreisau Circle", named after aristocrat Count Helmuth James von Moltke's Silesian estate. This was principally a discussion group of high-minded friends. As civilians, its opportunities for practical revolt were limited. Moltke, a Foreign Ministry official, was appalled at the way the war was being conducted by Germany. He noted in a letter to his wife of 21 October 1943: "In France extensive shootings are going on as I write. And all that is child's play compared to what is happening in Poland and Russia. How can I bear this and sit just the same in my warm room and drink teas? Don't I make myself an accomplice by doing so? What shall I say when someone asks me, 'What did you do during this time?'"

There was also a group of conservative and nationalists gathered around Carl Goerdeler, the former mayor of Leipzig and General Ludwig Beck, the former army chief of staff. Von Hassell was one of this group. Goerdeler made desperate efforts to recruit senior sol-

diers to the anti-Hitler cause. In a letter to Field Marshal von Kluge on 23 July 1943, he outlined his repugnance of the regime and the pointlessness of the war: "We must stop permitting fools to impose their illusions and lies on the German people, to claim that a war of conquest born of desire to dominate is really a defensive war. We have no need to fear Bolshevism or the Anglo-Saxons ... They are too dependent on our strength and abilities. But it must once more be decent Germans who are representing German interests."

Above right: Colonel-General Erich Höppener, one of the 20 July Bomb Plot conspirators. Sentence – death.
Right: Johannes Popitz (second from right), Prussian Minister of Finance, another conspirator. Sentence – death.

Finally, there was the group of younger military men such as Klaus Schenk von Stauffenberg, Henning von Tresckow and Friedrich Olbricht, with no pronounced ideological ties yet who added a much-needed dynamism to the movement. Tresckow made a number of attempts on Hitler's life, including an effort to destroy Hitler's plane at Smolensk in March 1943. Stauffenberg, a decorated war hero who had lost his right hand and left eye in Tunisia, had become sickened by the destruction: "I could never look the wives and children of the fallen in the eye if I did not do something to stop this senseless slaughter." He was aware of the dilemma he faced: "It is now time that something was done. But who has the courage to do something must do so in the knowledge that he will go down history as a traitor. If he does not do it, however, he will be a traitor to his conscience." He was a conservative monarchist who initially supported the Nazi movement, but by 1943 he was describing Hitler to his associates as being the Anti-Christ!

Stauffenberg, Beck and Goerdeler finally decided in the summer of 1944 that they must take decisive action: "The assassination must be attempted at any cost. We must prove to the world that men of the German resistance dared to take the decisive step and hazard their lives upon it. Compared to this object, nothing else matters."

Stauffenberg drew up the plan, which he called Valkyrie. This was to assassinate Hitler, set up a military government in Berlin, neutralize the *Gestapo* and the *SS* and sue for peace. He decided he would undertake the assassination himself. He was well placed to do this because as chief of staff of the Replacement Army he had frequent access to Hitler's headquarters in East Prussia. On 20 July 1944, Stauffenberg placed a briefcase contain-

Below: Field Marshal Erwin von Witzleben, a Bomb Plot conspirator, struggles to hold up his trousers. No indignity was spared him during the trial. Sentence – death.

Right: "I want them to be hanged, strung up like butchered cattle," Hitler told Freisler. The conspirators were strangled by wire while suspended from meat hooks.

ing a kilogram of plastic explosive beneath the table at which Hitler was holding his morning conference. He then slipped out of the room to "make a telephone call". Herbert Büchs was a *Luftwaffe* staff officer and was present at the meeting: "I went over and stood at Hitler's left on the far left-hand side of the huge briefing table. Hitler had the door to his back. I remember it was 12:37 hours. The briefing had begun punctually at 12:30 hours, so I had only missed the first few minutes. Stauffenberg must have already left the room by then. There was an explosion, a bright yellow flash that forced everyone down. It was total chaos. I saw Lieutenant-Colonel John von Freyend, who was standing near the window, jump out. Since no one knew what was going on, I jumped out of the window too."

THE PLOT FAILS

Hitler was severely shaken, lost his trousers and was lightly wounded, but he was not killed. Three of his staff died, but most of the bomb's force was absorbed by the heavy wooden table and also dissipated through the flimsy wooden hut's thin walls. A concrete bunker would have contained the shock waves of the explosion. Stauffenberg, having seen the hut explode, was confident that Hitler was dead and took a plane to Berlin. When he arrived, he set the rest of Valkyrie in train. However, the commander of the *Grossdeutschland* battalion in Berlin sent to arrest Göbbels was persuaded by the latter that Hitler was alive, and thus took his battalion to arrest the conspirators instead. "What followed was a brief exchange of gunfire and utter chaos," recalled one of the conspirators, Friedrich Georgi. "In the confusion, you could hear officers asking other officers 'are you for or against the Führer?'" Stauffenberg was shot

dead that night. He was lucky. Hitler's survival had ensured that the plot failed. As he told Mussolini: "I was standing here by this table. The bomb went off just in front of my feet ... it is obvious that nothing is going to happen to me; undoubtedly it is my fate to continue on my way and bring my task to completion ... What happened here today is the climax! Having now escaped death ... I am more than ever convinced that the great cause which I serve will be brought through its present perils and that everything will be brought to a good end."

He was able to use this plot as a pretext to execute almost 5000 opponents, whether implicated or not (it is estimated another 10,000 were sent to concentration camps). Every conspirator mentioned above in the context of the July plot was executed. There was a wild wave of arrests followed by torture, show trials conducted by Roland Freisler, President of the People's Court, and the death sentences were quickly carried out. In many cases these were by slow strangulation by piano wire while the victims were hanged from meat hooks. Hitler is said to have had these executions filmed and to have enjoyed watching them as they died. The legacy of these men has provided future generations of Germans with a symbol of resistance to Nazism.

GENOCIDE

Above: "Let not the land cover up their blood." The monument to the victims of Belsen erected outside the camp by British Jews in 1946.

Below: In addition to the 10,000 unburied dead, the British found a mass grave containing 40,000 bodies.

In the winter of 1944 Christabel Bielenberg, wife of a member of the "Kreisau Circle", shared a railway carriage with a young Latvian *SS* man who recounted his experiences in Poland: "'Well, they told us that we could revenge ourselves on our enemies and they sent us to Poland. Not to fight the Poles, oh no, they had been defeated long ago – but to kill Jews. We just had the shooting to do, others did the burying,' he drew a deep, sighing breath. 'Do you know what it means – to kill Jews, men, women, and children as they stand in a semi-circle around the machine guns? I belonged to what is called an *Einsatzkommando*, an extermination squad – so I know. What do you say when I tell you that a little boy, no older than my youngest brother, before such a killing, stood there to attention and asked me "Do I stand straight enough, Uncle?" Yes, he asked that of me; and once, when the circle stood round us, an old man stepped out of the ranks, he had long hair and a beard, a priest of some sort I suppose. Anyway, he came towards us slowly across the grass, slowly step by step, and within a few feet of the guns he stopped and looked at us one after another, a straight, deep, dark and terrible look. "My children," he said, "God is watching what you do." He turned from us and then someone shot him in the back before he had gone a few steps. But I – I could not forget that look, even now it burns me.'"

The Latvian *SS* man was obviously deeply troubled by the terrible acts he had committed, yet at some level he remained a considerate human being. Bielenberg fell asleep in the carriage: "I awoke twice before reaching Tuttlingen.

Once, when the train jerked to a stop at a half-lit station, I realized that I was warmer and that my head was resting on something hard and uncomfortable. The man had moved and was sitting beside me, he had placed his greatcoat over my knees and my head had fallen on to his shoulder. His *SS* shoulder tabs had been pressing into my cheek. In the half-light I saw his face for the second time: perhaps I had been mistaken about the twitching nerve; it looked peaceful enough, almost childlike ... The next time I woke, the carriage was empty and the train was moving."

There are disturbing questions raised by this account; how did ordinary men and women come to commit such crimes and, given the numbers involved in the extermination of the Jews, did the German public really not know what was happening to Europe's Jewish population?

Above: Jewish women sealed in cattle trucks on their way to Auschwitz. Those inside the so-called "Special Resettlement Trains" feared the worst as to their destination.

Almost as soon as Hitler came to power the Nazis began to enact discriminatory legislation against Germany's Jews. The Nazi Party had pledged to create a Germany in which Jews would be set apart from their fellow Germans and denied their place in German life and culture. Jews were expelled from a number of smaller towns and forced to move to larger towns or cities, or emigrate. In the interwar years the Nazi state continued to exclude its Jewish population from mainstream life, and encourage its emigration out of Germany. During this period the mass murder of Germany's Jews was not envisaged. Indeed, the number of Jews who died in Germany's concentration camp system, designed to punish the opponents of the regime and that killed many thousands of communists, social democrats and other undesirables numbered less than 100 between 1933 and 1938. However, the level of violence increased as war approached – in November 1938, for example, 91 Jews were murdered on a night of burning and looting known as "The Night of Broken Glass". In the following six months the numbers of Jews dying in Germany's concentration camps began to increase.

SYSTEMATIC SLAUGHTER

The outbreak of war led to a change in approach. Following in the wake of the victorious army were the *Einsatzgruppen* (these were special battalion-sized units who carried out executions whilst attached to the regular army; their task was to round up communist functionaries, "Asiatic inferiors" and Jews and liquidate them), which began systematically murdering elements of the Polish intelligentsia, leaders, clergy and also Polish Jews. Admiral Wilhelm Canaris, the anti-Nazi head of the German Military Intelligence Service, reported that *SS* commanders were boasting of 200 killings a day. Of the 10,000 Poles murdered, some 3000 were Jews. This, however, was not part of a concerted plan of extermination. From spring 1940 the Germans began to concentrate Poland's Jews into ghettoes in a number of

major cities. A blatantly anti-semitic population facilitated such treatment, far more extreme than anything so far experienced by German Jews. By 1941, the process of ghettoization was as complete as human ingenuity could make it and despite a deliberate policy of food rationing, which led to starvation, the mass of Polish Jews continued to survive in the ghettos.

The attack on the Soviet Union, however, led to an escalation of the persecution of Europe's Jews. Hitler warned his generals that the war would be fought on racial lines – "We are talking about a war of annihilation." Before the attack in June 1941, he issued the Commissar Order requiring the shooting of any Soviet commissars captured. The *Einsatzgruppen*, commanded by Reinhard Heydrich of the *SS*, were instructed to kill only "Jews in the service of party and State". However, there can be little doubt that the orders were interpreted as an instruction to kill all Jews. It led within six months to the murder of as many as one million Jews. They were killed in circumstances very similar to that described by the Latvian *SS* man in the opening quote. The *Einsatzgruppen* units numbered a mere 3000 men, which raises the question of how they killed so many in such a short period of time. The answer is that required the collaboration of the army. When the Commissar Order was passed on to Hitler's commanders, few, if any, objected. General Hermann Hoth, commander of the Fourth Panzer Army, declared: "The annihilation of those same Jews who support Bolshevism and its organization for murder, the partisans, is a measure of self-preservation."

Shortly before taking command of the Eleventh Army, General von Manstein said that: "The Jewish-Bolshevik system must be rooted

Left: *"Kristallnacht"* – "The Night of Broken Glass", 9–10 November 1938. The Synagogue at Magdeburg after the night of Nazi looting and burning of Jewish property.

out once and for all." Field Marshal von Reichenau's order to the Sixth Army of 10 October 1941 clearly makes the *Wehrmacht* responsible for the atrocities against Jews in the Ukraine: "In this eastern theatre of war, the soldier is not only a man fighting in accordance with the rules of war, but also the ruthless standard-bearer of national ideals and the avenger of all the bestialities perpetrated on the German peoples. For this reason the soldier must fully appreciate the necessity for the severe but just retribution that must be meted out to the sub-human species of Jewry." His troops' duty was to "free the German people forever from the Jewish-Asiatic threat". When handling large populations, it was inevitable that the regular German troops were involved. Dorothea Schlösser, part of an entertainment troupe touring *Wehrmacht* groups, recalled: "Soldiers told me about the horrible things happening to the Jews while I was in Poland singing with a road-show to entertain the troops. Everyone seemed to be talking about the truckloads of Jews who were being brought in and killed. The soldiers cried like children when they talked about it. I will never forget one experience I had while I was in Warsaw. I was standing off stage waiting for my appearance when I noticed some young soldiers in the audience. There were dancers on stage and one of the soldiers began to laugh hysterically and said, 'I already saw some people dancing tonight – the Jews we took away!' Then he suddenly began to sob, 'Why don't they defend themselves?'"

Not all were as traumatized as the young soldiers mentioned above. The Sixth Army was forced

Above right: Adolf Eichmann, head of the Race and Resettlement Office of the Reich Security Main Office Amt IV.
Right: Reinhard Heydrich, Himmler's deputy and head of the Reich Security Main Office of the *SS*.

Slav and anti-Semitic propaganda, even if few of them consciously acted at the time out of Nazi values. The nature of the war produced emotions that were both primitive and complex. Although there were cases of soldiers reluctant to carry out executions when most natural pity for civilians was transmuted into an incoherent anger based on the feeling that women and children had no business to be in a battle zone."

BRAVE PROTEST

Some did protest. Martin Koller, a *Luftwaffe* officer, had a very similar conversation to that of Christabel Bielenberg when returning by train from leave: "We talked about all kinds of things, everyday subjects, war and private life. And then he said he'd taken part in shooting Jews somewhere in the Baltic. There had been more than 3000 of them. They had to dig their own grave 'as big as a soccer field'. He told me this with a certain pride. I was completely at a loss and asked stupid questions like, 'Is it really true?' 'How was it done?' 'Who led this operation?' And I got precise answers to each. It was true, anyone could check; with twelve men armed with machine pistols and one machine gun. The ammunition had been officially provided by the *Wehrmacht*, and a German *SS* lieutenant, whose name he didn't remember, had been in command. I became confused and started to sweat. This just didn't fit into the whole picture – of me, of my country, of the world, of the war. It was so monstrous that I couldn't grasp it. 'Can I see your identification?' I asked, and 'Do you mind if I note it down?' He didn't

to issue the following instruction in August 1941: "In various places within the army's area of responsibility, organs of the *SD*, of the *Reichsführer's SS* and chiefs of the German police have been carrying out necessary executions of criminal, Bolshevik and mostly Jewish elements. There have been cases of off-duty soldiers volunteering to help the *SD* with their executions, or acting as spectators and taking photographs." Such orders prove the awareness of much of the *Wehrmacht* chain of command of the policy of extermination. Despite the above instruction, troops continued to be involved in anti-Jewish actions. Antony Beevor explained why: "German soldiers were bound to mistreat civilians after nine years of the regime's anti-mind and was just as proud of what he had done as I was of the planes I had shot down. And while I scribbled his … name down on a cigarette package, my thoughts somersaulted: either what he's told me is true, in which case I can't wear a German uniform any longer, or he's lying in which case he can't wear a German uniform any longer. What can, what should I do? My military instinct told me, 'Report it!'"

Koller did make a report and a senior officer quashed it. Yet there can be no doubt knowledge of the fate of the Jews did circulate, despite the regime's efforts to keep it secret. Conservative resister Helmuth von Moltke, a friend of Bielenberg's husband, spoke to a nurse from an *SS* sanatorium for men who had broken down shooting Jewish women and children. Racial policies and atrocities were discussed openly in military and governmental circles. Nor was the knowledge restricted to the small policy making élites. The White Rose group of Munich University students led by the Scholls included in one of their anti-Nazi pamphlets: "Since the conquest of Poland 300,000 Jews ave

Below: Jews in France are rounded up for deportation to a concentration camp. The Germans deported and murdered 83,000 Jews from France alone.

Above: Inside the Warsaw Ghetto. By 1941, the daily food ration in the ghetto was 184 calories, compared to 669 for a Pole and 2163 for a German.

have been murdered ... in the most bestial way. Here we see the most frightful crime against human dignity, a crime that is unparalleled in our whole history." Rumours abounded in Frankfurt and Berlin in the summer of 1943 that deported Jews were being gassed.

German authorities moved from the slaughter of Jews behind the lines on the Eastern Front to what was known as the "Final Solution" of the Jewish Question. That solution, formalized at the Wannsee Conference in January 1942, was the extermination of all European Jewry. Jews living throughout Europe, whether confined to ghettos in Poland or still living in their own homes, were to be rounded up, detained in local holding camps before being deported by train to distant camps where they would either be worked to death or murdered by gas. Such a large-scale undertaking had to draw upon a lot more than just military support. This enforced mass movement of Jews from Germany and elsewhere in Europe required the involvement of many civilians. The latter often later claimed to have had no knowledge of their role in the "Final Solution".

The following is a post-war interview with a senior railway official:

"Interviewer: Why were there more special trains during the war than before or after it?

Railway Official (RO): I see what you're getting at. You're referring to the so-called resettlement trains.

Interviewer: 'Resettlement'. That's it.

RO: That's what they are called. Those trains were ordered by the Ministry of Transport of the Reich. You needed an order from the ministry.

Interviewer: In Berlin.

RO: Correct. And as for the implementation of those orders, the Head Office of Eastbound Traffic in Berlin dealt with it.

Interviewer: Yes, I understand

RO: Is that clear?

Interviewer: Perfectly. But mostly, at the time, who was being 'resettled'?

RO: No! We didn't know that. Only when we were fleeing from Warsaw ourselves, did we learn that they could have been Jews, or criminals, or similar people.

Interviewer: Jews, criminals?

RO: Criminals. All kinds.

Interviewer: Special trains for criminals?

RO: No, that was just an expression. You couldn't talk about that. Unless you were tired of life, it was best not to mention that.

Interviewer: But you knew that the trains to Treblinka or Auschwitz were –

RO: Of course we knew. I was the last district; without me these trains couldn't reach their destination.

Below: Jews are rounded up in the Warsaw Ghetto in 1943. When the Germans began to clear the ghetto in April 1943, they were met by extremely stiff resistance.

Concentration Camps – HELL ON EARTH

1 The gas chambers at Dachau. The inmates, selected for death, were killed in specially designed gas chambers. The process of gassing was usually disguised; many gas chambers were labelled "shower room".

2 Jews disembark from their train. They were then selected for work or immediate gassing.

3 Female guards at Belsen concentration camp. The one in the centre is Irma Grese, "the beast of Belsen" and mistress of the camp commandant, Josef Kramer,

4 Electrified fences, guard towers and searchlights at Strutthof Concentration Camp near Danzig.

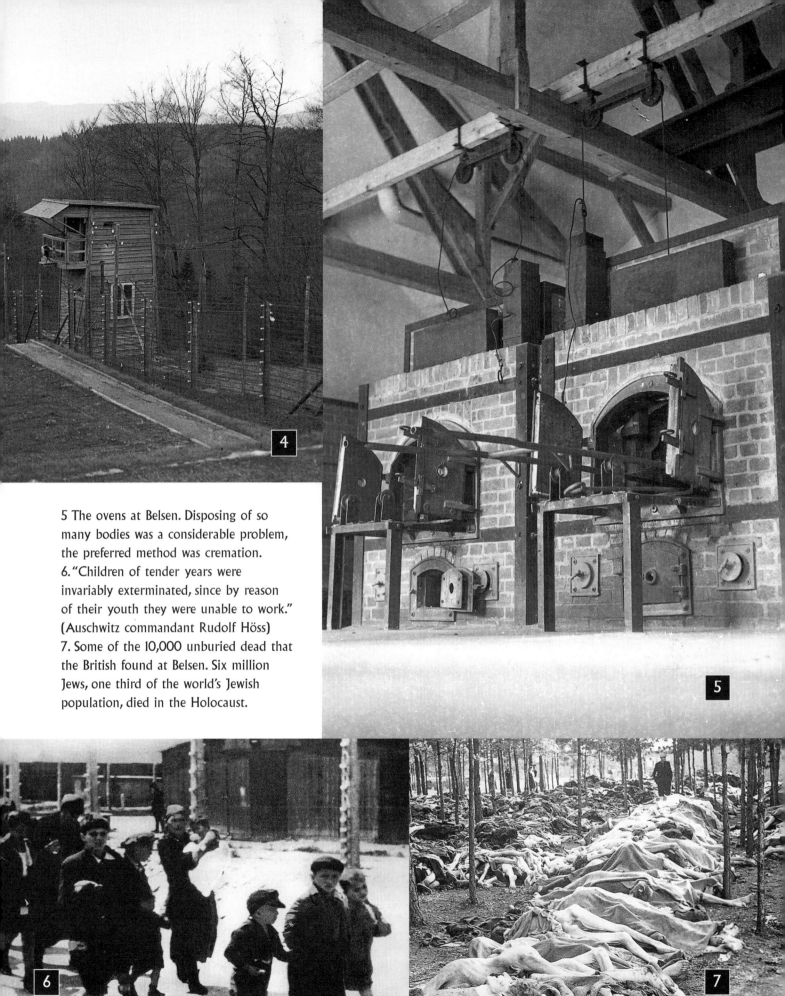

5 The ovens at Belsen. Disposing of so many bodies was a considerable problem, the preferred method was cremation.

6. "Children of tender years were invariably exterminated, since by reason of their youth they were unable to work." (Auschwitz commandant Rudolf Höss)

7. Some of the 10,000 unburied dead that the British found at Belsen. Six million Jews, one third of the world's Jewish population, died in the Holocaust.

Above: Belsen concentration camp after its liberation. More than half of the inmates died in the weeks that followed of malnutrition, typhus and dysentery.

For instance, a train that started in Essen had to go through the districts of Wuppertal, Hanover, Magdeburg, Berlin, Frankfurt/-Oder, Posen, Warsaw etc. So I had to...

Interviewer: Did you know that Treblinka meant extermination?

RO: Of course not!

Interviewer: You didn't know?

RO: Good God, no! How could we know? I never went to Treblinka. I stayed in Krakow, in Warsaw, glued to my desk.

Interviewer: You were a...

RO: I was strictly a bureaucrat!

Interviewer: I see. But it's astonishing that people in the department of special trains never knew about the 'Final Solution'.

RO: We were at war.

Interviewer: Because there were others who worked for the railroads who knew. Like the train conductors.

RO: Yes, they saw it. They did. But as to what happened, I didn't.

Interviewer: What was Treblinka for you? Treblinka or Auschwitz?

RO: Yes, for us Treblinka, Belzec and all that were concentration camps.

Interviewer: A destination.

RO: Yes, that's all.

Interviewer: But, not death?

RO: No, no... "

It is possible that this man was not lying and lacked the insight to conclude what his role was in the process of the "Final Solution". Given the rumours at the time and the fact that the trains never brought anyone back, it is reasonable to presume that German transport officials, and there were many thousands of them, had some knowledge of what was going on. Recent historical studies, such as Daniel Goldhagen's *Hitler's Willing Executioners*, have persuasively argued this case. Transport workers were not the only people involved, doctors and nurses checked the Jews before departure, and postal workers delivered the initial messages to German Jews ordering their deportation. Normal policemen were often responsible for round-ups in Germany, and Jews were often moved through the streets in broad daylight in preparation for their deportation. Also, the examples of Christabel Bielenberg and Martin Koller prove there were plenty of those directly involved at the most brutal end of the process who were willing to talk about it. Although it was wise not to voice such tales too openly, there must have been many conversations in train carriages or bars as people tried to unburden themselves. The most likely explanation seems to be that even if much of the German population did not precisely and categorically know that the systematic extermination of the Jews was being undertaken, they still must have suspected that something was happening. The only conclusion is that, perhaps partially due to the penalties for non-conformism in Hitler's Germany, the vast majority of Germans were indifferent to the fate of the Jews who had been around them until recently.

As for those German Jews who were rounded up by their fellow Germans and sent aboard German-run trains to the German-run death and concentration camps, a grim fate awaited them. "We had," Auschwitz commandant Rudolf Höss explained, "two *SS* doctors on duty to examine the incoming prisoners. These would be marched by one of the doctors, who would make spot decisions. Those who were fit to work were sent into the camp. Others were sent immediately to the extermination plants.

Below: A concentration camp survivor sorts through a pile of rags after liberation. The extermination continued until the camps were overrun by the advancing Allies.

Children of tender years were invariably exterminated, since by reason of their youth they were unable to work."

It was a terrifying ordeal for those who arrived at the death camps. The routine at Treblinka was similar to that in other camps. As soon as the cattle-wagon doors were unbolted the camp guards would use whips and dogs to herd those inside into the open. Men and women were separated, made to undress and then hand in their valuables. The old and infirm were led off towards the infirmary, but then arrived at a mass grave where each one was shot in the back of the head and thrown in. Men were sent to the gas chamber first as they took

Below: British troops supervise the distribution of food at Belsen. When US troops liberated Dachau, they were so disgusted that they killed 122 of the SS guards on the spot.

less time – women had to have their hair shorn in the chamber itself by a team of Jewish barbers working at a rate of two minutes per person. Then the doors to the chamber were closed.

Dr Kurt Gerstein was a disinfection officer at Belzec and witnessed a "typical" gassing: "Even in death one knows the families. They squeeze each other's hands, clenched in death, so that there is difficulty tearing them apart in order to evacuate the chamber for the next consignment. The cadavers, damp with sweat and urine, legs splattered with excrement and blood, are hurled outside. Children's corpses fly through the air ... Two dozen dentists open the jaws with hooks and look for gold. Gold left, without gold right. Other dentists break the gold teeth and crowns from the jaws with pliers and hammers."

ney. You couldn't help but notice it. It burned night and day. People came from Hungary, and we said, 'Tonight the Hungarians are burning. When is it going to be our turn?'"

By April 1944 there were 13 parent camps and 500 sub-camps operating in German-controlled territory. The biggest death camp was located at Auschwitz in Upper East Silesia. Originally opened as a camp for mostly Polish political prisoners, it was rapidly expanded as a work camp and then as a site for extermination. The camp itself was divided into three parts: Auschwitz 1, the original camp, Auschwitz 2 at Birkenau, built to accommodate 200,000 victims, was the death camp, and Auschwitz 3, the industrial centre. It is estimated that around two million Jews were murdered at the Auschwitz complex alone.

THE DEATH CAMPS

The *SS* had estimated the need to exterminate 11 million Jews, and so other death camps were set up to deal with the numbers being sent for annihilation. In early 1942, therefore, four were established in Poland: Belzec, Lublin, Sobibor and Treblinka, with two others being established in "Greater Germany": Chelmno and Auschwitz. Belzec had a killing capacity of 15,000 a day, while Treblinka and Lublin could boast a capacity of 25,000 a day. Of course, there were other concentration camps, and although they were not death camps atrocities and murders took place in all of them over a long period of time, and the conditions for inmates were horrendous. Their names have since become associated with all the evils of Nazism: Dachau, Sachsenhausen, Buchenwald, Ravensbrück, Mauthausen, Bergen-Belsen, Theresienstadt, Flossenbürg and Natzweiler.

Six million Jews died at the hands of the Nazis during World War II. Rudolf Würster, a young *Luftwaffe* recruit, provides a suitable conclusion. He witnessed the murder of Jews in Poland but kept the information to himself, and "confided only to my closest friends my feelings that we were going to have a lot to answer for if we lost the war."

Above: Ilse Koch, widow of the commandant of Buchenwald, on trial at Dachau for crimes against humanity in 1947, including having lampshades made of human skin.

Those that were "lucky" enough to pass the selection faced death through starvation and overwork, or even at the hands of the camp guards, who were mostly recruited for their indifference to suffering and their willingness to carry out the most inhumane orders. Dora Völkel recalled: "We were beaten a lot and hardly given anything to eat. You could watch human beings turn into animals. Many people lost all sense of human dignity … We were forced to carry heavy rocks from one place to another. We had to carry a rock about a kilometre, set it down, pick up another rock, and carry that back to where we had originally come from. And of course, there was the fire, the bright fire rising from the chim-

Above: Bomb damage. It took years before reconstruction in Germany was complete – this picture dates from 1948. Below: Damaged Cologne Cathedral. Countless art and architectural treasures were destroyed in World War II.

GERMANY DEFEATED

"That from the bottom of my heart I express my thanks to you all is just as self-evident as my wish that you should, because of that, on no account give up the struggle, but rather continue it against the enemies of the Fatherland, no matter where ... From the sacrifice of our soldiers and from my own unity with you unto death will in any event spring up in the history of Germany the seed of a radiant renaissance of the National Socialist movement and thus of a true community of nations."

Political Testament of Adolf Hitler, 29 April 1945.

Hitler killed himself the following day. The commander of Berlin, General Weidling, surrendered the city on 2 May. British commander Field Marshal Montgomery accepted the capitulation of Germany's forces in the north and west on 4 May. The Western Allies Supreme Commander, Dwight D. Eisenhower, took the surrender of Germany at Rheims on 7 May. Finally, the act of surrender was repeated in the presence of representatives of the Soviet Union on 8 May. It became effective the following day.

PEACE AGAIN

The citizens and soldiers of Germany emerged from their cellars, shelters, foxholes and trenches into peace, but it remained a very dangerous world. Brunhilde Pomsel emerged from her shelter with a group of her colleagues from the Propaganda Ministry and walked to Templehof about 5.5km (three and half miles) away: "The war had just come to an end. The walk through Berlin was horrible – dead horses and dead people everywhere. Russian military policewomen were already out directing the traffic." There seems to have been a difference between the treatment of German civilians by the first line troops and those that followed.

Jürgen Graf was a teenager in Berlin and the first Russian troops he met "were very friendly and sometimes brought us things to eat". His family's relationship with them "went well for exactly 48 hours" and then: "The next wave of Russian troops arrived and they settled in to stay. These Russians were really bad. Their main problem was liquor, and they were the ones who started the period of rape and destruction in Berlin." They indulged in an orgy of destruction and destroyed Graf's father's art collection, using his "paintings as dartboards", smashing his precious porcelain and burning his carved wooden statues. Graf summed it up thus:

"That's what living with the Soviets was like. The first troops were friendly and gave us food. They had officers with them who spoke German very well and told us to be calm, that everything would be all right. These officers explained that first they would take Berlin, and then a form of self-administration could be set up to replace Nazi rule. All of this was very encouraging. Just 48 hours later, houses were burned, women raped and people who had gone underground, who had worked against the fascists for years, were taken away and shot."

Brunhilde Pomsel concurred: "The Russians didn't touch a hair on our heads. I wasn't raped either. We were lucky to have been captured by these particular soldiers, who were part of Zhukov's troops. They were very disciplined and treated us correctly." She also provided an interesting anecdote about the young troops guarding her and her fellow prisoners: "Young Soviet soldiers constantly kept coming in to see us. We presumed they were our guards. I was still young, and at first naturally thought they were interested in me. But they came because they wanted to talk to Frau Junius [an elderly translator who had worked for the Germany News Agency], the White

Above: The wrecked statue on top of the Brandenburg Gate in Berlin, 1945. The city was bombed, fought over and finally divided into four by the victorious Allies.

Russian. They always came with vodka and onions. They set everything down on the table and got out the water glasses. I had to pour the vodka and drink along with them. They sat and talked with Frau Junius for hours. When they left, I always asked Frau Junius what they talked about. She said: 'They are all such nice boys. They wanted to know what living in Russia under the Czar was like.'"

The experience of German soldiers when they surrendered varied considerably. It was an extremely dangerous moment and contained a considerable risk of being shot out of hand or badly beaten. Conversely, many were pleasantly surprised by the humane treatment they received, particularly as they had been continuously told by Nazi propaganda that they were likely to be executed immediately. A number of Germans had their racial preconceptions seriously challenged by contact with Allied troops following their capture. Lothar Loewe surrendered on 5 May and was understandably worried: "The squad that took us prisoner lined us up against the wall of a shed where there were two dead civilians lying on the ground. I was sure we were going to be shot.

Below: A column of German prisoners is marched to the rear near Giesen, Germany, in late March 1945 as tanks and trucks of the US 6th Armored Division roll by.

There was a big discussion with one of the officers, and then suddenly they came up to us and took our rings and watches. But I also found myself with two packs of cigarettes I hadn't had before – the Russians pressed two packs of German cigarettes into my hands."

He and his colleagues had their wounds treated and were then fed. Loewe had no equipment and "it was this Bolshevik, this person I'd always believed to be a monster, that lent me, the Nordic German, his mess kit and spoon to eat with." He had seen the German treatment of Soviet POWs, who were uniformly badly cared for and underfed and "were made to look like the subhumans we imagined them to be". He was taken aback:

Above: The moment of surrender was a dangerous time. Prisoners might be shot out of hand, treated with casual indifference or quite often considerable kindness.

"The idea that a German soldier would give a Russian prisoner his mess kit and spoon to eat from was simply unimaginable to me. And the fact that this Soviet gave me his, voluntarily, happily, because he felt sorry for me, shook the foundations of my image of them. That's when I told myself that maybe the Soviets were much different from what they had told us to believe. This was my first encounter with Soviet people and I'll never forget it for the rest of my life."

Wolfgang Kasak surrendered to Poles fighting with the Soviets: "I was led away by a very nice Polish soldier. Without saying a word, he made it clear that I would be interrogated and that everything would be taken from me, so why didn't I give him my watch."

Kurt Meyer-Grell was captured by the Red Army on 7 May 1945: "We were all beset by a sense of doom ... Because we were afraid of being put at the mercy of the Russians. Even in 1945, many of us believed the Russians didn't take pris-

oners. And I remember very clearly that when we were marched out and loaded into trucks, many of us expected to be taken into the nearest ditch and shot ... At first we were very decently treated; there's no other way to put it. I saw Russian officers salute us as we marched past them through streets full of rubble. "

Wolfgang Schöler was captured "along with the rest of my company, by Czech partisans. We were handed over to the Russians. I must say that, under the circumstances, we were treated pretty well."

Similarly, Bruno Weik, who was captured at Danzig, recalled that: "The Russians didn't mistreat us. They gave us dressings for our wounds. They showed no hate, and they didn't threaten us. A young Russian doctor treated us very well ...

They shared drinks with us. Most of the time they didn't even know what was in the bottles. They had French cognac and let everyone have a shot … They did the best they could. You can't say they are third-class people, or that they are inferior."

Similar stories are told about being captured by the Americans. Robert Vogt was held at Rouen where he saw black American soldiers for the first time: "When we saw them we were scared stiff and thought, 'Oh Lord, now we're done for.' This feeling came from – and here I must say that we were lied to in the Third Reich – being told these people were subhuman, barbarians etc. Even at

Below: The "Big Three" – Churchill, Roosevelt and Stalin – at Yalta in February 1945, where they agreed on the postwar division of Germany into four zones of occupation.

school we were told that. So we were terribly afraid. But my fear disappeared twenty minutes later, after I'd spoken with a black American."

When he told the soldier that he was hungry, the man drove him to a field kitchen and together they loaded the jeep with food and took it back to the other German prisoners. Like Lothar Loewe when shown kindness by a Red Army soldier, Vogt was forced to reassess many things he had been taught to believe: "I must say that I came to consider these black soldiers as our protectors, which is when I began to have serious doubts about the Third Reich's propaganda. Here I had proof that we had been lied to … they weren't brutes. We liked them better than the white Americans. They said to us, 'We're black slaves, you're white slaves.' They were very kind to us. This major

experience with blacks made me wonder: 'If what they told us about blacks was a lie, what else had they lied to us about?'"

Surrendering Germans were just as likely to be met with violence or, at best, indifference. Badly wounded Rudolf Vilter recalled that "we thought that the Russians would come and shoot us and they did indeed come very soon, but they didn't harm us. On the other hand, they didn't help us either." Wolfgang Kasak, however, experienced perhaps a more typical example of capture: "One thing I will never forget about the march into captivity was the shooting of a 15-year-old boy right before my very eyes. He simply couldn't walk any

more, so a Russian soldier took potshots at him. The boy was still alive when some officers came over and fired his gun into the boy's ear. It took all of our strength to stay in the middle of the extremely slow-moving herds being driven east. We kept hearing the submachine guns whenever a straggler was shot."

At the Yalta Conference in February 1945, the leaders of the three major Allied powers – Winston Churchill, Franklin Roosevelt and Josef Stalin –

Above: A Nazi staged photograph of the so-called "Werewolves" – fanatical Nazis who roamed the forests of central Europe after the end of the war, to no effect.

had agreed to divide Germany into four zones of occupation: British, American, Soviet and French. Military governments were established in each. The long-term treatment of German prisoners depended very much on which zone they were held in. The Western Allies had tried to maintain reasonable standards of internment for the increasingly vast numbers of Germans that they captured. It was a daunting task. British Field Marshal Montgomery described the situation facing the British zone under his control:

"In the area occupied ... there were appalling civilian problems to be solved. Over one million civilian refugees had fled into the area before the advancing Russians. About one million German wounded were in hospital in the area, with no medical supplies. Over one and half million unwounded German fighting men had surrendered ... and were now Prisoners of War, with all that entailed. Food would shortly be exhausted. The transport and communication services had ceased to function, and industry and agriculture were largely at a standstill."

He had roughly 20 million Germans on his hands who had to be fed and housed, and Montgomery readily admitted that: "Tremendous problems would be required to be handled and if they were not solved before winter began, many Germans would die of starvation, exposure and disease."

The Allied authorities in the French, American and Soviet zones faced almost exactly the same problems. Thus while Josef Hühnerbach might have judged his period in Allied captivity as "great", men captured later faced a very different situation as Allied logistics became over-strained. The quality of treatment declined rapidly in the face of such huge numbers. Conditions were exceedingly grim and many, many Germans died of starvation and exposure in all the Allied zones. American Captain Frederick Siegfriedt, appalled by the conditions former *SS* men were kept in a camp near Zimming in eastern France, said that the operation of the camp CCE 27 seemed "typical of the entire system". He continued: "When an enclosure got a bunch of prisoners they didn't know what do do with, or could not otherwise handle, they were shipped unannounced to another enclosure … I have no idea how many died nor where they were buried. I am sure the Americans did not bury them and we had no such thing as a

bulldozer. I can only assume a detail of German PWs [Prisoners of War] would bury them. I could look out of the window of my office and tell if the body being carried was alive or dead by whether or not there was a fifth man following with the man's personal possessions. The number could have been from five to twenty a day."

He concluded: "Obviously we, the US Army, were not prepared to deal with so many prisoners". The Americans had allowed the camps to fall below the level required by the Geneva Convention. Lieutenant-Colonel Henry W. Allard, in charge of the US camps in France in 1945, said: "The standards of PW camps in the ComZ [the US Army's rear zone] in Europe compare as only

Below: The Allies found themselves in charge of vast numbers of prisoners. As the sheer volume of men swamped the system, camp conditions deteriorated.

slightly better or even worse than the living conditions of the Japanese PW camps our men tell us about, and unfavourably with the German ones."

This American assessment is borne out by German accounts. Hermann Blocksdorff gives a chilling account of life at the Sinzig camp which is worth quoting at length: "Each group of 10 was given the outdoor space of a medium-sized living room. We had to live like this for three months, no roof over our heads. Even the badly wounded only got a bundle of straw. And it rained on the Rhine. For days. And we were always in the open. People died like flies. Then we got our first rations, and I swear to God, I'm telling the truth: we got one slice of bread for 10 men. Each man got a tiny strip of that one slice. In addition to that we got, per 10 men, a tablespoon of milk powder, coffee, grape-

fruit powder, and one tablespoon of sugar. Per man, that was a strip of bread and a teaspoon of the above-mentioned powders. And this went on for three long months. I only weighed 27kg [90lb]. The dead were carried out every day. Then a voice would come over the loudspeaker: 'German soldiers, eat slowly. You haven't had anything to eat in a long time. When you get your rations today from the best-fed army in the world, you'll die if you don't eat slowly."'

By the time he was released in June 1945, he and his comrades "looked like scarecrows". Blocksdorff was delighted to return home and he recalled: "How happy I was that it was still standing! When I rang the bell, Americans came to the door – my wife's new friends. They asked me what the hell I wanted."

Left: US infantrymen pass the St Severin Church in Cologne, March 1945. Of the city's population of over one million, only 150,000 remained at this time.

Germany –
A NATION LAID LOW

1 The centre of Hitler's power; the gutted remains of the reception room at the Reich Chancellery. The "Thousand Year Reich" ended in the rubble of Berlin after only 12.
2 These people on their way towards relatives in the Cologne-Aachen area are very lucky, as they have access to a truck.
3 The shattered remains of Shell House in Berlin after the War. Women – the *Trümmerfrau* – steadily cleared the rubble.
4 Refugees crowd into West Berlin. Many Berliners chose to flee the Soviet-occupied zone.

5 The struggle to survive. Food remained in short supply. Here, German civilians strip the carcass of a dead horse lying on the roadside for meat.

6 A German housewife hunts for anything that will burn in Halberstadt. In an estimated 95 percent of German towns, wood was the only fuel available.

7 With much of Germany's utilities destroyed, basic necessities such as drinking water had to be provided. Here, people queue for water at Lüneberg.

Above: With the collapse of government, people had to fend for themselves as best they could. Here, a crowd of hungry Germans board a freight train in Frankfurt.

The major difference between the treatment of German prisoners by the Americans and Soviets lay not in the conditions the Germans had to endure, but in how long they were held. The Western Allies were keen to repatriate the German soldiers in their hands as soon as possible. Once it was established that the men were not members of the *SS*, *Gestapo* or wanted for war crimes, the British and Americans were eager to release them. The Soviets were determined to have retribution on those who had wreaked such havoc on Soviet territory. When it came to making German prisoners work, the actual production

gained was slightly less than the cost of keeping them, but did not stop widespread Soviet exploitation of the vast numbers of German soldiers captured. On the whole, the experience was grim. Wolfgang Kasak was shipped to somewhere on the River Volta where "we had to build our own camp". Nonetheless, he had to admit that "even starving prisoners couldn't help but admire the scenery". Wolfgang Schöler recalled that: "Frankly I don't think anyone needs to tell us about living conditions in concentration camps, because they weren't much different from ours. For example – just to name some numbers – initially there were approximately 9000 of us and within a very short time, at least 1800 had died very unpleasantly. We were physically exploited through bad treatment and the sub-tropical climate."

Joseph Lücking, despite a horrendous journey eastwards in which one in 10 of his comrades died, reckoned of his ration of three drinking cups of flour soup a day: "That was it and it stayed that way for weeks on end. But the situation wasn't much different on the other side, either. To be honest, the Russians were suffering horribly from hunger themselves. I mean, I saw for myself in Moscow that the Russians would say that they'd picked up so and so many dead off the streets that day, people who'd died from malnutrition in 1945."

Even Wolfgang Schöler admitted that despite the mistreatment that he endured in Soviet custody: "I experienced something which confirms the kindness of the people in Russia: I was taken to a Russian hospital and cared for by Russian doctors and nurses. And I never had the impression that they would have treated us any differently had we been their own."

Those Germans shipped out into the Soviet Gulag system, where they worked as forced labour, were returned home haphazardly, those who survived, that is. Some were released after a year or so, others had to endure until 1956 when Konrad Adenauer's West German Government finally negotiated the survivors' return. Many thousands died in the Soviet Union.

A small hard core of Nazis wanted to fight on. In the last months of the war the Nazi leadership had attempted to establish "Werewolf" guerrilla groups to continue the struggle. Herbert Mittelstädt recounted what was probably a fairly typical example of the attempt to recruit volunteers: "On 1 May 1945, our lieutenant approached the 25 of us and gravely announced, 'I no longer

Below: A mother and child wait for transport to a displaced and homeless persons centre. A quarter of Germany's population was in a similar situation in 1945.

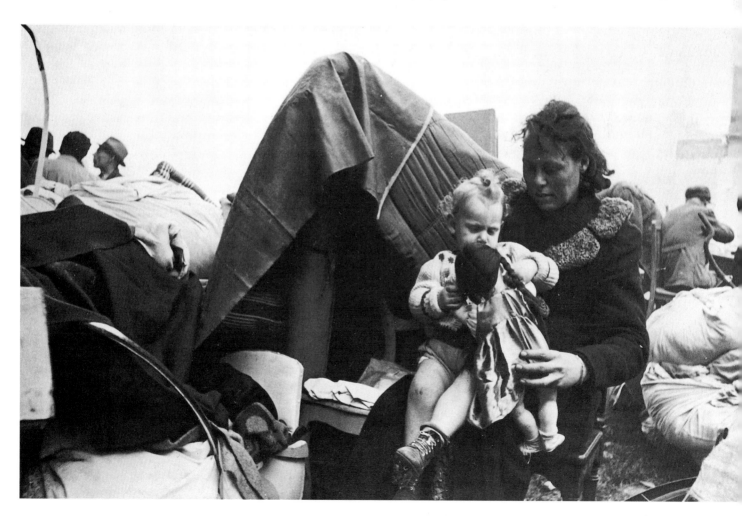

believe that there is any way possible for us to win this war. I am going to discharge you, and whoever wants to can continue to fight with me as a Werewolf.' Only one guy raised his hand. His family was in East Prussia, and the possibility of his ever returning was extremely slim. Since the lieutenant only had a single ally, he said, 'The whole thing is not worth it. I'm going to discharge myself as well!'"

Klaus Messmer was an active member, and he and his group attempted to sabotage and blow up French military vehicles, but even he saw little point in continuing: "We soon realized that our efforts to resist had done absolutely nothing to change anything. A new era had begun and there was nothing we could do about it."

With most of the men either dead or in some sort of prison camp, the initial clearing up was left to the women who lived in the cities. Anna Mittelstädt was in Berlin when the war ended and was drafted as a *Trümmerfrau* – a woman organized to clear rubble:

"After the Russians arrived, women were employed by civilian firms to remove the ruins and to clean up the streets. We worked like dogs. There were no men around. They were either dead or prisoners in some camp. We had to walk long distances to reach our work area. A few fortunate ones were able to use the *S-Bahn* [the elevated train system] which amazingly, in spite of all the bombing, was still intact and operating. I organized and led the *Trümmerfrau*-Brigade in Berlin."

Some 50,000 women were involved in the enterprise which gained them extra rations. One of the best descriptions of this is provided in a work of fiction by Günter Grass's *My Century*: "Brick dust. Brick dust everywhere, let me tell you. In the air you breathe, the clothes you wear, between teeth – you name it. But you think that it got us down? Not us women. Main thing was the war was over … It was hard work shovelling rubble. And the bricks that were still whole we stacked up nice and neat … Piecework they called it … And you should've seen us! Overalls out of old army blankets, sweaters from wool scraps, and kerchiefs round our heads, tied up top to keep the dust out. Fifty thousand rubble women there was in Berlin … Not a man in the bunch."

Germany's women were the true force behind Germany's reconstruction in the first months of peace after May 1945. They were the ones who believed that they had endured too much to give up now. The men, if they came back at all, were often broken physically or mentally. Eventually those men who did return

Left: Forced to face the truth. As part of the Allied denazification programme, Germans were made to watch newsreels showing Nazi atrocities.

tried to rebuild their families and lives. Renate Hoffmann, having endured terrible treatment when cut off by the Soviet advance, made her way to Munich to meet her terribly burned husband: "We fell into another's arms. We talked and I immediately realized it was the same voice, nothing had changed. My husband got out of bed and put on his robe – the same motions, the same movements, the same figure. But it had still been a shock, because the face was no longer there – it was gone."

Tellingly, it was she who brought the family back together: "We quickly agreed that I should go back to the Soviet zone to get the children and return to Munich as soon as possible. That is exactly what I did, and in the autumn of 1945 we were reunited as a family once again."

Germany faced massive problems in the immediate post-war period. The cost to her in human terms had been staggering: 2,850,000 military dead and 500,000 civilian dead. The damage to the nation's infrastructure had also been immense. Of the 19 million dwellings in Germany, 2,750,000 had been completely destroyed and a further

Above: Refugees make their west into the British-occupied zone of Germany. Few civilians wished to remain in the zone occupied by the vengeful Red Army.

1,250,000 heavily damaged. The losses among individual towns and cities was horrendous: Hamburg had lost 53 percent of its homes, Cologne 70 percent, Dortmund 66 percent, Munich 33 percent, Dresden 60 percent and Berlin, perhaps surprisingly, 37 percent. More than 16 million Germans were refugees from the east, and there were 4,500,000 displaced persons in Germany – foreign labourers – plus two million prisoners of war of different nationalities. Public transport, especially the railways, was wrecked, as were public utilities.

A kind of numbness gripped those who still lived, as they battled on a daily basis with destruction, destitution and starvation. Under Hitler's leadership the German people had come close to committing national suicide – never in modern times had a major power been brought so low. For those citizens who remained in the rubble of the Third Reich, survival was the main aim.

GLOSSARY

Aryan Term first used by the linguistic scholar Friedrich Max Müller to describe a group of peoples who migrated into northwest Europe in ancient history. As seen by the Nazis, the "Nordic" peoples of Europe formed the heartland of the so-called "Aryan race".

Blitzkrieg "Lightning War". A strategic concept of waging war developed by the German Army in the 1920s, using mass armoured formations, supported by overwhelming air power, to paralyze, surround and then annihilate enemy armies. Speed, surprise and terror were integral to the *Blitzkrieg*, plus bold and imaginative leadership by corps and divisional commanders. The *Blitzkrieg* was stunningly successful in 1939–41.

Der Stürmer Semi-pornographic and violently antisemitic Nazi Party weekly newspaper edited by Julius Streicher.

Einsatzgruppen *SS* Special Action Groups. First organized by Himmler and Heydrich in 1939, they followed the armies into Poland to murder national leaders and round up Jews to put them in ghettos (they also murdered many Jews doing so). During the invasion of Russia the *Einsatzgruppen* were split into four units of 3000 each. By the end of March 1943 they had killed an estimated 633,300 Jews, and went on to murder another 100,000 more in 1944–45.

Freikorps Private units of ex-soldiers raised by their former officers at the end of World War I. These right-wing, paramilitary groups, such as the *Ehrhardt* Brigade, were secretly funded by Captain von Schleicher of the Political Department of the Germany Army to protect Germany's eastern borders and then put down revolution at home. Hitler witnessed the brutal suppression of the communist government of Bavaria by the *Freikorps* in 1919. Munich became a refuge for *Freikorps* members, and many later joined the ranks of the *SA*.

Gauleiter Senior Nazi Party administrative figure in a *Gau* (District). In 1938 there were 32 Nazi Party districts; by 1942 there were 40.

Labour Front The sole labour union organization in the Third Reich. Set up in 1933, it came to control all aspects of the German workforce.

Gestapo *Geheime Staatspolizei*. The secret police of the Third Reich, that used terror to keep control of the state and its population. Its activities extended into occupied countries during the war years. At its height, in 1943, there were 45,000 *Gestapo* members controlling 60,000 agents and 100,000 informers. The organization was headed by Heinrich Müller.

KPD Communist Party of Germany. The strongest communist party in the world outside the Soviet Union until its destruction by the Nazis in 1933. During the 1920s the *KPD* believed the Nazis to be part of the ruling bourgeoisie, and viewed the Socialist Party as the real enemy. This led to the Nazis and *KPD* working together on numerous occasions to break up Socialist Party meetings.

"Night of the Long Knives" The purging of the *SA* by Hitler and the *SS* in June 1934. Following Hitler's coming to power, Röhm and the *SA* leadership talked of a second revolution in which the old traditional power groups would be swept away, stating that the *SA* was the true defender of the nation. On 30 June Hitler, ordered the *SS* to begin executing those individuals considered to be "enemies of the regime". Some 1000 were killed, including Röhm and Gregor Strasser.

Nuremberg Laws A series of anti-Jewish laws drafted by Wilhelm Stukart, made public at the

1935 Nuremberg Rally and enforced from September of that year. The first Reich Law of Citizenship recognized two degrees of humanity: the *Reichsbürger*, the citizen of pure German blood; and, for all other categories of person, the *Staatsengehörige*, the subject of the state. Some 250 decrees followed these laws, which excluded Jews from economic life and forced them to wear the Star of David.

Reichsarbeitsdienst (*RAD*) Labour service. By a law of 26 June 1933, the RAD enforced six months' labour service for all males between the ages of 19 and 25. This was later extended to women also.

Reichstag The home of the German parliament in Berlin. After it was burnt down in February 1933, the parliament met in Berlin's Kroll Opera House.

Reichstag Fire One month after Hitler became Chancellor, the *Reichstag* building burnt to the ground. The next day President Hindenburg suspended all civil liberties, and this decree became law in March. This made Hitler dictator and Germany de facto a police state. Though the communist Marius van der Lubbe was tried, convicted and executed for the crime, it is suspected that an *SA* detachment may have started the fire.

Reichswehr The army of 100,000 men allowed to the Weimar Republic by the Versailles Treaty.

SA *Sturmabteilung*. The Brownshirts – uniformed Nazi Party supporters recruited from 1921 by Ernst Röhm. Mostly ex-soldiers and ex-*Freikorps* members, they grew in number until banned after the Munich "Beer Hall Putsch" in 1923. However, following the reformation of the party the *SA* rose in numbers. When Hitler became Chancellor in 1933, the *SA* numbered 500,000. Hitler, fearing Röhm and the *SA* would become a rival power base, ordered the *SS* to emasculate the *SA* during the "Night of the Long Knives".

SD *Sicherheitsdienst*. The Nazi Party's own intelligence and security body. Headed by Reinhard Heydrich, it had a wide range of functions,

including internal state security after the Nazis came to power in 1933, and foreign intelligence.

SS *Schutz Staffel*. Protection Squad. Originally the personal bodyguard of Adolf Hitler, under Heinrich Himmler the *SS* became a state within a state, an army within an army. It eventually developed into an organization with many branches, such as the *Waffen-SS* (armed *SS*), concentration camps, the Race and Resettlement Office, and numerous business enterprises. At the Nuremberg Tribunal, the *SS* was declared a criminal organization.

"Strength through Joy" Successful and popular Nazi scheme for the leisure and pleasure of workers. Sports and leisure activities gave ordinary Germans access to foreign travel, tourist areas and entertainment. It was of great propaganda value to the Third Reich.

Versailles Treaty The peace treaty signed in June 1919 that ended World War I. It established the League of Nations and the states of Czechoslovakia, Poland, Hungary and Lithuania, as well as the "free city" of Danzig. The German Army was reduced to 100,000 men, the navy became a rump and the air force was disbanded.

Volkssturm Last-ditch defence units of the Third Reich, formed in October 1944. All males between the ages of 16 and 60 were organized in their districts, though they were given little training and had few weapons or uniforms.

Wannsee Conference The meeting in the *SS* Reich Chief Security Office headquarters at Wannsee, Berlin, in January 1942 that decided upon the Final Solution (extermination of the Jewish people). The meeting, which was attended by 15 *SS* and government officials, was chaired by Reinhard Heydrich.

Weimar Republic The German Republic that governed between 1919 and 1933. The National Assembly met in Weimar, a town 240km (150 miles) southwest of Berlin.

FURTHER READING

Führer Conferences on Naval Affairs, 1939-45 (Greenhill, London, 1990)

Bacque, James, *Crimes and Mercies: The Fate of German Civilians under Allied Occupation, 1944-50* (Warner, London, 1997)

Beevor, Antony, *Stalingrad* (Viking, London, 1998)

Bessel, Richard (ed.), *Life in the Third Reich* (OUP, Oxford, 1987)

Bielenberg, Christabel, *The Past is Myself* (Corgi, London, 1968)

Blandford, Edmund, *Serving the Third Reich* (Airlife, Shrewsbury, 1996)

Bullock, Alan, *Hitler: a study in tyranny* (Penguin, London, 1990)

Bullock, Alan, *Hitler and Stalin: parallel lives* (Fontana Press, London, 1998)

Calvocoressi, Peter; Wint, Guy and Pritchard, John, *Total War* (Penguin, London, 1972)

Carell, Paul, *Invasion! They're Coming!* (Schiffer, Atglen, PA, 1995)

Cooper, Matthew, *Panzer: The Armoured Force of the Third Reich* (Macdonald and Jane's, London, 1976)

Craig, Gordon, *Germany, 1866-1945* (Oxford Paperbacks, Oxford, 1981)

Deighton, Len, *Blitzkrieg* (Grafton, London, 1979)

Dear, I.C.B. and Foot, M.R.D., *The Oxford Companion to the Second World War* (OUP, Oxford, 1995)

Fest, Joachim, *The Face of the Third Reich* (Penguin, London, 1991)

Fest, Joachim, *The Face of the Third Reich* (Penguin, London, 1970)

Fest, Joachim, *Plotting Hitler's Death* (Phoenix, London, 1994)

Fischer, Klaus, *Nazi Germany: a new history* (Constable, London, 1996)

Gilbert, Martin, *The Holocaust: The Jewish Tragedy* (Fontana Collins, Glasgow, 1987)

Grass, Günter, *My Century* (Faber and Faber, London, 1999)

Guderian, Heinz, *Panzer Leader,* (Macdonald Futura, Heinz, 1952)

Goldhagen, Daniel, *Hitler's Willing Executioners* (Little, Brown & Company, London, 1996)

Hastings, Max, *Overlord* (Pan, London, 1984)

Höss, Rudolf, *Commandant of Auschwitz* (Weidenfeld and Nicolson, London, 1951)

Housden, Martyn, *Resistance and Conformity in the Third Reich* (Routledge, London, 1997)

Kersaudy, François, *Norway 1940* (Arrow, London, 1990)

Kershaw, Ian, *Popular Opinion and Political Dissent in the Third Reich: Bavaria 1933-45* (Clarendon, Oxford, 1983)

Kershaw, Ian, *Hitler, 1889-1936: hubris* (Penguin, London, 1998)

Koonz, Claudia, *Mothers in the Fatherland* (Methuen, London, 1986)

Liddell Hart, Basil, *The Other Side of the Hill* (Pan, London, 1948, revised 1951)

Lochner, Louis (ed.), *The Goebbel's Diaries* (Hamish Hamilton, London, 1948)

Lucas, James, *Germany's Elite Panzer Force: Grossdeutschland* (Macdonald and Jane's, London, 1978)

Mason, Tim, *Women in Germany, 1925–1940: family, welfare and work*, History Workshop Journal I, pp.74-113 (1976)

Maschmann, Melita, *Account Rendered* (Abelard-Schuman, London, 1964)

Merson, Allan, *Communist Resistance in Nazi Germany* (Lawrence and Wishart, London, 1985)

Noakes, Jeremy (ed.), *Nazism 1919-45 Volume 4, The German Home Front in World War II* (University of Exeter Press, Exeter, 1998)

Overy, Richard, *Why the Allies Won* (Jonathon Cape, London, 1995)

Overy, Richard, *The Nazi Economic Recovery* (Cambridge University Press, Cambridge, 1996)

Posner, Gerald, *Hitler's Children: Inside the Families of the Third Reich* (Mandarin, London, 1991)

Rees, Laurence, *The Nazis: a warning from history* (BBC Books, London, 1997)

Sereny, Gitta, *Albert Speer: His Battle with Truth* (Picador, London, 1995)

Shirer, William, *The Rise and Fall of the Third Reich* (Arrow, London, 1991)

Speer, Albert, *Inside the Third Reich* (Weidenfeld and Nicolson, London, 1970)

Steinert, Marlis, *Hitler's War and the Germans* (Ohio University Press, Athens, 1977)

Steinhoff, Johannes; Pechel, Peter and Showalter, Dennis, *Voices from the Third Reich: An Oral History* (Da Capo Press, New York, 1989)

Toland, John, *Hitler* (Wordsworth, Ware, 1997)

Trevor-Roper, Hugh, *The Last Days of Hitler* (Papermac, London, 1995)

Trevor-Roper, Hugh, *Hitler's Table Talk, 1941–44* (Phoenix Press, London, 1988)

INDEX